Mom! I Learn Division Using Math-Chess-Puzzles Connection

棋谜式除法

Frank Ho   Amanda Ho

何数棋谜 培训

Ho Math Chess Learning Centre

Mom! I Learn Division Using Math-Chess-Puzzles Connection

Ho Math Chess   何数棋谜   妈!我会棋谜式除法啦!

Frank Ho, Amanda Ho © 2004 – 2020, all rights reserved.

Student's Name _____ Date _____

Table of Contents

***** Part 1 Worksheets using math-chess-puzzles connection ***** 8

Chess pieces and their mathematical values 9

IQ math chess puzzles 10

Memory and computation training 11

Frankho Maze 何数棋谜宫 12

Trace the path from ▨ to ✳ 12

Movement direction is shown by a darker line segment. 12

***** Review of times table ***** 13

Multiplication of 2 13

Multiplication of 3 14

Multiplication 4 15

Multiplication 5 16

Multiplication of 6 17

Multiplication of 7 18

Multiplication of 8 19

Multiplication of 9 20

Multiplication of 10 21

Learning multiplication and division 22

Numerical ability assessment 30

Frankho Eight Diagrams Math™ 31

Assessment of multiplication 32

Assessment of multiplication (order of operation) 34

Addition, subtraction, multiplication and division of 2 35

Addition, subtraction, multiplication and division of 3 36

Addition, subtraction, multiplication and division of 4 37

Addition, subtraction, multiplication and division of 5 38

Addition, subtraction, multiplication and division of 6 39

Addition, subtraction, multiplication and division of 7 40

Addition, subtraction, multiplication and division of 8 41

Addition, subtraction, multiplication and division of 9 42

Mom! I Learn Division Using Math-Chess-Puzzles Connection

Ho Math Chess 何数棋谜 妈!我会棋谜式除法啦!

Frank Ho, Amanda Ho © 2004 – 2020, all rights reserved.

Student's Name _____ Date _____

Addition, subtraction, multiplication and division of 10's power or multiples of 10	43
Learning multiplication by pattern	44
Addition, subtraction, and division of 11	45
Addition, subtraction, and division of 12	46
Addition, subtraction, and division of 13	47
Addition, subtraction, and division of 14	48
Addition, subtraction, and division of 15	49
Addition, subtraction, and division of 16	50
Addition, subtraction, and division of 17	51
Addition, subtraction, and division of 18	52
Reverse Subtraction	53
Reverse Addition	54
Reverse Multiplication	55
Reverse Division	57
Learning division from multiplication (Concept used for % and getting one factor)	59
Paired whole numbers	61
Adding with convergent thinking	63
Intelligent math worksheet	67
Spatial relation and subtraction operation	74
Intelligent worksheets of division and remainder	83
Division with minimum quotient and no remainder	111
Reduce the following fractions.	113
dd divided by dd	122
***** Part 2 Multiplication Review *****	145
dd × dd multiplication concepts	146
dd × dd with carrying	148
ddd × dd with carrying	160
ddd	161
ddd × dd without carrying	164
d0d × dd	168
***** Part 3 Traditional worksheets *****	170

No part of this publication can be copied, duplicated, or reproduced.

Mom! I Learn Division Using Math-Chess-Puzzles Connection

Ho Math Chess 何数棋谜 妈!我会棋谜式除法啦!

Frank Ho, Amanda Ho © 2004 – 2020, all rights reserved.

Student's Name _____ Date _____

Less than or equal ≤	171
Division notations	172
Divisible by 2	173
Divisible by 3	174
Divisible by 4	175
Divisible by 5	176
Divisible by 6	177
Divisible by 9	178
Divisible by 10	179
Dividing by relating	183
From multiplication to division procedure	185
From multiplication to division (d ÷ d)	186
dd ÷ d with 1-digit quotient and no remainder	188
From multiplication to division	190
dd ÷ d with 1-digit quotient and no remainder	197
dd ÷ d with remainder vs. no remainder	198
From multiplication to division	204
Multiplication and division facts	212
Use the following array	214
Division math minutes	216
dd ÷ d with 2-digit quotient and no remainder	218
dd ÷ d with 2-digit quotient and remainder	224
ddd ÷ d with three-digit quotient and no remainder	226
ddd ÷ d with three-digit quotient and remainder	230
Short Division	233
Rounding whole number (5 up, 4 down)	235
Trailing zeros in the dividend	239
Trailing zeros in the dividend and divisor	240
Zeros in the middle of quotient	244
Quotient with leading, middle, and training zeros	246
d0...0d. ÷ dd0… with no remainder	247

No part of this publication can be copied, duplicated, or reproduced.

Mom! I Learn Division Using Math-Chess-Puzzles Connection

Ho Math Chess 何数棋谜 妈!我会棋谜式除法啦!

Frank Ho, Amanda Ho © 2004 – 2020, all rights reserved.

Student's Name _____ Date _____

÷ by multiples of 10's (equivalent to × by multiples of 0.1)	248
Estimating quotient of ddd ÷ dd	249
ddd ÷ dd with 2-digit quotient	250
Estimating ddd ÷ dd with 1-digit quotient	258
ddd ÷ dd with 1-digit quotient	259
ddd ÷ dd with 1-digit quotient and remainder	263
Estimating of 2-digit(s) quotient by rounding	267
Estimating quotient of 2-digit or more divisors by rounding	268
ddd ÷ dd = q with no remainder	270
ddd ÷ dd = qq with no remainder	271
ddddd ÷ ddd	276
Addition and subtraction	279
Multiplication and addition	285
Multiplication and subtraction	289
Division and addition	292
Division and subtraction	302
Multiplication and division	303
***** Part 4 Decimal division *****	304
ddd ÷ dd. Round the answers to the nearest hundredth.	307
dddd ÷ dd. Round the answers to the nearest hundredth.	309
ddd ÷ ddd. Round the answers to the nearest hundredth.	311
dddd ÷ ddd. Round the answers to the nearest hundredth.	312

Mom! I Learn Division Using Math-Chess-Puzzles Connection

Ho Math Chess 何数棋谜 妈!我会棋谜式除法啦!

Frank Ho, Amanda Ho © 2004 – 2020, all rights reserved.

Student's Name _____ Date _____

About Ho Math Chess™ Math Workbooks

I have taught students from grade 1 to grade 12 since I opened the Vancouver *Ho Math Chess* Learning Centre in 1995. I have personally witnessed on how some students suffered because they could not master some very basic computational skills. I do not want to create a workbook, which is about practice, practice, and more practice of computational skills. This has motivated me to create a workbook that would be very different from the conventional ones in terms of the way the questions are presented to the students. I wanted students to learn basic computation skills by using the carefully designed worksheets so that students can master basic computation skills in an intuitive way. These worksheets were being designed while I watched student's work and modified accordingly to their responses.

I had an idea to create a computational workbook, which integrates chess knowledge, puzzles, and math in such a way that students could learn how to transfer abstract symbols into numerical values and then calculating the results by using puzzles-like problems. This idea may sound very simple, but the result is much more profound – not only students learn to do math in multi-step, they also learn how to process information by converting abstract symbols into numerical values, which is important in learning critical thinking skill.

One very noticeable computation format in *Ho Math Chess* math workbooks is the way computation directions are presented - it is no longer just a linear fashion; instead, students work on computations in all kinds of directions: top-down, bottom up, left to eight, right to left, diagonally, and even circular motion. For example, the multiplication workbook computation format is designed in such a way that it takes the boredom out by using the format of multi-direction computation and multi-concept learning. Students could be introduced division computation procedure while working on multiplication and even equivalent fractions but without realizing that they are working on advanced math concepts and mechanic computation procedure beyond their grade level. One other example is that the factoring procedure is introduced while students are working on multiplication. These many embedded computational procedures included in the elementary level of math workbook will benefit students when they go to higher grades.

Mom! I Learn Division Using Math-Chess-Puzzles Connection

Ho Math Chess 何数棋谜 妈!我会棋谜式除法啦!

Frank Ho, Amanda Ho © 2004 – 2020, all rights reserved.

Student's Name _____ Date _____

My idea of using multi-direction, multi-operation, multi-procedure, multi-concept learning style is the very distinct and innovative way of creating these workbooks. Students found them less boring and even willing to do the same worksheets the second time if they did not master the first time.

I am hoping by working through these addition, subtraction, multiplication workbooks, the division would be just a matter of fine-tuning its computation procedure.

In 2014, all computation workbooks have taken major upgrades to include truly math and chess integrated material, this idea is a world first and these worksheets formats are also world first. With these releases of many new and innovative workbooks, the math teaching and tutoring has taken the entire math tutoring to a revolutionary stage. Because of the creation of integrated math, chess, and puzzles integrated workbooks, Ho Math Chess has made the dream of fun math teaching becomes true.

Students at Ho Math Chess have enjoyed math even more than the previous workbooks and we see dramatic changes in student's attitude, they are happier and more willing to work on math.

Frank Ho
Amanda Ho

July 2014

Mom! I Learn Division Using Math-Chess-Puzzles Connection

Ho Math Chess 何数棋谜 妈!我会棋谜式除法啦!

Frank Ho, Amanda Ho © 2004 – 2020, all rights reserved.

Student's Name _____ Date _____

***** Part 1 Worksheets using math-chess-puzzles connection *****

Mom! I Learn Division Using Math-Chess-Puzzles Connection

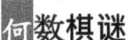 Math Chess　何数棋谜　妈!我会棋谜式除法啦!

Frank Ho, Amanda Ho © 2004 − 2020, all rights reserved.

Student's Name _____ Date _____

Chess pieces and their mathematical values

Symbols of chess pieces	Names of chess pieces	Mathematical values
♛ ♛ ♕ ♕	Queen	9
♜ ♜ ♖ ♖	Rook	5
♝ ♝ ♗ ♗	Bishop	3
♞ ♞ ♘ ♘	Knight	3
♟ ♟ ♙ ♙	Pawn	1
♚ ♚ ♔ ♔	King	0

Mom! I Learn Division Using Math-Chess-Puzzles Connection

Ho Math Chess　何数棋谜　妈!我会棋谜式除法啦!

Frank Ho, Amanda Ho © 2004 − 2020, all rights reserved.

Student's Name _____ Date _____

IQ math chess puzzles

You are a chess piece located at (e, 5).

6	(a, 3)	(b, 3)	(c, 3)
5	(a, 2)	**4 1 / 2 3**	(c, 2)
4	(a, 1)	(b, 1)	(c, 1)
	d	e	f

Rule: All the digits 1 to 3 must appear exactly once in every row and column.

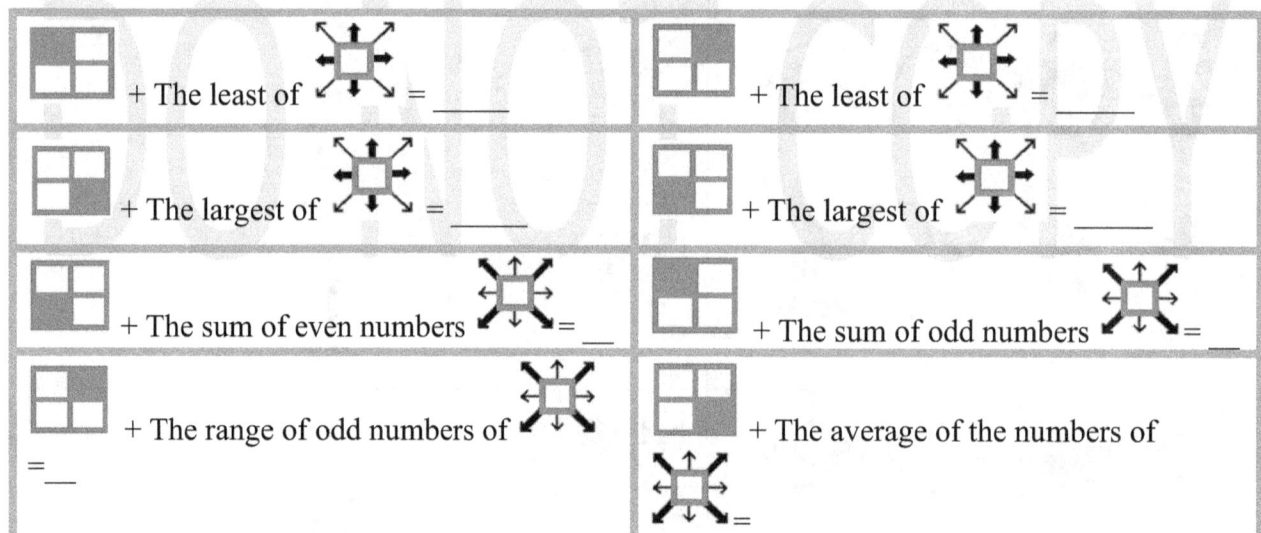

+ The least of ⟐ = _____   + The least of ⟐ = _____

+ The largest of ⟐ = _____   + The largest of ⟐ = _____

+ The sum of even numbers ⟐ = __   + The sum of odd numbers ⟐ = __

+ The range of odd numbers of ⟐ = __   + The average of the numbers of ⟐ = __

Mom! I Learn Division Using Math-Chess-Puzzles Connection

Ho Math Chess 何数棋谜 妈!我会棋谜式除法啦!

Frank Ho, Amanda Ho © 2004 – 2020, all rights reserved.

Student's Name _____ Date _____

Memory and computation training

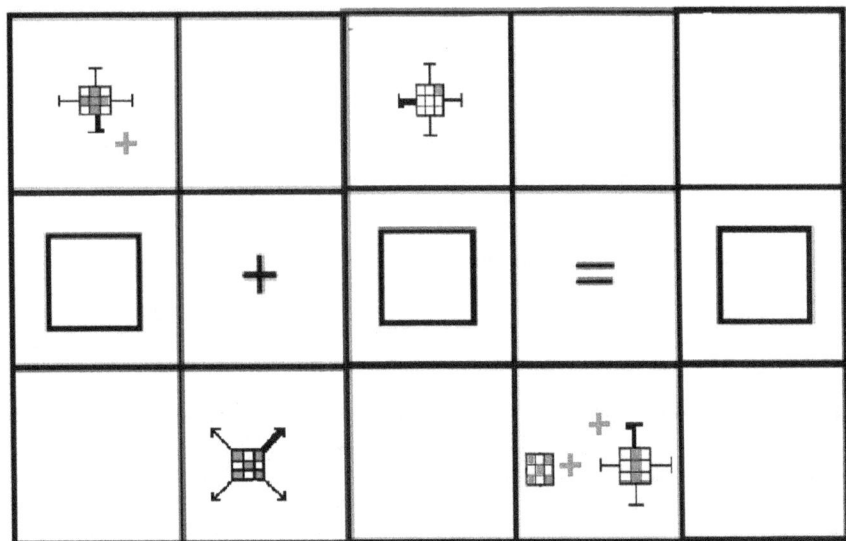

answer

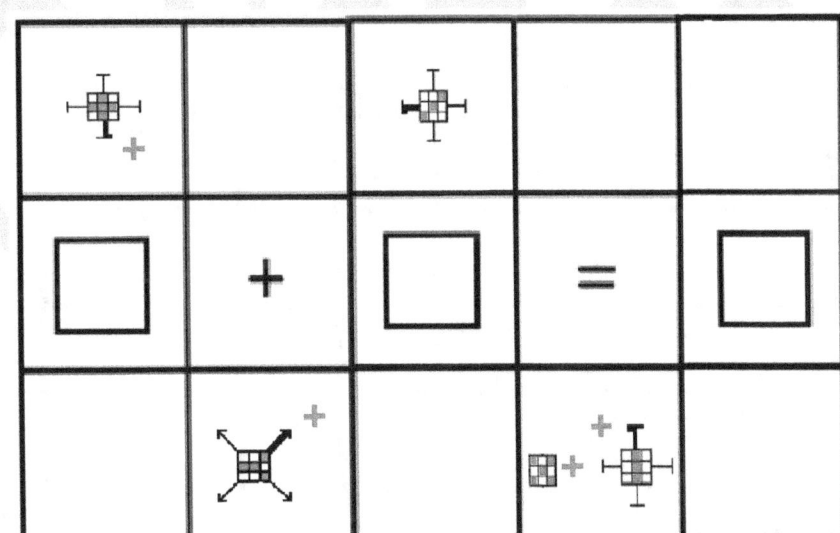

Mom! I Learn Division Using Math-Chess-Puzzles Connection

Ho Math Chess 何数棋谜 妈!我会棋谜式除法啦!

Frank Ho, Amanda Ho © 2004 − 2020, all rights reserved.

Student's Name _____ Date _____

Frankho Maze 何数棋谜宫

Trace the path from/to ✷.

Movement direction is shown by a darker line segment.

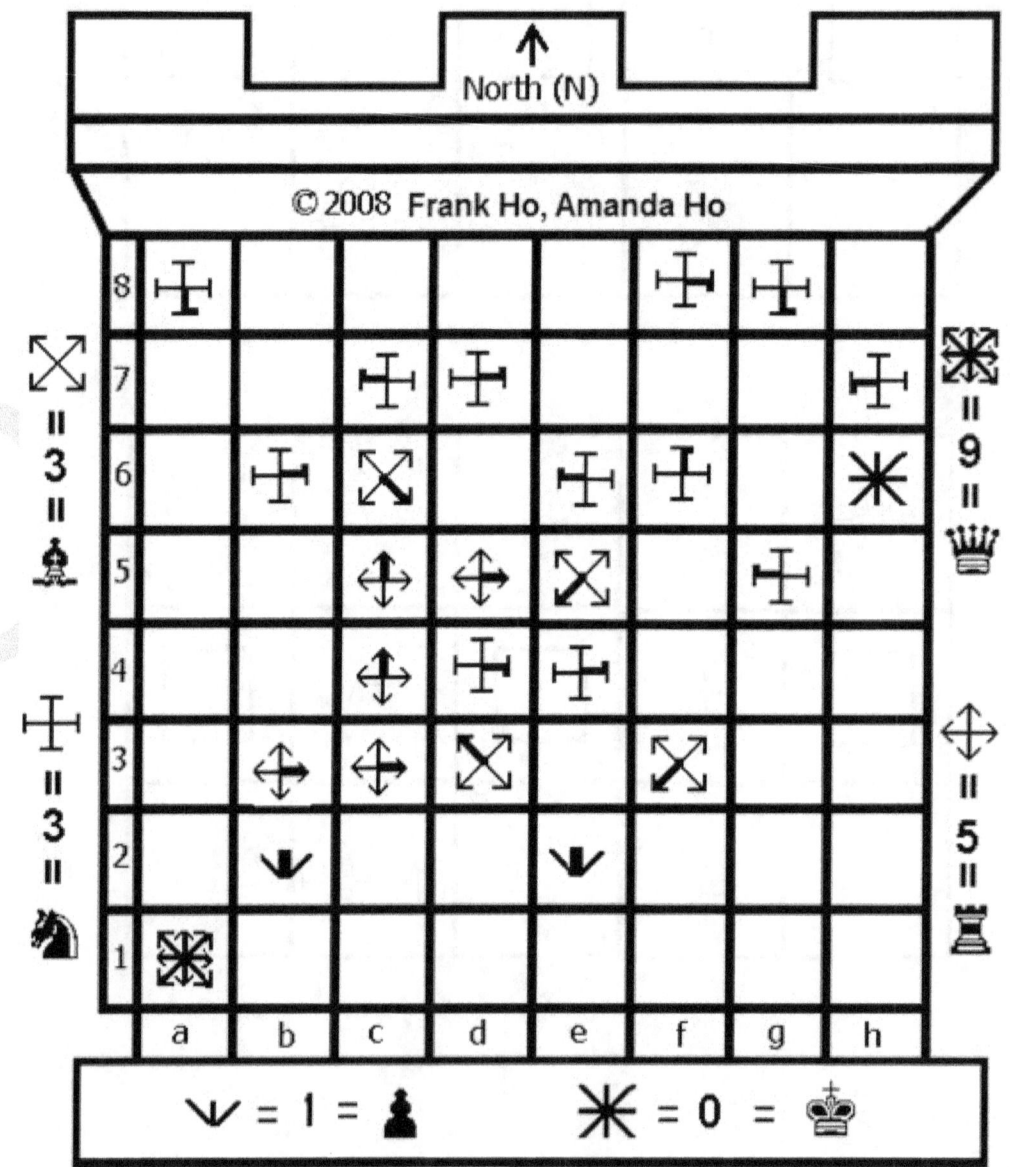

Mom! I Learn Division Using Math-Chess-Puzzles Connection

Ho Math Chess 何数棋谜 妈!我会棋谜式除法啦!

Frank Ho, Amanda Ho © 2004 − 2020, all rights reserved.

Student's Name _____ Date _____

***** Review of times table *****

Multiplication of 2

9	2	3
8	2	4
7	6	5

Mom! I Learn Division Using Math-Chess-Puzzles Connection

Ho Math Chess　何数棋谜　妈!我会棋谜式除法啦!

Frank Ho, Amanda Ho © 2004 – 2020, all rights reserved.

Student's Name _____ Date _____

Multiplication of 3

9	2	3
8	3	4
7	6	5

Mom! I Learn Division Using Math-Chess-Puzzles Connection

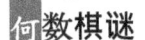 Math Chess   何数棋谜   妈!我会棋谜式除法啦!

Frank Ho, Amanda Ho © 2004 – 2020, all rights reserved.

Student's Name _____ Date _____

Multiplication 4

9	2	3
8	4	4
7	6	5

Mom! I Learn Division Using Math-Chess-Puzzles Connection

Ho Math Chess 何数棋谜 妈!我会棋谜式除法啦!

Frank Ho, Amanda Ho © 2004 − 2020, all rights reserved.

Student's Name _____ Date _____

Multiplication 5

9	2	3
8	5	4
7	6	5

9	2	3
8	5	4
7	6	5

Page 16

Mom! I Learn Division Using Math-Chess-Puzzles Connection

Ho Math Chess 何数棋谜 妈!我会棋谜式除法啦!

Frank Ho, Amanda Ho © 2004 – 2020, all rights reserved.

Student's Name _____ Date _____

Multiplication of 6

9	2	3
8	6	4
7	6	5

Page 17

Mom! I Learn Division Using Math-Chess-Puzzles Connection

Ho Math Chess 何数棋谜 妈!我会棋谜式除法啦!

Frank Ho, Amanda Ho © 2004 − 2020, all rights reserved.

Student's Name _____ Date _____

Multiplication of 7

9	2	3
8	7	4
7	6	5

Mom! I Learn Division Using Math-Chess-Puzzles Connection

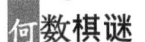
Math Chess 何数棋谜 妈!我会棋谜式除法啦!

Frank Ho, Amanda Ho © 2004 − 2020, all rights reserved.

Student's Name _____ Date _____

Multiplication of 8

9	2	3
8	8	4
7	6	5

Page 19

Mom! I Learn Division Using Math-Chess-Puzzles Connection

Ho Math Chess 何数棋谜 妈!我会棋谜式除法啦!

Frank Ho, Amanda Ho © 2004 − 2020, all rights reserved.

Student's Name _____ Date _____

Multiplication of 9

9	2	3
8	9	4
7	6	5

Page 20

Mom! I Learn Division Using Math-Chess-Puzzles Connection

Ho Math Chess 何数棋谜 妈!我会棋谜式除法啦!

Frank Ho, Amanda Ho © 2004 – 2020, all rights reserved.

Student's Name _____ Date _____

Multiplication of 10

9	2	3
8	10	4
7	6	5

Mom! I Learn Division Using Math-Chess-Puzzles Connection

Ho Math Chess 何数棋谜 妈!我会棋谜式除法啦!

Frank Ho, Amanda Ho © 2004 – 2020, all rights reserved.

Student's Name _____ Date _____

Learning multiplication and division

5	2	3	4	6	6
4	9	6	3	5	8
3	5	7	7	2	4
2	2	4	9	3	5
1	7	4	3	6	6
	a	B	c	d	e

You are at c3 = ☐.

Find out all factors of 7 = _____ 1, 7

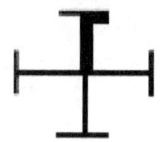

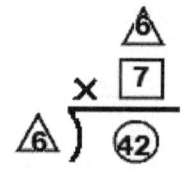

□7 × △6 = ○42   △6 = ○42 ÷ □7

△6 × □7 = ○42   □7 = ○42 ÷ △6

□7 × ? < ○42, ? = < 6

△6 × ? < ○42, ? = < 7

○42 ÷ ? < △6, ? = > 7

○42 ÷ ? < □7, ? = > 6

Mom! I Learn Division Using Math-Chess-Puzzles Connection

Ho Math Chess　何数棋谜　妈!我会棋谜式除法啦!

Frank Ho, Amanda Ho © 2004 − 2020, all rights reserved.

Student's Name _____　Date _____

Learning multiplication and division

5	2	3	4	7	6
4	9	6	3	5	8
3	5	7	7	2	4
2	2	4	9	3	5
1	7	4	3	6	6
	a	b	c	d	e

You are at c3 = ☐.

Find out all factors of 7 = _____.

$\square \times \triangle = \bigcirc \qquad \triangle = \bigcirc \div \square$

$\triangle \times \square = \bigcirc \qquad \square = \bigcirc \div \triangle$

$\square \times ? < \bigcirc, ? = $ _____

$\triangle \times ? < \bigcirc, ? = $ _____

$\bigcirc \div ? < \triangle, ? = $ _____

$\bigcirc \div ? < \square, ? = $ _____

Mom! I Learn Division Using Math-Chess-Puzzles Connection

Ho Math Chess   何数棋谜   妈!我会棋谜式除法啦!

Frank Ho, Amanda Ho © 2004 – 2020, all rights reserved.

Student's Name _____   Date _____

Learning multiplication and division

5	2	3	4	7	6
4	9	6	3	5	8
3	5	7	7	2	4
2	2	4	9	3	5
1	7	4	3	6	6
	a	b	c	d	e

You are at c3 = ☐ .

Find out all factors of 7 = _____ .

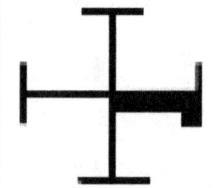

$$\square\overline{)\bigcirc}^{\square \times \triangle} \qquad \triangle\overline{)\bigcirc}^{\triangle \times \square}$$

$\square \times \triangle = \bigcirc \qquad \triangle = \bigcirc \div \square$

$\triangle \times \square = \bigcirc \qquad \square = \bigcirc \div \triangle$

$\square \times ? < \bigcirc, ? =$ _____

$\triangle \times ? < \bigcirc, ? =$ _____

$\bigcirc \div ? < \triangle, ? =$ _____

$\bigcirc \div ? < \square, ? =$ _____

Mom! I Learn Division Using Math-Chess-Puzzles Connection

Ho Math Chess 何数棋谜 妈!我会棋谜式除法啦!

Frank Ho, Amanda Ho © 2004 − 2020, all rights reserved.

Student's Name _____ Date _____

Learning multiplication and division

5	2	3	4	7	6
4	9	6	3	5	8
3	5	7	7	2	4
2	2	4	9	3	5
1	7	4	3	6	6
	a	b	c	d	e

You are at c3 = ☐.

Find out all factors of 7 = _____.

□ × △ = ○   △ = ○ ÷ □

△ × □ = ○   □ = ○ ÷ △

□ × ? < ○, ? = _____

△ × ? < ○, ? = _____

○ ÷ ? < △, ? = _____

○ ÷ ? < □, ? = _____

Mom! I Learn Division Using Math-Chess-Puzzles Connection

Ho Math Chess 何数棋谜 妈!我会棋谜式除法啦!

Frank Ho, Amanda Ho © 2004 − 2020, all rights reserved.

Student's Name _____ Date _____

Learning multiplication and division

5	2	3	4	7	6
4	9	6	3	5	8
3	5	7	7	2	4
2	2	4	9	3	5
1	7	4	3	6	6
	a	b	c	d	e

You are at c3 = ☐.

Find out all factors of 7 = _____.

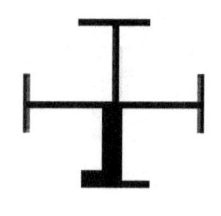

$$\square \overline{)\stackrel{\times \triangle}{\bigcirc}} \qquad \triangle \overline{)\stackrel{\times \square}{\bigcirc}}$$

☐ × △ = ○   △ = ○ ÷ ☐
△ × ☐ = ○   ☐ = ○ ÷ △

☐ × ? < ○, ? = _____

△ × ? < ○, ? = _____

○ ÷ ? < △, ? = _____

○ ÷ ? < ☐, ? = _____

Mom! I Learn Division Using Math-Chess-Puzzles Connection

Ho Math Chess 何数棋谜 妈!我会棋谜式除法啦!

Frank Ho, Amanda Ho © 2004 – 2020, all rights reserved.

Student's Name _____ Date _____

Learning multiplication and division

5	2	3	4	7	6
4	9	6	3	5	8
3	5	7	7	2	4
2	2	4	9	3	5
1	7	4	3	6	6
	a	b	c	d	e

You are at c3 = ☐.

Find out all factors of 7 = _____.

$$\square \overline{)\bigcirc}^{\times \triangle \atop \square} \qquad \triangle \overline{)\bigcirc}^{\times \square \atop \triangle}$$

☐ × △ = ○   △ = ○ ÷ ☐
△ × ☐ = ○   ☐ = ○ ÷ △

☐ × ? < ○, ? = _____

△ × ? < ○, ? = _____

○ ÷ ? < △, ? = _____

○ ÷ ? < ☐, ? = _____

Mom! I Learn Division Using Math-Chess-Puzzles Connection

Ho Math Chess 何数棋谜 妈!我会棋谜式除法啦!

Frank Ho, Amanda Ho © 2004 – 2020, all rights reserved.

Student's Name _____   Date _____

Learning multiplication and division

5	2	3	4	7	6
4	9	6	3	5	8
3	5	7	7	2	4
2	2	4	9	3	5
1	7	4	3	6	6
a	b	c	d	e	

You are at c3 = ☐.

Find out all factors of 7 = _____.

$\square \times \triangle = \bigcirc \qquad \triangle = \bigcirc \div \square$

$\triangle \times \square = \bigcirc \qquad \square = \bigcirc \div \triangle$

$\square \times ? < \bigcirc, ? = $ _____

$\triangle \times ? < \bigcirc, ? = $ _____

$\bigcirc \div ? < \triangle, ? = $ _____

$\bigcirc \div ? < \square, ? = $ _____

Page 28

Mom! I Learn Division Using Math-Chess-Puzzles Connection

Ho Math Chess   何数棋谜   妈!我会棋谜式除法啦!

Frank Ho, Amanda Ho © 2004 − 2020, all rights reserved.

Student's Name _____ Date _____

Learning multiplication and division

5	2	3	4	7	6
4	9	6	3	5	8
3	5	7	7	2	4
2	2	4	9	3	5
1	7	4	3	6	6
	a	b	c	d	e

You are at c3 = ☐.

Find out all factors of 7 = _____.

$\square \times \triangle = \bigcirc \qquad \triangle = \bigcirc \div \square$

$\triangle \times \square = \bigcirc \qquad \square = \bigcirc \div \triangle$

$\square \times ? < \bigcirc, ? =$ _____

$\triangle \times ? < \bigcirc, ? =$ _____

$\bigcirc \div ? < \triangle, ? =$ _____

$\bigcirc \div ? < \square, ? =$ _____

Mom! I Learn Division Using Math-Chess-Puzzles Connection

Ho Math Chess　何数棋谜　妈!我会棋谜式除法啦!

Frank Ho, Amanda Ho © 2004 – 2020, all rights reserved.

Student's Name _____　Date _____

Numerical ability assessment

1	3 + 9		12 × 2		One hour is how many minutes	
2	9 + 3		22 × 2		One hour 20 minutes is how many minutes	
3	12 − 3		33 × 2		15 minutes is how many hours?	
4	12 − 9		44 × 2		30 minutes is how many hours?	
5	2 × 2		55 × 2		121 × 2	
6	3 × 3		11 × 3		242 × 2	
7	4 × 4		22 × 3		123 × 2	
8	6 × 6		44 × 3		321 × 2	
9	5 × 5		55 × 3		213 × 2	
10	9 × 9		8 × 3		312 × 2	
11	8 × 8		8 × 9		231 × 2	
12	11 × 11		9 × 6		321 × 2	
13	10 × 10		7 × 6		121 × 3	
14	7 × 7		5 × 6		232 × 3	
15	12 × 12		2 × 6		123 × 3	
16	13 × 13		1 × 1 × 1 × 1		321 × 3	
17	14 × 14		1 ÷ 1		213 × 3	
18	15 × 15		23 ÷ 1		312 × 3	
19	25 × 25		24 ÷ 2		231 × 3	
20	35 × 35		22 ÷ 1		321 × 3	
21	55 × 55		48 ÷ 2		121 × 3	
22	19 − 2		48 ÷ 4		242 × 3	
23	14 − 5		48 ÷ 3		25 ÷ 5	
24	12 − 8		48 ÷ 12		2555 ÷ 5	
25	13 − 6		48 ÷ 6		250 ÷ 5	
26	11 − 4		48 ÷ 48		2500 ÷ 5	
27	10 − 9		72 ÷ 2		2505 ÷ 5	
28	10 − 4		72 ÷ 3		25050 ÷ 5	
29	18 − 9		72 ÷ 4		100 ÷ 5	
30	17 − 8		72 ÷ 12		1000 ÷ 5	
31	17 − 9		72 ÷ 6		500 ÷ 5	
32	11 − 2		72 ÷ 36		100 ÷ 50	
33	13 − 4		1 ÷ 2		100 ÷ 100	
34	15 − 8		2 ÷ 4		100 ÷ 10	
35	17 − 9		$\frac{1}{2} + \frac{1}{2}$		1000 ÷ 10	
36	14 − 9		One dollar is how many cents?		1 ÷ 0.1	
37	13 − 4		One dollar 10 cents is how many cents?		10 ÷ 0.1	

Mom! I Learn Division Using Math-Chess-Puzzles Connection

Ho Math Chess 何数棋谜 妈!我会棋谜式除法啦!

Frank Ho, Amanda Ho © 2004 – 2020, all rights reserved.

Student's Name_____ Date_____

Frankho Eight Diagrams Math™

只见棋谜不见题 劝君迷路不哭涕 数学象棋加谜题 健脑思维眞神奇

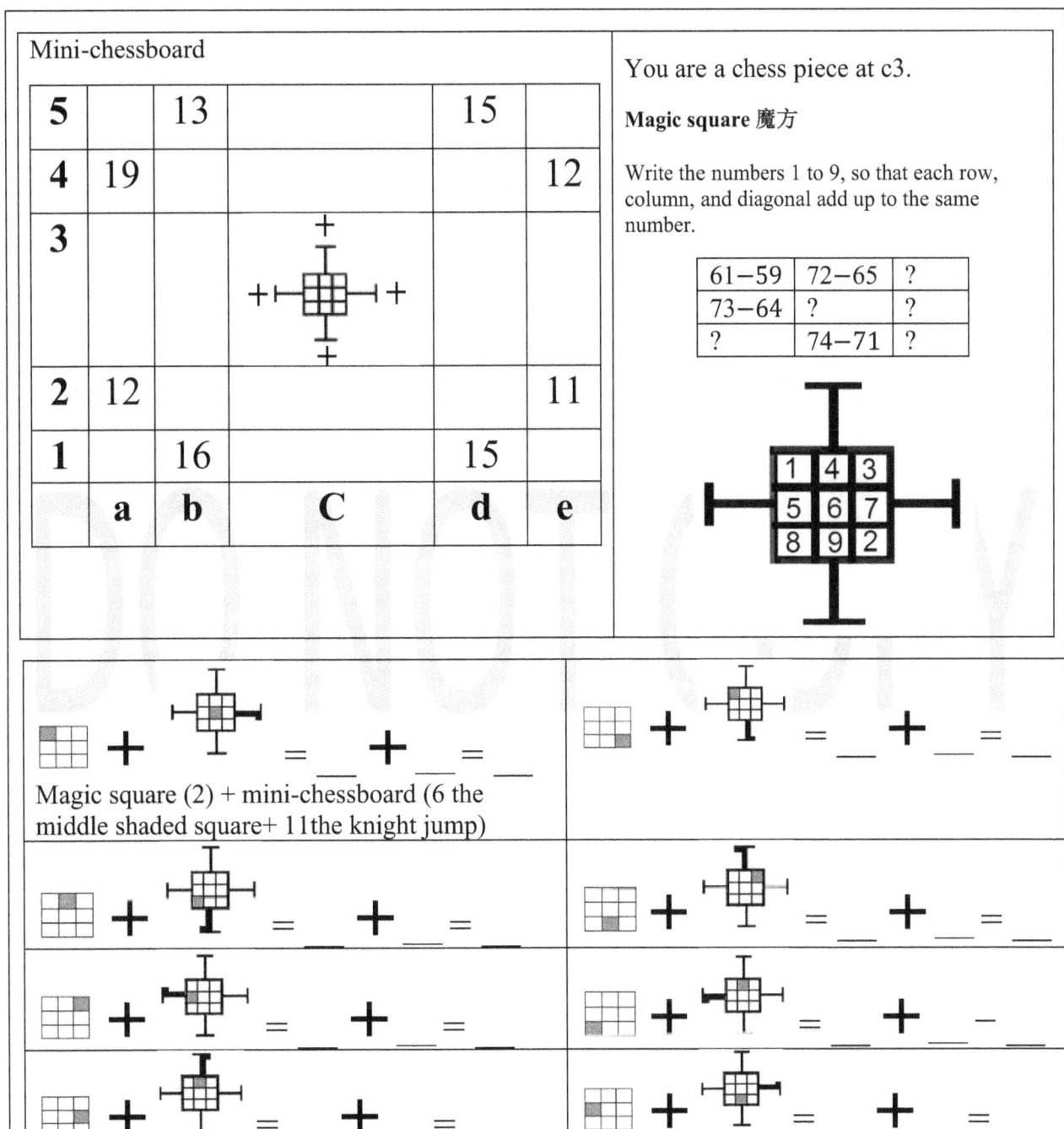

Mom! I Learn Division Using Math-Chess-Puzzles Connection

Ho Math Chess 何数棋谜 妈!我会棋谜式除法啦!

Frank Ho, Amanda Ho © 2004 − 2020, all rights reserved.

Student's Name _____ Date _____

Assessment of multiplication

Fill in each ? by a number such that $a_1 \times a_2 = a_3$ and $b_1 \times b_2 = b_3$.

↘ = $a_1 \times b_2$, ↙ = $b_1 \times a_2$.

Example

	a	b
3	6	1
2	?2	?1
1	?3	?1

$3 \times 2 = 6, 1 \times 1 = 1$

↘ + ↙ = _3_ + _2_ = 5

$3 \times 1 + 1 \times 2 = 5$

↘ − ↙ = _3_ − _2_ = 1

$3 \times 1 − 1 \times 2 = 3 − 2 = 1$

---

	a	b
3	6	2
2	?	?
1	?	?

↘ + ↙ = __ + __ = 13

↘ − ↙ = __ − __ = 11

---

	a	b
3	6	2
2	?	?
1	?	?

↘ + ↙ = __ + __ = 8

↘ − ↙ = __ − __ = 4

No part of this publication can be copied, duplicated, or reproduced.

Mom! I Learn Division Using Math-Chess-Puzzles Connection

Ho Math Chess　何数棋谜　妈!我会棋谜式除法啦!

Frank Ho, Amanda Ho © 2004 – 2020, all rights reserved.

Student's Name _____　　　　Date _____

Assessment of multiplication

Fill in each ? by a number such that $a1 \times a2 = a3$ and $b1 \times b2 = b3$.

$\searrow = a1 \times b2$, $\swarrow = b1 \times a2$.

	3	6	2
	2	?	?
	1	?	?
		a	b

$\searrow + \swarrow = \_\_ + \_\_ = 7$

$\searrow - \swarrow = \_\_ - \_\_ = 1$

	3	6	3
	2	?	?
	1	?	?
		a	b

$\searrow + \swarrow = \_\_ + \_\_ = 19$

$\searrow - \swarrow = \_\_ - \_\_ = 17$

	3	6	3
	2	?	?
	1	?	?
		a	b

$\searrow + \swarrow = \_\_ + \_\_ = 11$

$\searrow - \swarrow = \_\_ - \_\_ = \_\_ = 7$

Mom! I Learn Division Using Math-Chess-Puzzles Connection

Ho Math Chess 何数棋谜 妈!我会棋谜式除法啦!

Frank Ho, Amanda Ho © 2004 – 2020, all rights reserved.

Student's Name _____ Date _____

Assessment of multiplication (order of operation)

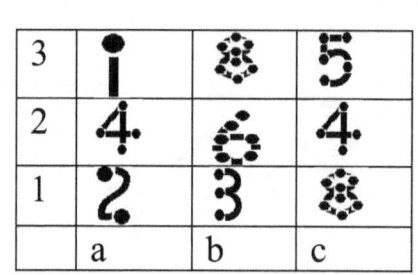

You are at b2 = ☐..

☐ + ✥ × (☐ – 1) = ___ + ___ × ___ = ___

☐ + ✥ × (☐ – 1) = ___ + ___ × ___ = ___

☐ + ✥ × (☐ – 1) = ___ + ___ × ___ = ___

☐ + ✥ × (☐ – 1) = ___ + ___ × ___ = ___

☐ + ✕ × (☐ – 1) = ___ + ___ × ___ = ___

☐ + ✕ × (☐ – 1) = ___ + ___ × ___ = ___

☐ + ✕ × (☐ – 1) = ___ + ___ × ___ = ___

Mom! I Learn Division Using Math-Chess-Puzzles Connection

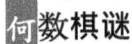 Math Chess   何数棋谜   妈!我会棋谜式除法啦!

Frank Ho, Amanda Ho © 2004 – 2020, all rights reserved.

Student's Name _____   Date _____

Addition, subtraction, multiplication and division of 2

28	39	48
29	2	58
78	18	19

11	21	31
41	2	51
61	71	81

13	19	15
18	2	14
17	12	16

12	16	18
14	2	10
6	8	4

39 + 2 = 41   21 − 2 = 19   19 × 2 = 38   16 ÷ 2 = 8

___ + ___ = ___   ___ − ___ = ___   ___ × ___ = ___   ___ ÷ ___ = ___

___ + ___ = ___   ___ − ___ = ___   ___ × ___ = ___   ___ ÷ ___ = ___

___ + ___ = ___   ___ − ___ = ___   ___ × ___ = ___   ___ ÷ ___ = ___

___ + ___ = ___   ___ − ___ = ___   ___ × ___ = ___   ___ ÷ ___ = ___

___ + ___ = ___   ___ − ___ = ___   ___ × ___ = ___   ___ ÷ ___ = ___

___ + ___ = ___   ___ − ___ = ___   ___ × ___ = ___   ___ ÷ ___ = ___

___ + ___ = ___   ___ − ___ = ___   ___ × ___ = ___   ___ ÷ ___ = ___

Mom! I Learn Division Using Math-Chess-Puzzles Connection

Ho Math Chess 何数棋谜 妈!我会棋谜式除法啦!

Frank Ho, Amanda Ho © 2004 – 2020, all rights reserved.

Student's Name _____ Date _____

Addition, subtraction, multiplication and division of 3

27	39	48
29	3	57
76	18	16

12	21	33
41	3	54
62	73	83

13	19	15
18	3	14
17	12	16

12	15	27
21	3	33
24	36	39

Page 36

Mom! I Learn Division Using Math-Chess-Puzzles Connection

Ho Math Chess 何数棋谜 妈!我会棋谜式除法啦!

Frank Ho, Amanda Ho © 2004 – 2020, all rights reserved.

Student's Name _____ Date _____

Addition, subtraction, multiplication and division of 4

27	39	48
29	4	57
76	18	16

12	21	33
41	4	54
62	73	83

13	19	15
18	4	14
17	12	16

12	16	28
20	4	32
24	28	36

___ + ___ = ___   ___ − ___ = ___   ___ × ___ = ___   ___ ÷ ___ = ___

Mom! I Learn Division Using Math-Chess-Puzzles Connection

Ho Math Chess 何数棋谜 妈!我会棋谜式除法啦!

Frank Ho, Amanda Ho © 2004 – 2020, all rights reserved.

Student's Name _____ Date _____

Addition, subtraction, multiplication and division of 5

28	39	46
27	5	58
76	19	17

12	21	34
44	5	53
61	73	82

13	19	15
18	5	14
17	12	16

10	15	20
35	5	40
30	35	45

Page 38

Mom! I Learn Division Using Math-Chess-Puzzles Connection

Ho Math Chess   何数棋谜   妈!我会棋谜式除法啦!

Frank Ho, Amanda Ho © 2004 − 2020, all rights reserved.

Student's Name _____   Date _____

Addition, subtraction, multiplication and division of 6

28	39	45
26	6	57
76	18	19

13	21	32
45	6	54
63	72	81

13	19	15
18	6	14
17	12	16

12	18	24
42	6	30
36	48	54

___ + ___ = ___   ___ − ___ = ___   ___ × ___ = ___   ___ ÷ ___ = ___

Page 39

Mom! I Learn Division Using Math-Chess-Puzzles Connection

Ho Math Chess 何数棋谜 妈!我会棋谜式除法啦!

Frank Ho, Amanda Ho © 2004 − 2020, all rights reserved.

Student's Name _____ Date _____

Addition, subtraction, multiplication and division of 7

28	39	45
26	7	57
74	18	19

13	21	36
45	7	54
63	72	80

13	19	15
18	7	14
17	12	16

14	21	28
42	7	35
49	56	63

Mom! I Learn Division Using Math-Chess-Puzzles Connection

Ho Math Chess 何数棋谜 妈!我会棋谜式除法啦!

Frank Ho, Amanda Ho © 2004 – 2020, all rights reserved.

Student's Name _____ Date _____

Addition, subtraction, multiplication and division of 8

28 | 39 | 44 26 | 8 | 57 73 | 15 | 14	13 | 21 | 32 45 | 8 | 54 66 | 77 | 81	13 | 19 | 15 18 | 8 | 14 17 | 12 | 16	32 | 16 | 24 40 | 8 | 48 56 | 48 | 72
_39_ + _8_ = _47_	_21_ − _8_ = _13_	_19_ × _8_ = _152_	_16_ ÷ _8_ = _2_
__ + __ = __	__ − __ = __	__ × __ = __	__ ÷ __ = __
__ + __ = __	__ − __ = __	__ × __ = __	__ ÷ __ = __
__ + __ = __	__ − __ = __	__ × __ = __	__ ÷ __ = __
__ + __ = __	__ − __ = __	__ × __ = __	__ ÷ __ = __
__ + __ = __	__ − __ = __	__ × __ = __	__ ÷ __ = __
__ + __ = __	__ − __ = __	__ × __ = __	__ ÷ __ = __
__ + __ = __	__ − __ = __	__ × __ = __	__ ÷ __ = __

No part of this publication can be copied, duplicated, or reproduced.

Mom! I Learn Division Using Math-Chess-Puzzles Connection

Ho Math Chess   何数棋谜   妈!我会棋谜式除法啦!

Frank Ho, Amanda Ho © 2004 − 2020, all rights reserved.

Student's Name _____   Date _____

Addition, subtraction, multiplication and division of 9

28	39	44
26	9	57
73	15	14

13	21	32
45	9	54
66	77	81

13	19	15
18	9	14
17	12	16

36	18	27
45	9	24
33	11	32

___ + ___ = ___   ___ − ___ = ___   ___ × ___ = ___   ___ ÷ ___ = ___

Mom! I Learn Division Using Math-Chess-Puzzles Connection

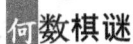 Math Chess   何数棋谜   妈!我会棋谜式除法啦!

Frank Ho, Amanda Ho © 2004 – 2020, all rights reserved.

Student's Name _____   Date _____

Addition, subtraction, multiplication, and division of 10's power or multiples of 10

8	9	4
6	10	7
3	5	1

13	21	32
45	100	54
66	77	81

13	19	15
18	30	14
17	12	16

36	18	27
45	50	24
33	11	32

_9_ + _1_ = 10   _21_ + _79_ = 100   _19_ + _11_ = 30   _18_ + _32_ = 50

___ + ___ = ___

___ + ___ = ___

___ + ___ = ___

___ + ___ = ___

___ + ___ = ___

___ + ___ = ___

___ + ___ = ___

Mom! I Learn Division Using Math-Chess-Puzzles Connection

Ho Math Chess 何数棋谜 妈!我会棋谜式除法啦!

Frank Ho, Amanda Ho © 2004 – 2020, all rights reserved.

Student's Name _____ Date _____

Learning multiplication by pattern

3	2	3	4
2	5	8	6
1	7	8	9
	a	b	c

The original square is at b2.

b2 × ⇕ = __ × __ = ◯, ◯ ÷ b2 = △, △ × b2 = ◯, ◯ ÷ ⇕ = __

b2 × ⇔ = __ × __ = ◯, ◯ ÷ b2 = △, △ × b2 = ◯, ◯ ÷ ⇔ = __

b2 × ⇕ = __ × __ = ◯, ◯ ÷ b2 = △, △ × b2 = ◯, ◯ ÷ ⇕ = __

b2 × ⇕ = __ × __ = ◯, ◯ ÷ b2 = △, △ × b2 = ◯, ◯ ÷ ⇕ = __

b2 × ⤢ = __ × __ = ◯, ◯ ÷ b2 = △, △ × b2 = ◯, ◯ ÷ ⤢ = __

b2 × ⤢ = __ × __ = ◯, ◯ ÷ b2 = △, △ × b2 = ◯, ◯ ÷ ⤢ = __

b2 × ⤡ = __ × __ = ◯, ◯ ÷ b2 = △, △ × b2 = ◯, ◯ ÷ ⤡ = __

b2 × ⤡ = __ × __ = ◯, ◯ ÷ b2 = △, △ × b2 = ◯, ◯ ÷ ⤡ = __

No part of this publication can be copied, duplicated, or reproduced.

Mom! I Learn Division Using Math-Chess-Puzzles Connection

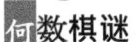 Math Chess   何数棋谜   妈!我会棋谜式除法啦!

Frank Ho, Amanda Ho © 2004 − 2020, all rights reserved.

Student's Name _____   Date _____

Addition, subtraction, and division of 11

2	3	4
5	11	6
7	8	9

3 + 8 = 11

11 − 3 = 8

7, 4
5, 6
2, 9
3, 8
4, 7
6, 5
9, 2

Page 45

Mom! I Learn Division Using Math-Chess-Puzzles Connection

Ho Math Chess 何数棋谜 妈!我会棋谜式除法啦!

Frank Ho, Amanda Ho © 2004 − 2020, all rights reserved.

Student's Name _____ Date _____

Addition, subtraction, and division of 12

4	3	4
5	12	6
7	8	9

$\underline{3} + \underline{9} = 12$

$12 - 3 = \underline{9}$

___ + ___ = ___

___ − ___ = ___

Page 46

Mom! I Learn Division Using Math-Chess-Puzzles Connection

Ho Math Chess 何数棋谜 妈!我会棋谜式除法啦!

Frank Ho, Amanda Ho © 2004 − 2020, all rights reserved.

Student's Name_____ Date_____

Addition, subtraction, and division of 13

4	5	6
5	13	6
7	8	9

4	5	6
5	13	6
7	8	9

4	5	6
5	13	6
7	8	9

4	5	6
5	13	6
7	8	9

5 + 8 = 13

13 − 5 = 8

Page 47

Mom! I Learn Division Using Math-Chess-Puzzles Connection

Ho Math Chess 何数棋谜 妈!我会棋谜式除法啦!

Frank Ho, Amanda Ho © 2004 − 2020, all rights reserved.

Student's Name _____   Date _____

Addition, subtraction, and division of 14

8	5	7
5	14	6
7	8	9

8	5	7
5	14	6
7	8	9

8	5	7
5	14	6
7	8	9

8	5	7
5	14	6
7	8	9

$5 + 9 = 14$

$14 - 5 = 9$

Page 48

Mom! I Learn Division Using Math-Chess-Puzzles Connection

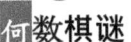 Math Chess   何数棋谜   妈!我会棋谜式除法啦!

Frank Ho, Amanda Ho © 2004 − 2020, all rights reserved.

Student's Name _____   Date _____

Addition, subtraction, and division of 15

6	7	8
9	15	6
7	8	9

6	7	8
9	15	6
7	8	9

6	7	8
9	15	6
7	8	9

6	7	8
9	15	6
7	8	9

$\underline{7} + \underline{8} = 15$

$15 - 7 = \underline{8}$

Page 49

Mom! I Learn Division Using Math-Chess-Puzzles Connection

Ho Math Chess 何数棋谜 妈!我会棋谜式除法啦!

Frank Ho, Amanda Ho © 2004 – 2020, all rights reserved.

Student's Name _____ Date _____

Addition, subtraction, and division of 16

7	8	9
8	16	7
7	8	9

7	8	9
8	16	7
7	8	9

7	8	9
8	16	7
7	8	9

7	8	9
8	16	7
7	8	9

$\underline{8} + \underline{8} = 16$

$16 - 8 = \underline{8}$

Page 50

Mom! I Learn Division Using Math-Chess-Puzzles Connection

Ho Math Chess 何数棋谜 妈!我会棋谜式除法啦!

Frank Ho, Amanda Ho © 2004 — 2020, all rights reserved.

Student's Name _____ Date _____

Addition, subtraction, and division of 17

8	9	8
9	17	8
9	8	9

8	9	8
9	17	8
9	8	9

8	9	8
9	17	8
9	8	9

8	9	8
9	17	8
9	8	9

$\underline{9} + \underline{8} = 17$

$\underline{17} - 9 = \underline{8}$

___ + ___ = ___

___ − ___ = ___

Page 51

Mom! I Learn Division Using Math-Chess-Puzzles Connection

Ho Math Chess 何数棋谜 妈!我会棋谜式除法啦!

Frank Ho, Amanda Ho © 2004 – 2020, all rights reserved.

Student's Name _____   Date _____

Addition, subtraction, and division of 18

9	9	9
9	18	9
9	9	9

9	9	9
9	18	9
9	9	9

9	9	9
9	18	9
9	9	9

9	9	9
9	18	9
9	9	9

$\underline{9} + \underline{8} = 18$

$\underline{18} - 9 = \underline{9}$

Page 52

Mom! I Learn Division Using Math-Chess-Puzzles Connection

Reverse Subtraction

62	20	17
59		8
44	25	9

□ = ?

62 − 45 = 17

Mom! I Learn Division Using Math-Chess-Puzzles Connection

Ho Math Chess 何数棋谜 妈!我会棋谜式除法啦!

Frank Ho, Amanda Ho © 2004 – 2020, all rights reserved.

Student's Name _____ Date _____

Reverse Addition

62	33	17
59		8
44	25	9

□ = ?

□ − ▦ = ▦
79 − 17 = 62

□ − ▦ = ▦

□ − ▦ = ▦

□ − ▦ = ▦

□ − ▦ = ▦

□ − ▦ = ▦

62 − 45 = □ − ▦ = ▦

□ − ▦ = ▦

Mom! I Learn Division Using Math-Chess-Puzzles Connection

Ho Math Chess　何数棋谜　妈!我会棋谜式除法啦!

Frank Ho, Amanda Ho © 2004 − 2020, all rights reserved.

Student's Name _____ Date _____

Reverse Multiplication

18	12	14
10	2	6
8	4	16

□ = ?, ✳ = central square

□ × ✳ = ✳ → 9 × 2 = 18

□ × ✳ = ✳

□ × ✳ = ✳

□ × ✳ = ✳

□ × ✳ = ✳

□ × ✳ = ✳

□ × ✳ = ✳

□ × ✳ = ✳

Mom! I Learn Division Using Math-Chess-Puzzles Connection

Ho Math Chess 何数棋谜 妈!我会棋谜式除法啦!

Frank Ho, Amanda Ho © 2004 − 2020, all rights reserved.

Student's Name _____ Date _____

Reverse Multiplication

18	12	14
10	2	6
8	4	16

□ = ?, ✶ = central square

2 × 9 = 18

Page 56

Mom! I Learn Division Using Math-Chess-Puzzles Connection

Ho Math Chess 何数棋谜 妈!我会棋谜式除法啦!

Frank Ho, Amanda Ho © 2004 – 2020, all rights reserved.

Student's Name _____ Date _____

Reverse Division

18	12	14
10	2	6
8	4	16

□ = ?, ✹ = central square

$\dfrac{12}{6} = 2$

Page 57

Mom! I Learn Division Using Math-Chess-Puzzles Connection

Ho Math Chess 何数棋谜 妈!我会棋谜式除法啦!

Frank Ho, Amanda Ho © 2004 – 2020, all rights reserved.

Student's Name _____ Date _____

Reverse Division

9	2	3
8	2	4
7	6	5

□ = ?, ✷ = central square

Mom! I Learn Division Using Math-Chess-Puzzles Connection

Ho Math Chess 何数棋谜 妈!我会棋谜式除法啦!

Frank Ho, Amanda Ho © 2004 – 2020, all rights reserved.

Student's Name_____ Date_____

Learning division from multiplication (Concept used for % and getting one factor)

5		9		2	
4	8	9	2	3	3
3		8	6	4	
2	7	7	6	5	4
1		6		5	
	a	b	c	d	e

You are ✺ at C3, ☐ = ?.

✺ × c4 = ☐, ☐ ÷ c4 = ✺, ☐ ÷ ✺ = c4

✺ × d3 = ☐, ☐ ÷ d3 = ✺, ☐ ÷ ✺ = d3

✺ × c2 = ☐, ☐ ÷ c2 = ✺, ☐ ÷ ✺ = c2

✺ × b3 = ☐, ☐ ÷ b3 = ✺, ☐ ÷ ✺ = b3

✺ × d4 = ☐, ☐ ÷ d4 = ✺, ☐ ÷ ✺ = d4

✺ × d2 = ☐, ☐ ÷ d2 = ✺, ☐ ÷ ✺ = d2

✺ × b2 = ☐, ☐ ÷ b2 = ✺, ☐ ÷ ✺ = b2

✺ × b4 = ☐, ☐ ÷ b4 = ✺, ☐ ÷ ✺ = b4

Mom! I Learn Division Using Math-Chess-Puzzles Connection

Ho Math Chess 何数棋谜 妈!我会棋谜式除法啦!

Frank Ho, Amanda Ho © 2004 − 2020, all rights reserved.

Student's Name _____ Date_____

Learning division from multiplication (Concept used for % and getting one factor)

5		9		2	
4	8	9	2	3	3
3			8	6	4
2	7	7		6	5	4
1		6		5	
	a	b	c	d	e

You are ✧ at C3, □ = ?.

✧ × d5 = □, □ ÷ d5 = ✧, □ ÷ ✧ = d5

✧ × b5 = □, □ ÷ b5 = ✧, □ ÷ ✧ = b5

✧ × e4 = □, □ ÷ e4 = ✧, □ ÷ ✧ = e4

✧ × e2 = □, □ ÷ e2 = ✧, □ ÷ ✧ = e2

✧ × d1 = □, □ ÷ d1 = ✧, □ ÷ ✧ = d1

✧ × b1 = □, □ ÷ b1 = ✧, □ ÷ ✧ = b1

✧ × a4 = □, □ ÷ a4 = ✧, □ ÷ ✧ = a4

✧ × a2 = □, □ ÷ a2 = ✧, □ ÷ ✧ = a2

Mom! I Learn Division Using Math-Chess-Puzzles Connection

Ho Math Chess 何数棋谜 妈!我会棋谜式除法啦!

Frank Ho, Amanda Ho © 2004 − 2020, all rights reserved.

Student's Name _____ Date _____

Paired whole numbers

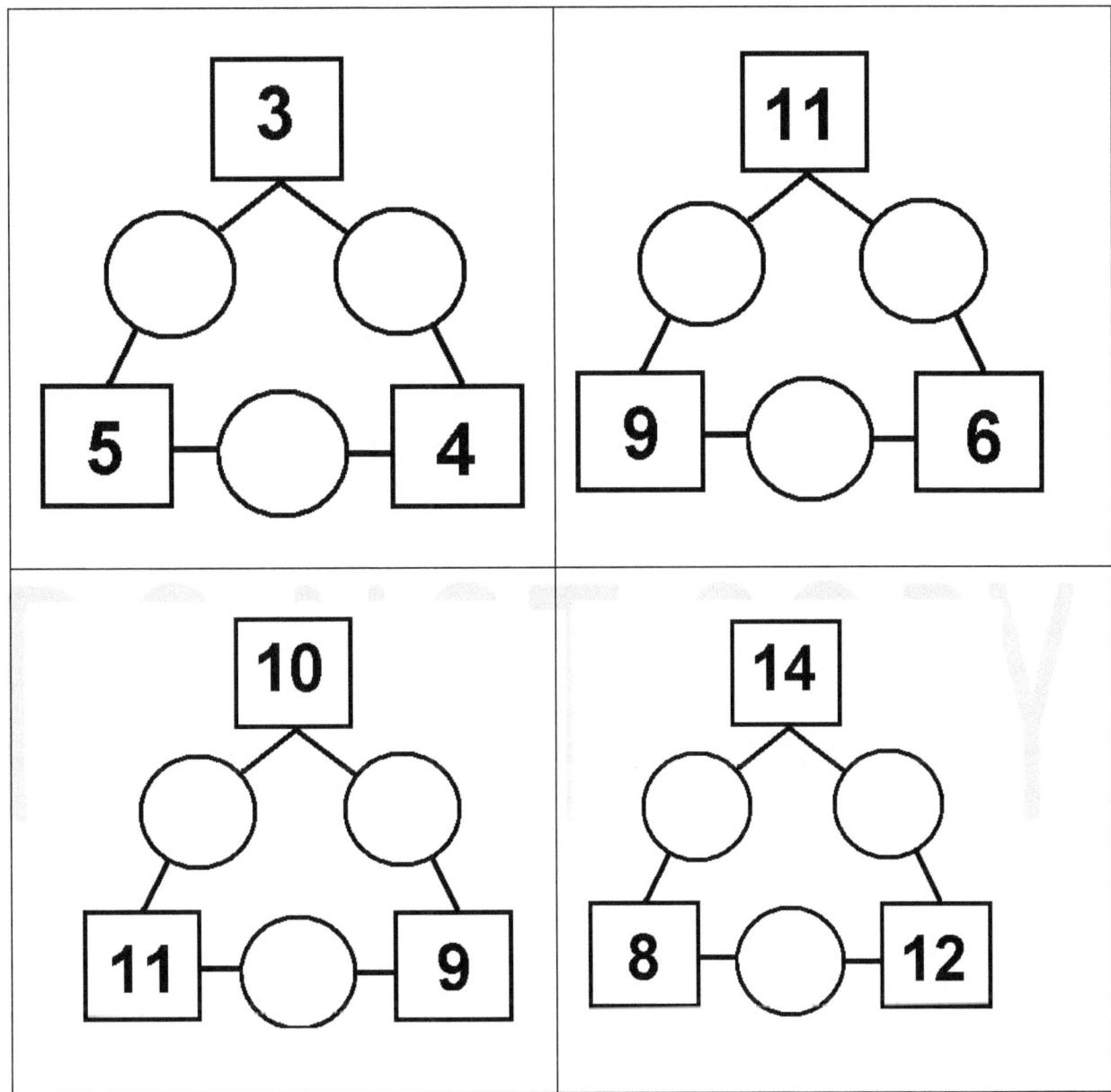

Mom! I Learn Division Using Math-Chess-Puzzles Connection

Ho Math Chess 何数棋谜 妈!我会棋谜式除法啦!
Frank Ho, Amanda Ho © 2004 – 2020, all rights reserved.

Student's Name _____ Date _____

Paired whole numbers

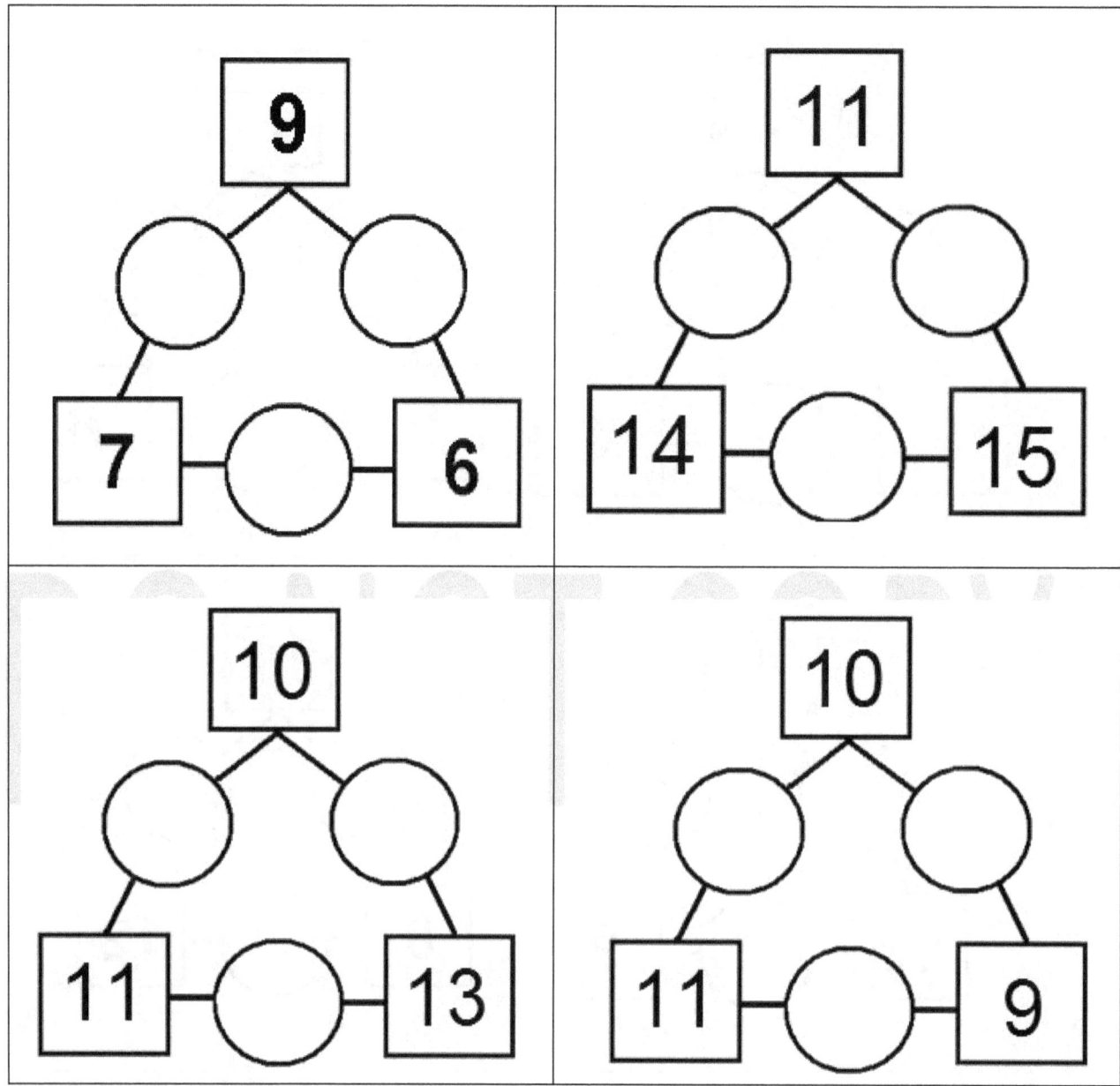

Mom! I Learn Division Using Math-Chess-Puzzles Connection

Ho Math Chess   何数棋谜   妈!我会棋谜式除法啦!

Frank Ho, Amanda Ho © 2004 – 2020, all rights reserved.

Student's Name _____   Date _____

Adding with convergent thinking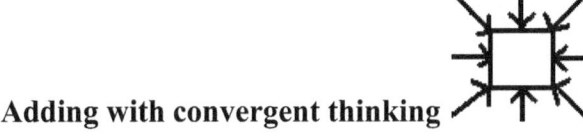

	a	b	c	d	e
5					
4					
3			6		
2					
1					

Answers may locate at different squares.

You are at c3 = ☐

Fill in each box with one number from 1 to 9 such that these 2 numbers adding in the direction of will have the sum of ☐. For example, 1 + 5 = 6.

Mom! I Learn Division Using Math-Chess-Puzzles Connection

Ho Math Chess 何数棋谜 妈!我会棋谜式除法啦!

Frank Ho, Amanda Ho © 2004 − 2020, all rights reserved.

Student's Name _____ Date _____

Adding with convergent thinking

	a	b	c	d	e
5					
4					
3			7		
2					
1					

Answers may locate at different squares.

You are at c3 = ☐

Fill in each box with one number from 1 to 9 such that these 2 numbers adding in the direction of ⟶☐⟵ will have the sum of ☐. For example, 1 + 6 = 7.

Mom! I Learn Division Using Math-Chess-Puzzles Connection

Ho Math Chess 何数棋谜 妈!我会棋谜式除法啦!

Frank Ho, Amanda Ho © 2004 – 2020, all rights reserved.

Student's Name _____ Date _____

Adding with convergent thinking

	a	b	c	d	e
5					
4					
3			8		
2					
1					

Answers may locate at different squares.

You are at c3 = ☐

Fill in each box with one number from 1 to 9 such that these 2 numbers adding in the direction of ⬒ will have the sum of ☐. For example, 1 + 7 = 8.

Mom! I Learn Division Using Math-Chess-Puzzles Connection

Ho Math Chess 何数棋谜 妈!我会棋谜式除法啦!

Frank Ho, Amanda Ho © 2004 – 2020, all rights reserved.

Student's Name _____ Date _____

Adding with convergent thinking

5					
4					
3			9		
2					
1					
	a	b	c	d	e

Answers may locate at different squares.

You are at c3 = ☐

Fill in each box with one number from 1 to 9 such that these 2 numbers adding in the direction of (convergent arrows) will have the sum of ☐. For example, 1 + 8 = 9.

Page 66

Mom! I Learn Division Using Math-Chess-Puzzles Connection

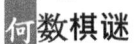 Math Chess   何数棋谜   妈!我会棋谜式除法啦!

Frank Ho, Amanda Ho © 2004 − 2020, all rights reserved.

Student's Name _____   Date _____

Intelligent math worksheet

5		7		0	
4	6	8	9	10	1
3		11	5, 6	12	
2	5	13	14	15	2
1		4		3	
	a	b	c	d	e

You are at c3 = ☐.

Pick a number = ____.

Use the picked number for all the following problems.

☐ + ↕↔ = ___ + ___ = ___

☐ + ↕↔ = ___ + ___ = ___

☐ + ↕↔ = ___ + ___ = ___

☐ + ↕↔ = ___ + ___ = ___

☐ + ✕ = ___ + ___ = ___

☐ + ✕ = ___ + ___ = ___

☐ + ✕ = ___ + ___ = ___

☐ + ✕ = ___ + ___ = ___

Mom! I Learn Division Using Math-Chess-Puzzles Connection

Ho Math Chess   何数棋谜   妈!我会棋谜式除法啦!

Frank Ho, Amanda Ho © 2004 – 2020, all rights reserved.

Student's Name _____ Date _____

5		7		0	
4	6	8	9	10	1
3		11	8, 9	12	
2	5	13	14	15	2
1			4	3	
	a	b	c	d	e

You are at c3 = ☐ .

Pick a number = ____ .

Use the picked number for all the following problems.

☐ + ✥ = ___ + ___ = ___

☐ + ✥ = ___ + ___ = ___

☐ + ✥ = ___ + ___ = ___

☐ + ✥ = ___ + ___ = ___

☐ + ✕ = ___ + ___ = ___

☐ + ✕ = ___ + ___ = ___

☐ + ✕ = ___ + ___ = ___

☐ + ✕ = ___ + ___ = ___

Mom! I Learn Division Using Math-Chess-Puzzles Connection

Ho Math Chess　何数棋谜　妈!我会棋谜式除法啦!

Frank Ho, Amanda Ho © 2004 − 2020, all rights reserved.

Student's Name _____ Date _____

5		7		0	
4	6	8	9	10	1
3		11	7, 8	12	
2	5	13	14	15	2
1			4		3
	a	b	c	d	e

You are at c3 = ☐.

Pick a number = ___.

☐ + ⬌ = ___ + ___ = ___

☐ + ⬌ = ___ + ___ = ___

☐ + ⬌ = ___ + ___ = ___

☐ + ⬌ = ___ + ___ = ___

☐ + ✕ = ___ + ___ = ___

☐ + ✕ = ___ + ___ = ___

☐ + ✕ = ___ + ___ = ___

☐ + ✕ = ___ + ___ = ___

Mom! I Learn Division Using Math-Chess-Puzzles Connection

Ho Math Chess　何数棋谜　妈!我会棋谜式除法啦!

Frank Ho, Amanda Ho © 2004 − 2020, all rights reserved.

Student's Name _____ Date _____

5		7		0	
4	6	8	9	10	1
3		11	9, 10	12	
2	5	13	14	15	2
1		4		3	
	a	b	c	d	e

You are at c3 = ☐ .

Pick a number = ____ .

☐ + ✥ = ___ + ___ = ___

☐ + ✥ = ___ + ___ = ___

☐ + ✥ = ___ + ___ = ___

☐ + ✥ = ___ + ___ = ___

☐ + ✕ = ___ + ___ = ___

☐ + ✕ = ___ + ___ = ___

☐ + ✕ = ___ + ___ = ___

☐ + ✕ = ___ + ___ = ___

Mom! I Learn Division Using Math-Chess-Puzzles Connection

Ho Math Chess 何数棋谜 妈!我会棋谜式除法啦!

Frank Ho, Amanda Ho © 2004 − 2020, all rights reserved.

Student's Name _____ Date _____

5		7		0	
4	6	8	9	10	1
3		11	11,12	12	
2	5	13	14	15	2
1		4		3	
	a	b	C	d	e

You are at c3 = ☐.

Pick a number = ____.

☐ + ✥ = __ + __ = __

☐ + ✥ = __ + __ = __

☐ + ✥ = __ + __ = __

☐ + ✥ = __ + __ = __

☐ + ✕ = __ + __ = __

☐ + ✕ = __ + __ = __

☐ + ✕ = __ + __ = __

☐ + ✕ = __ + __ = __

No part of this publication can be copied, duplicated, or reproduced. Page 71

Mom! I Learn Division Using Math-Chess-Puzzles Connection

Ho Math Chess　何数棋谜　妈!我会棋谜式除法啦!

Frank Ho, Amanda Ho © 2004 – 2020, all rights reserved.

Student's Name _____　Date _____

5		7		0	
4	6	8	9	10	1
3		11	16, 17	12	
2	5	13	14	15	2
1		4		3	
	A	b	c	d	e

You are at c3 = ☐.

Pick a number = ___.

☐ + ↔ = __ + __ = __

☐ + ↕ = __ + __ = __

☐ + ↔ = __ + __ = __

☐ + ↕ = __ + __ = __

☐ + ✗ = __ + __ = __

☐ + ✗ = __ + __ = __

☐ + ✗ = __ + __ = __

☐ + ✗ = __ + __ = __

Mom! I Learn Division Using Math-Chess-Puzzles Connection

Ho Math Chess   何数棋谜   妈!我会棋谜式除法啦!

Frank Ho, Amanda Ho © 2004 − 2020, all rights reserved.

Student's Name _____   Date _____

5	2	3	4	5	6
4	6	8	9	10	11
3	12	13		14	15
2	16	17	18	19	20
1	21	22	23	24	25
	a	b	c	d	e

You are at c3 = ☐.

$a_5 \times b_4 + \square = d_2 \times e_1$ __ × __ + __ = __ × __

$2 \times 8 + \square_{(443)} = 19 \times 25 = 459$

$a_3 \times b_3 + \square = d_3 \times e_3$ __ × __ + __ = __ × __

$d_4 \times e_5 + \square = a_1 \times b_2$ __ × __ + __ = __ × __

$c_4 \times c_5 + \square = c_1 \times c_2$ __ × __ + __ = __ × __

$a_5 \times b_4 + \square = a_1 \times b_2$ __ × __ + __ = __ × __

$a_3 \times b_3 + \square = d_2 \times e_1$ __ × __ + __ = __ × __

$c_4 \times c_5 + \square = d_4 \times e_5$ __ × __ + __ = __ × __

$d_4 \times e_5 + \square = c_1 \times c_2$ __ × __ + __ = __ × __

Mom! I Learn Division Using Math-Chess-Puzzles Connection

Ho Math Chess 何数棋谜 妈!我会棋谜式除法啦!

Frank Ho, Amanda Ho © 2004 − 2020, all rights reserved.

Student's Name _____ Date _____

Spatial relation and subtraction operation

7	8	3
6	11	5
2	9	4

7	2	4
6	11	5
9	8	3

4	9	5
8	12	11
7	3	6

11	4	7
5	12	9
3	8	6

$11 - 8 = 3$ $2 + 9 = 11$ $12 - 9 = 3$ $4 + 8 = 12$

___ − ___ = ___   ___ + ___ = ___   ___ − ___ = ___   ___ + ___ = ___

___ − ___ = ___   ___ + ___ = ___   ___ − ___ = ___   ___ + ___ = ___

___ − ___ = ___   ___ + ___ = ___   ___ − ___ = ___   ___ + ___ = ___

___ − ___ = ___   ___ + ___ = ___   ___ − ___ = ___   ___ + ___ = ___

___ − ___ = ___   ___ + ___ = ___   ___ − ___ = ___   ___ + ___ = ___

___ − ___ = ___   ___ + ___ = ___   ___ − ___ = ___   ___ + ___ = ___

___ − ___ = ___   ___ + ___ = ___   ___ − ___ = ___   ___ + ___ = ___

Mom! I Learn Division Using Math-Chess-Puzzles Connection

Ho Math Chess 何数棋谜 妈!我会棋谜式除法啦!

Frank Ho, Amanda Ho © 2004 – 2020, all rights reserved.

Student's Name _____ Date _____

Spatial relation and subtraction operation

7	8	11
6	13	5
12	9	4

7	12	4
6	13	5
9	8	11

13	9	5
8	14	12
7	11	6

11	6	7
5	14	9
12	8	13

13 − 8 = 5   12 + 1 = 13   14 − 9 = 5   6 + 8 = 14

__ − __ = __   __ + __ = __   __ − __ = __   __ + __ = __

__ − __ = __   __ + __ = __   __ − __ = __   __ + __ = __

__ − __ = __   __ + __ = __   __ − __ = __   __ + __ = __

__ − __ = __   __ + __ = __   __ − __ = __   14-11=3   __ + __ = __

__ − __ = __   __ + __ = __   __ − __ = __   __ + __ = __

__ − __ = __   __ + __ = __   __ − __ = __   __ + __ = __

__ − __ = __   __ + __ = __   __ − __ = __   __ + __ = __

Page 75

Mom! I Learn Division Using Math-Chess-Puzzles Connection

Ho Math Chess 何数棋谜 妈!我会棋谜式除法啦!

Student's Name ______________________ Date ______________

Spatial relation and subtraction operation

8	7	13
9	15	6
14	11	12

7	9	14
6	15	13
12	8	11

13	8	15
9	16	7
14	11	12

11	7	15
14	16	13
12	8	9

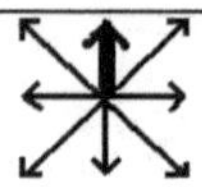 15 – 7 = 8	 9 + 6 = 15	 16 – 8 = 8	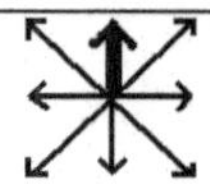 7 + 9 = 16
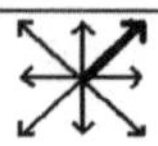 ___ – ___ = ___	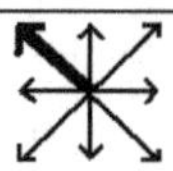 ___ + ___ = ___	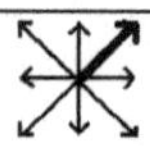 ___ – ___ = ___	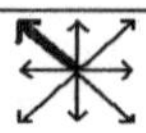 ___ + ___ = ___
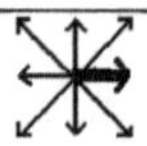 ___ – ___ = ___	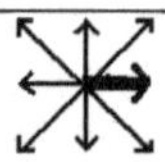 ___ + ___ = ___	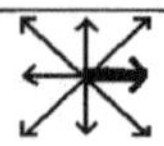 ___ – ___ = ___	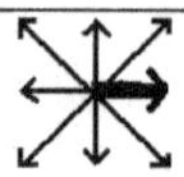 ___ + ___ = ___
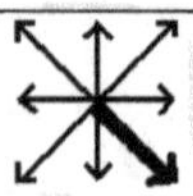 ___ – ___ = ___	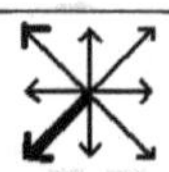 ___ + ___ = ___	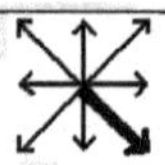 ___ – ___ = ___	 ___ + ___ = ___
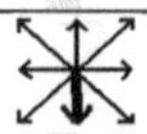 ___ – ___ = ___	 ___ + ___ = ___	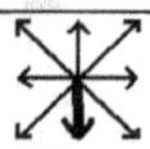 ___ – ___ = ___	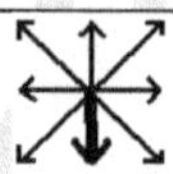 ___ + ___ = ___
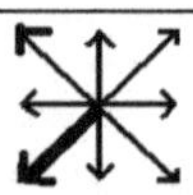 ___ – ___ = ___	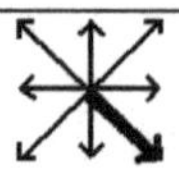 ___ + ___ = ___	 ___ – ___ = ___	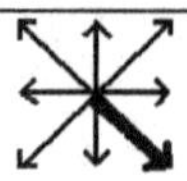 ___ + ___ = ___
 ___ – ___ = ___	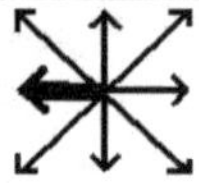 ___ + ___ = ___	 ___ – ___ = ___	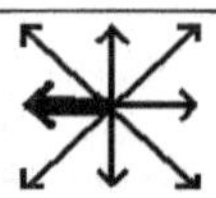 ___ + ___ = ___ 14+2=16
 ___ – ___ = ___	 ___ + ___ = ___	 ___ – ___ = ___	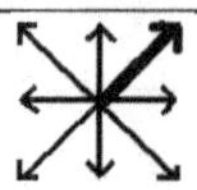 ___ + ___ = ___

Mom! I Learn Division Using Math-Chess-Puzzles Connection

Ho Math Chess 何数棋谜 妈!我会棋谜式除法啦!

Frank Ho, Amanda Ho © 2004 – 2020, all rights reserved.

Student's Name _____ Date _____

Spatial relation and subtraction operation

1

13	8	9
15	17	16
14	11	12

11	9	14
16	17	13
12	8	15

13	9	15
11	18	16
14	12	17

13	17	15
16	18	14
12	9	11

$\underline{17} - \underline{8} = \underline{9}$

$\underline{9} + \underline{8} = \underline{17}$

$\underline{18} - \underline{9} = 9$

$\underline{17} + \underline{1} = \underline{18}$

Page 77

Mom! I Learn Division Using Math-Chess-Puzzles Connection

Ho Math Chess 何数棋谜 妈!我会棋谜式除法啦!

Frank Ho, Amanda Ho © 2004 – 2020, all rights reserved.

Student's Name _____ Date _____

Spatial relation and subtraction operation

1

8	7	13
5	19	6
14	16	12

7	9	14
6	19	13
12	8	11

13	8	15
9	21	7
14	16	12

11	7	15
14	21	13
12	8	9

19 – 7 = 12   9 + 10 = 19   21 – 8 = 13   7 + 14 = 21

Page 78

Mom! I Learn Division Using Math-Chess-Puzzles Connection

Ho Math Chess 何数棋谜 妈!我会棋谜式除法啦!

Frank Ho, Amanda Ho © 2004 − 2020, all rights reserved.

Student's Name _____ Date _____

Spatial relation and multiplication operation

6	3	2
4	2	5
7	9	8

7	9	4
6	3	3
2	8	5

3	8	5
9	4	7
6	4	2

6	7	5
4	5	3
2	8	9

2 × 3 = 6

3 × 9 = 27

Mom! I Learn Division Using Math-Chess-Puzzles Connection

Ho Math Chess 何数棋谜 妈!我会棋谜式除法啦!

Frank Ho, Amanda Ho © 2004 − 2020, all rights reserved.

Student's Name _____ Date _____

Spatial relation and multiplication operation

6	3	2
4	6	5
7	9	8

7	9	4
6	7	3
2	8	5

3	8	5
9	8	7
6	4	2

6	7	5
4	9	3
2	8	9

6 × 3 = 18

7 × 9 = 63

Mom! I Learn Division Using Math-Chess-Puzzles Connection

Ho Math Chess 何数棋谜 妈!我会棋谜式除法啦!

Frank Ho, Amanda Ho © 2004 – 2020, all rights reserved.

Student's Name_____ Date_____

Spatial relation and multiplication operation

16	13	12
14	2	15
17	19	18

17	19	14
16	3	3
12	18	15

13	18	15
19	4	17
16	14	12

16	17	15
14	5	13
12	18	19

2 × 13 = 26

3 × 19 = 57

Mom! I Learn Division Using Math-Chess-Puzzles Connection

Ho Math Chess 何数棋谜 妈!我会棋谜式除法啦!

Frank Ho, Amanda Ho © 2004 − 2020, all rights reserved.

Student's Name _____ Date _____

Spatial relation and multiplication operation

16	13	12
14	6	15
17	19	18

17	19	14
16	7	3
12	18	15

13	18	15
19	8	17
16	14	12

16	17	15
14	9	13
12	18	19

2 × 13 = 26

3 × 19 = 57

Page 82

Mom! I Learn Division Using Math-Chess-Puzzles Connection

Ho Math Chess   何数棋谜   妈!我会棋谜式除法啦!

Frank Ho, Amanda Ho © 2004 – 2020, all rights reserved.

Student's Name _____   Date _____

Intelligent worksheets of division and remainder

Division and remainder

3	10	30	15
2	20	40	25
1	5	45	45
	a	b	c

You are at b2 = ☐.

3	1	2	3
2	4	5	6
1	7	8	9
	d	e	f

You are at e2 = ☐.

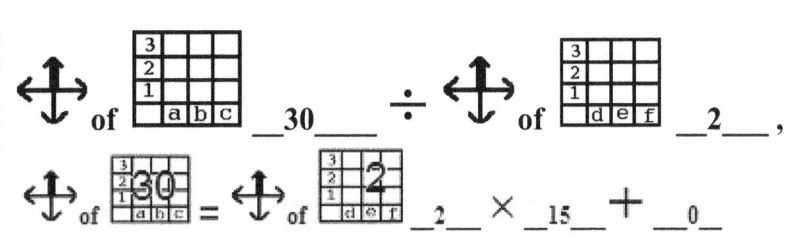

↕ of [abc] __30__ ÷ ↕ of [def] __2__ ,

↕ of [30/abc] = ↕ of [2/def] __2__ × __15__ + __0__

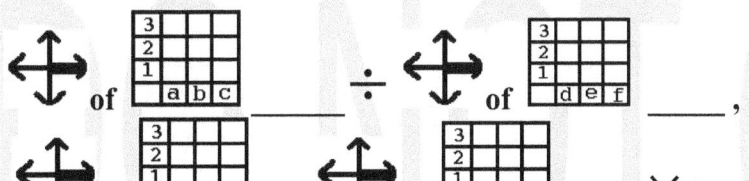

↕ of [abc] _____ ÷ ↕ of [def] _____ ,

↕ of [abc] = ↕ of [def] _____ × _____ + _____

Mom! I Learn Division Using Math-Chess-Puzzles Connection

Ho Math Chess   何数棋谜   妈!我会棋谜式除法啦!

Frank Ho, Amanda Ho © 2004 − 2020, all rights reserved.

Student's Name _____   Date _____

Division and remainder

3	10	30	15
2	20	40	25
1	5	45	45
	a	b	c

You are at b2 = ☐.

3	1	2	3
2	4	5	6
1	7	8	9
	d	e	f

You are at e2 = ☐.

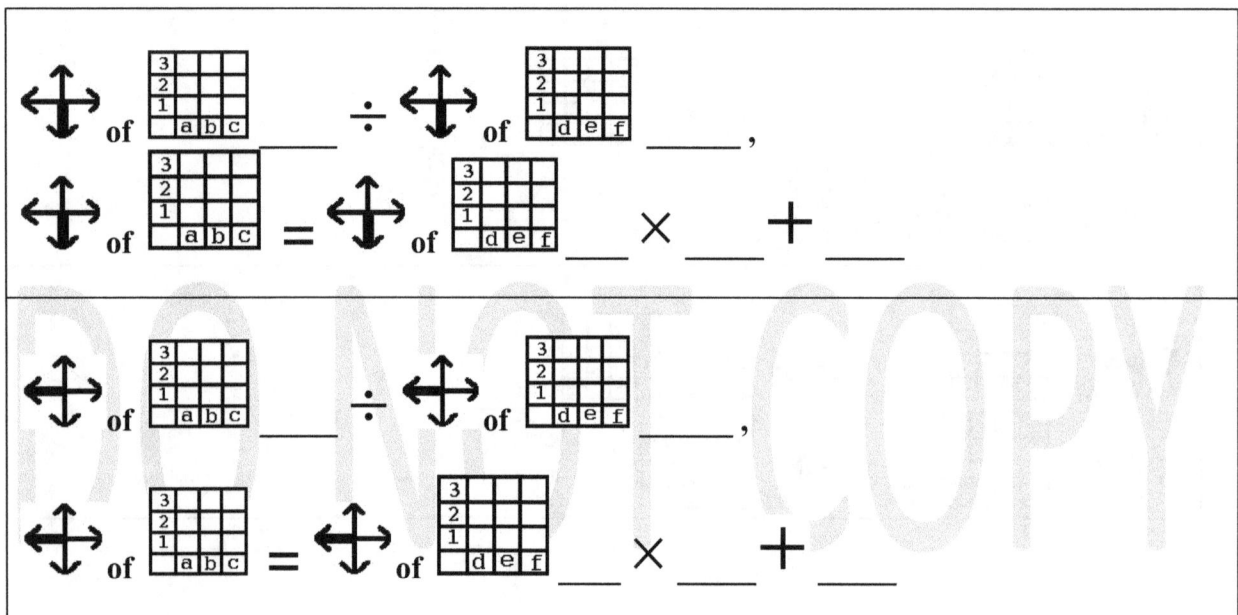

Mom! I Learn Division Using Math-Chess-Puzzles Connection

Division and remainder

3	10	30	15
2	20	40	25
1	5	45	45
	a	b	c

You are at b2 = ☐.

3	1	2	3
2	4	5	6
1	7	8	9
	d	e	f

You are at e2 = ☐.

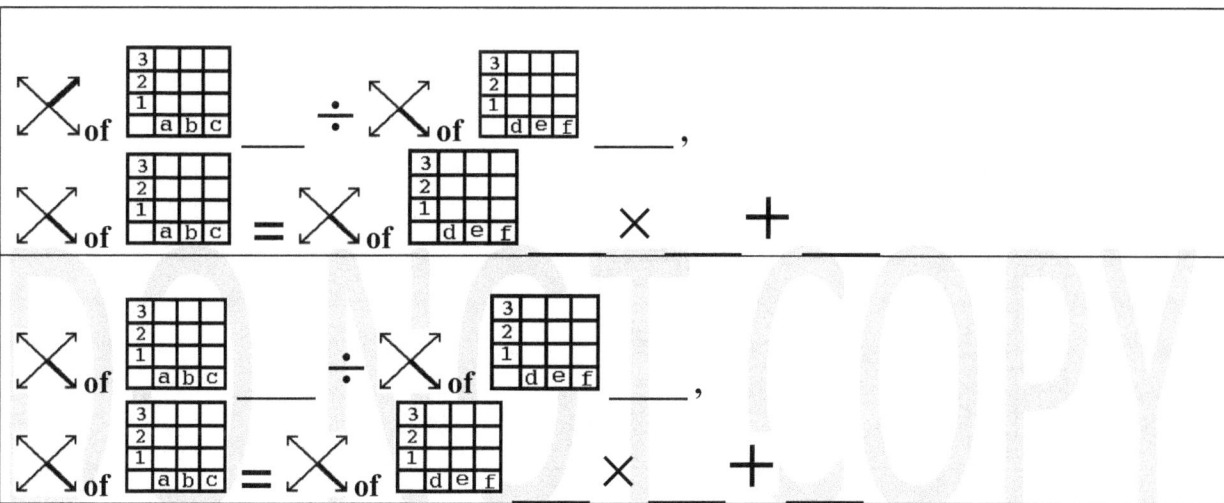

Mom! I Learn Division Using Math-Chess-Puzzles Connection

Division and remainder

3	10	30	15
2	20	40	25
1	5	45	45
	a	b	c

You are at b2 = ☐.

3	1	2	3
2	4	5	6
1	7	8	9
	d	e	f

You are at e2 = ☐.

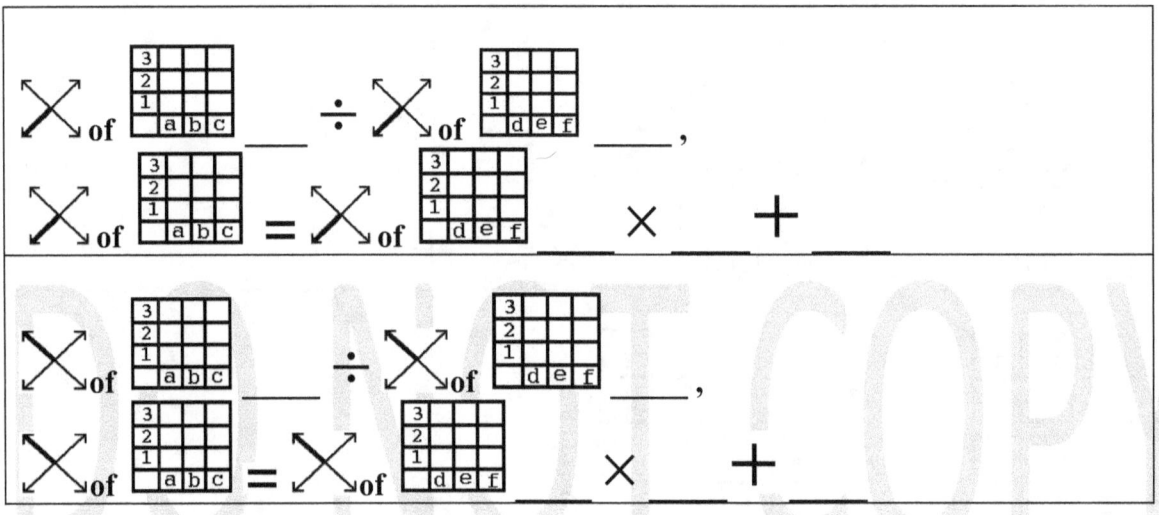

Mom! I Learn Division Using Math-Chess-Puzzles Connection

Ho Math Chess　何数棋谜　妈!我会棋谜式除法啦!

Frank Ho, Amanda Ho © 2004 – 2020, all rights reserved.

Student's Name _____　　Date _____

Division and remainder

3	12	54	24
2	48	6	36
1	18	30	42
	a	b	c

You are at b2 = ☐.

3	5	2	3
2	4	6	6
1	7	8	9
	d	e	f

You are at e2 = ☐.

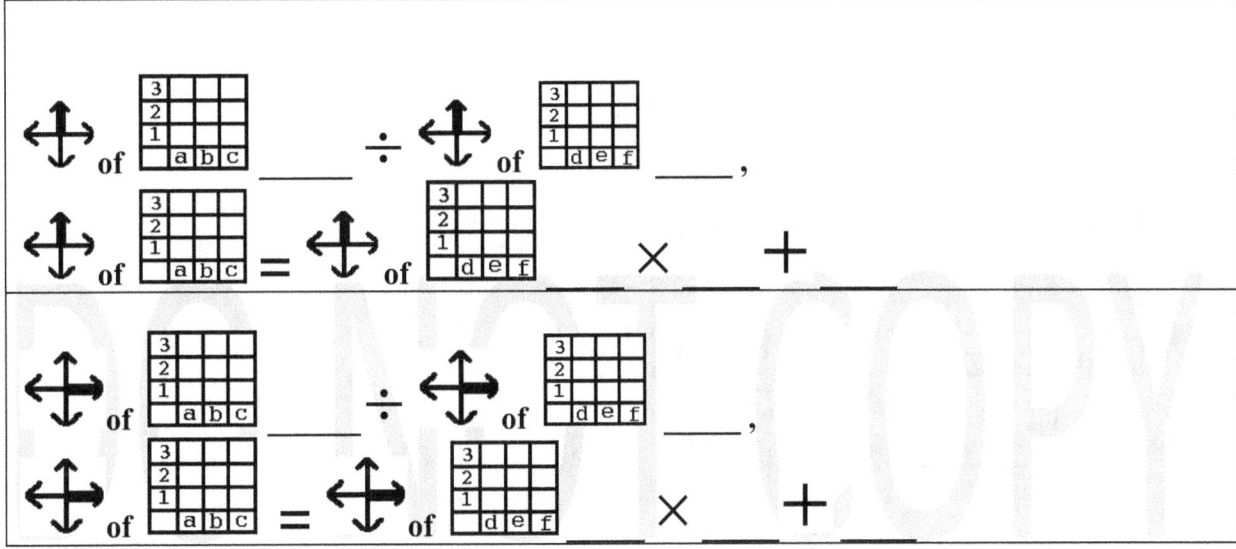

Mom! I Learn Division Using Math-Chess-Puzzles Connection

Ho Math Chess 何数棋谜 妈!我会棋谜式除法啦!

Frank Ho, Amanda Ho © 2004 − 2020, all rights reserved.

Student's Name _____ Date _____

Division and remainder

3	12	54	24
2	48	6	36
1	18	30	42
	a	b	c

You are at b2 = ☐.

3	5	2	3
2	4	6	6
1	7	8	9
	d	e	f

You are at e2 = ☐.

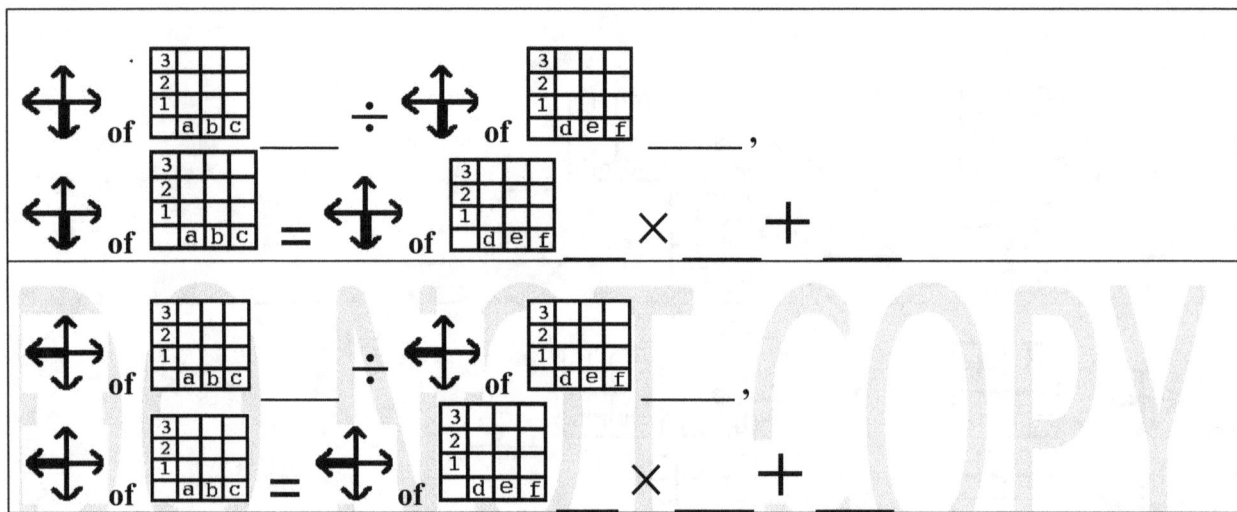

Page 88

Mom! I Learn Division Using Math-Chess-Puzzles Connection

Ho Math Chess 何数棋谜 妈!我会棋谜式除法啦!

Frank Ho, Amanda Ho © 2004 − 2020, all rights reserved.

Student's Name _____ Date _____

Division and remainder

3	12	54	24
2	48	6	36
1	18	30	42
	a	b	c

You are at b2 = ☐.

3	5	2	3
2	4	6	6
1	7	8	9
	d	e	f

You are at e2 = ☐.

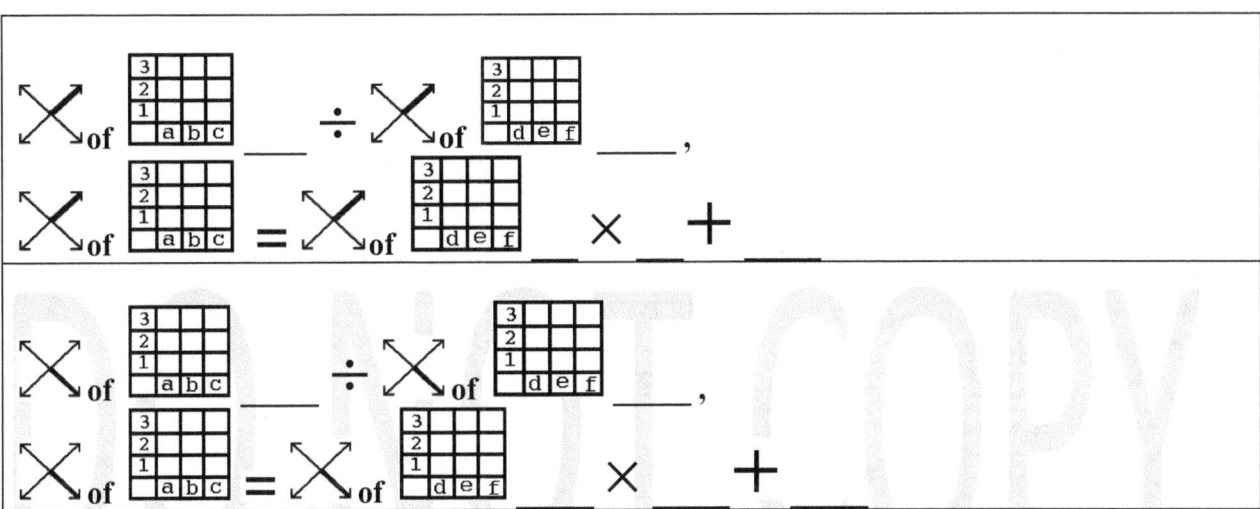

Page 89

Mom! I Learn Division Using Math-Chess-Puzzles Connection

Ho Math Chess 何数棋谜 妈!我会棋谜式除法啦!

Frank Ho, Amanda Ho © 2004 – 2020, all rights reserved.

Student's Name _____ Date _____

Division and remainder

3	12	54	24
2	48	6	36
1	18	30	42
	a	b	c

You are at b2 = ☐.

3	5	2	3
2	4	6	6
1	7	8	9
	d	e	f

You are at e2 = ☐.

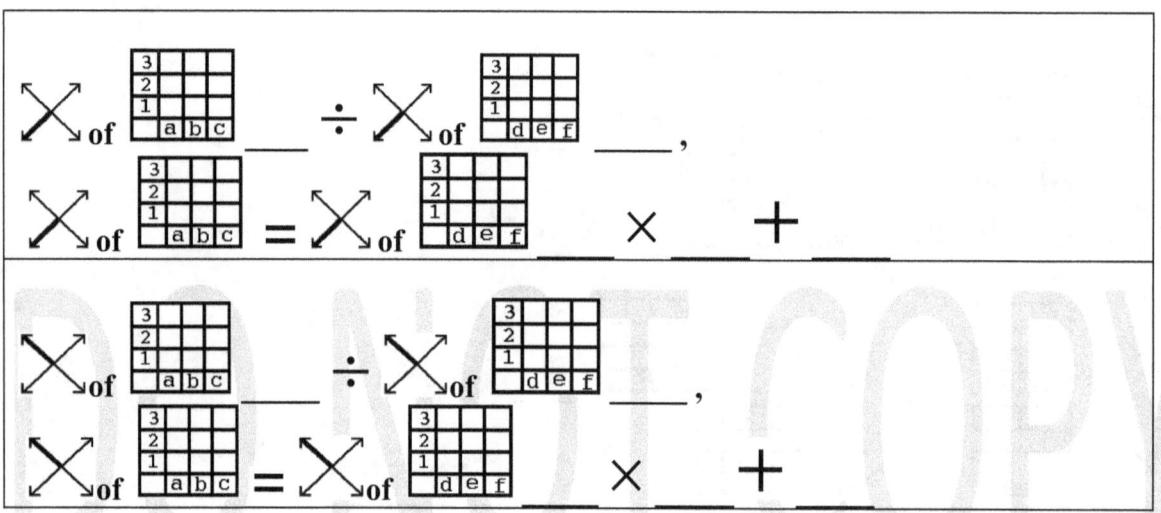

Mom! I Learn Division Using Math-Chess-Puzzles Connection

Ho Math Chess 何数棋谜 妈!我会棋谜式除法啦!

Frank Ho, Amanda Ho © 2004 − 2020, all rights reserved.

Student's Name _____   Date _____

Division and remainder

3	14	35	7
2	28	40	21
1	56	49	42
	a	b	c

You are at b2 = ☐.

3	1	2	3
2	4	7	6
1	5	8	9
	d	e	f

You are at e2 = ☐.

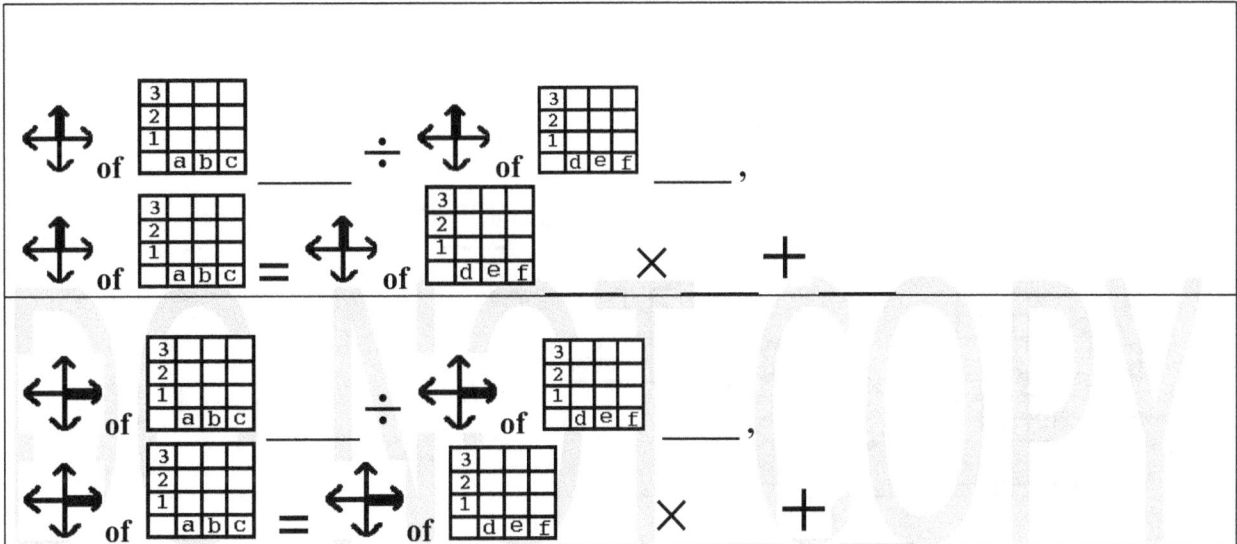

Page 91

Mom! I Learn Division Using Math-Chess-Puzzles Connection

Division and remainder

3	14	35	7
2	28	40	21
1	56	49	42
	a	b	c

You are at b2 = ☐.

3	1	2	3
2	4	7	6
1	5	8	9
	d	e	f

You are at e2 = ☐.

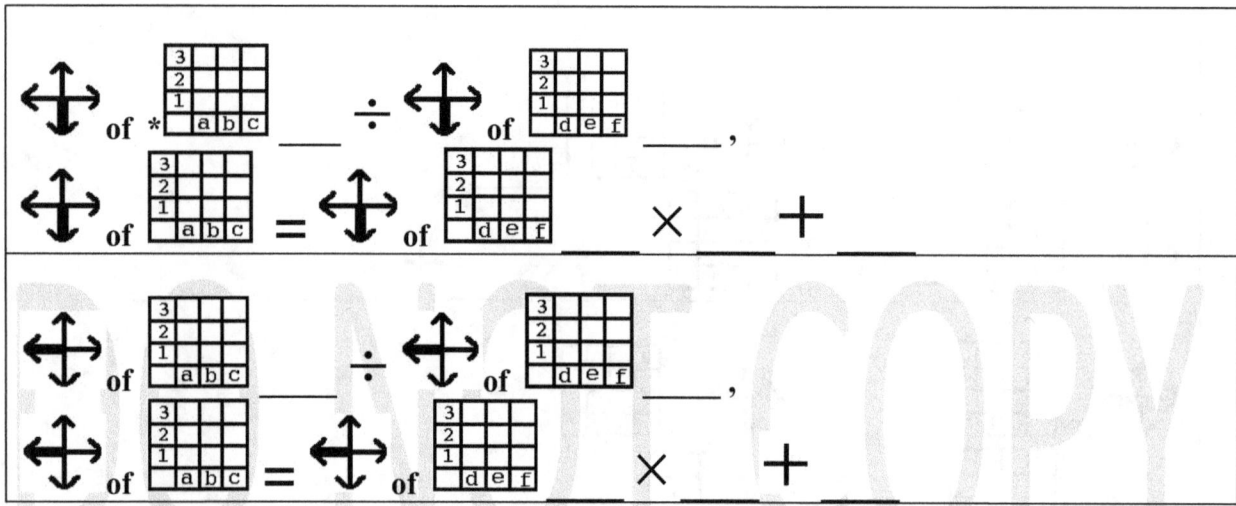

Mom! I Learn Division Using Math-Chess-Puzzles Connection

Ho Math Chess   何数棋谜   妈!我会棋谜式除法啦!

Frank Ho, Amanda Ho © 2004 – 2020, all rights reserved.

Student's Name _____   Date _____

Division and remainder

3	14	35	7
2	28	40	21
1	56	49	42
	a	b	c

You are at b2 = ☐.

3	1	2	3
2	4	7	6
1	5	8	9
	d	e	f

You are at e2 = ☐.

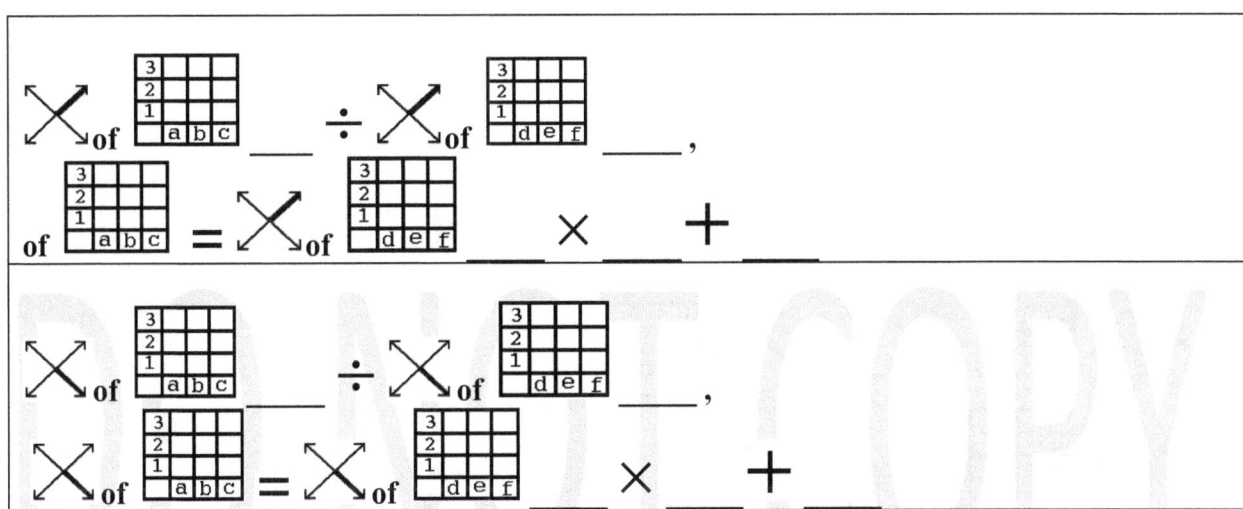

Page 93

Mom! I Learn Division Using Math-Chess-Puzzles Connection

Ho Math Chess 何数棋谜 妈!我会棋谜式除法啦!

Frank Ho, Amanda Ho © 2004 – 2020, all rights reserved.

Student's Name _____ Date _____

Division and remainder

3	14	35	7
2	28	40	21
1	56	49	42
	a	b	c

You are at b2 = ☐.

3	1	2	3
2	4	7	6
1	5	8	9
	d	e	f

You are at e2 = ☐.

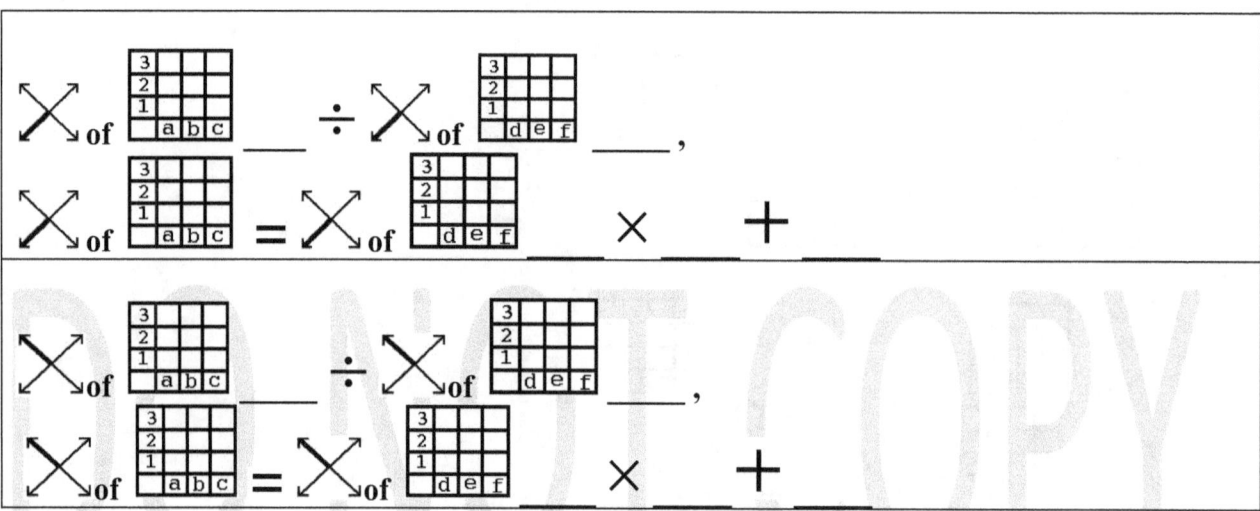

Page 94

Mom! I Learn Division Using Math-Chess-Puzzles Connection

Ho Math Chess 何数棋谜 妈!我会棋谜式除法啦!

Frank Ho, Amanda Ho © 2004 − 2020, all rights reserved.

Student's Name _____ Date _____

Division and remainder

3	24	32	56
2	16	40	64
1	8	72	48
	a	b	c

You are at b2 = ☐.

3	1	2	3
2	4	8	6
1	7	5	9
	d	e	f

You are at e2 = ☐.

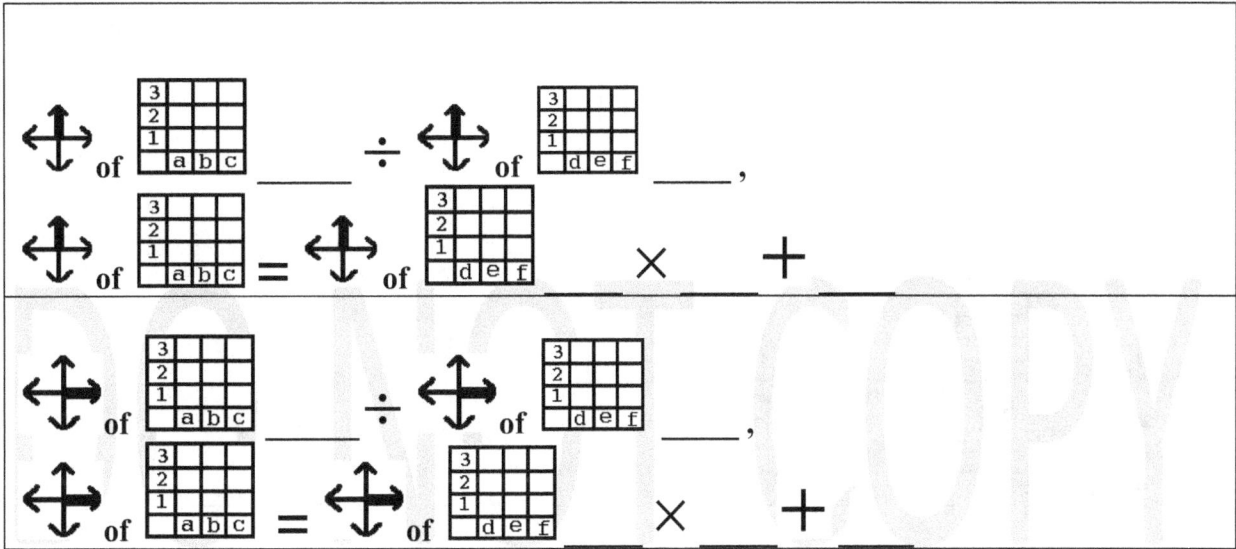

Page 95

Mom! I Learn Division Using Math-Chess-Puzzles Connection

Student's Name _____ Date _____

Division and remainder

3	24	32	56
2	16	40	64
1	8	72	48
	a	b	c

You are at b2 = ☐.

3	1	2	3
2	4	8	6
1	7	5	9
	d	e	f

You are at e2 = ☐.

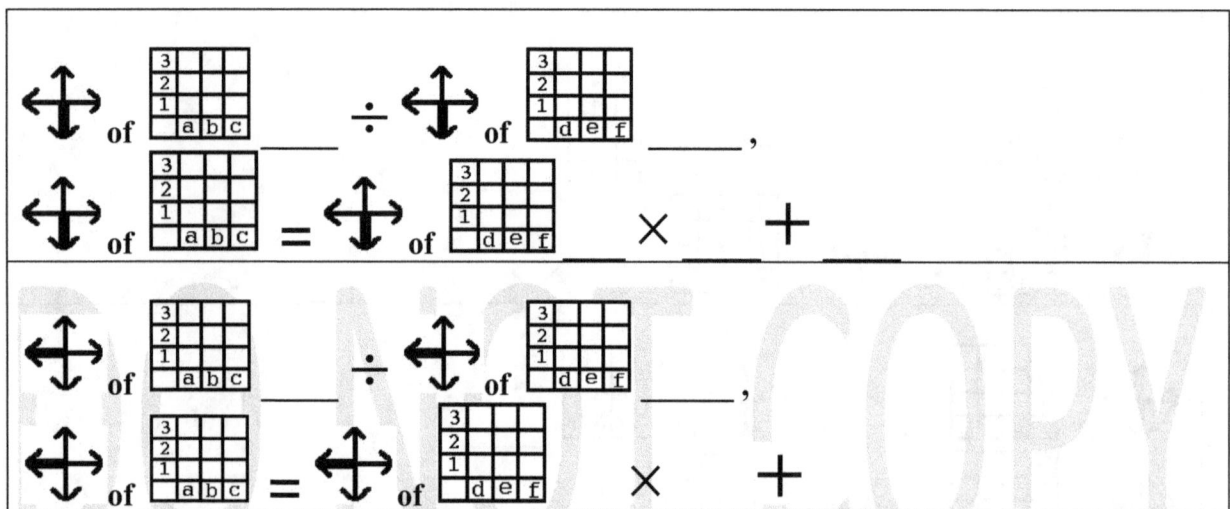

Mom! I Learn Division Using Math-Chess-Puzzles Connection

Ho Math Chess 何数棋谜 妈!我会棋谜式除法啦!

Frank Ho, Amanda Ho © 2004 − 2020, all rights reserved.

Student's Name _____ Date _____

Division and remainder

3	24	32	56
2	16	40	64
1	8	72	48
	a	b	c

You are at b2 = ☐.

3	1	2	3
2	4	8	6
1	7	5	9
	d	e	f

You are at e2 = ☐.

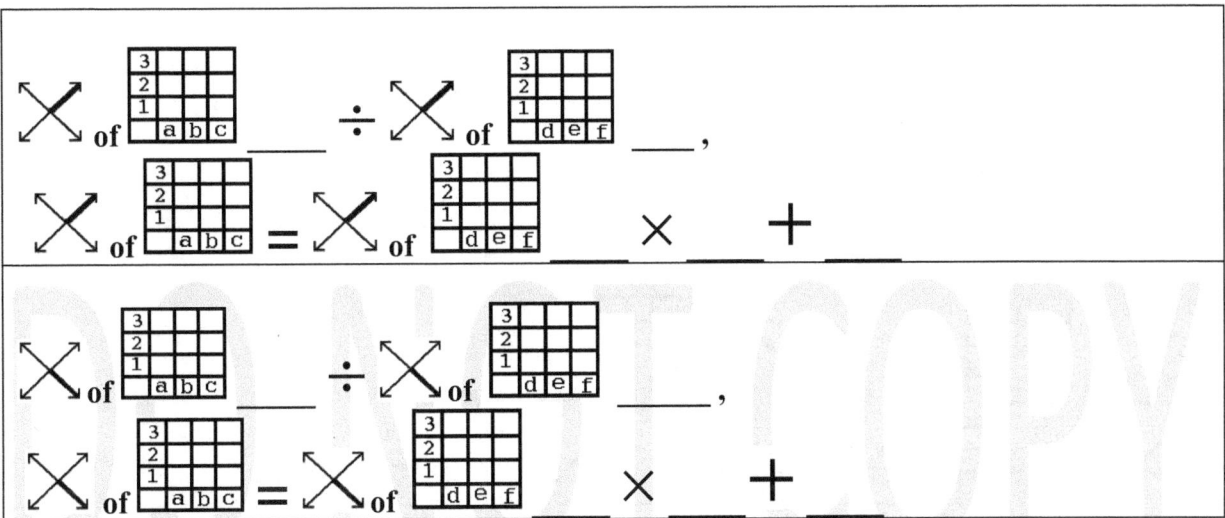

Page 97

Mom! I Learn Division Using Math-Chess-Puzzles Connection

Division and remainder

3	24	32	56
2	16	40	64
1	8	72	48
	a	b	c

You are at b2 = ☐.

3	1	2	3
2	4	8	6
1	7	5	9
	d	e	f

You are at e2 = ☐.

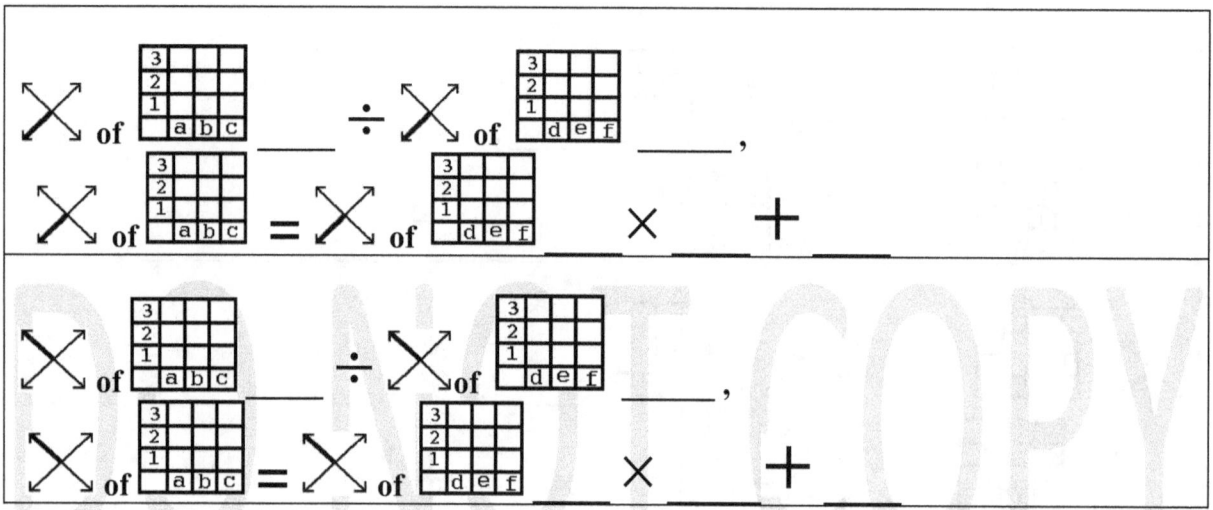

Mom! I Learn Division Using Math-Chess-Puzzles Connection

Ho Math Chess 何数棋谜 妈!我会棋谜式除法啦!

Frank Ho, Amanda Ho © 2004 − 2020, all rights reserved.

Student's Name _____ Date _____

Division and remainder

3	9	72	18
2	54	81	27
1	36	45	63
	a	b	c

You are at b2 = ☐.

3	1	2	3
2	4	9	6
1	7	8	5
	d	e	f

You are at e2 = ☐.

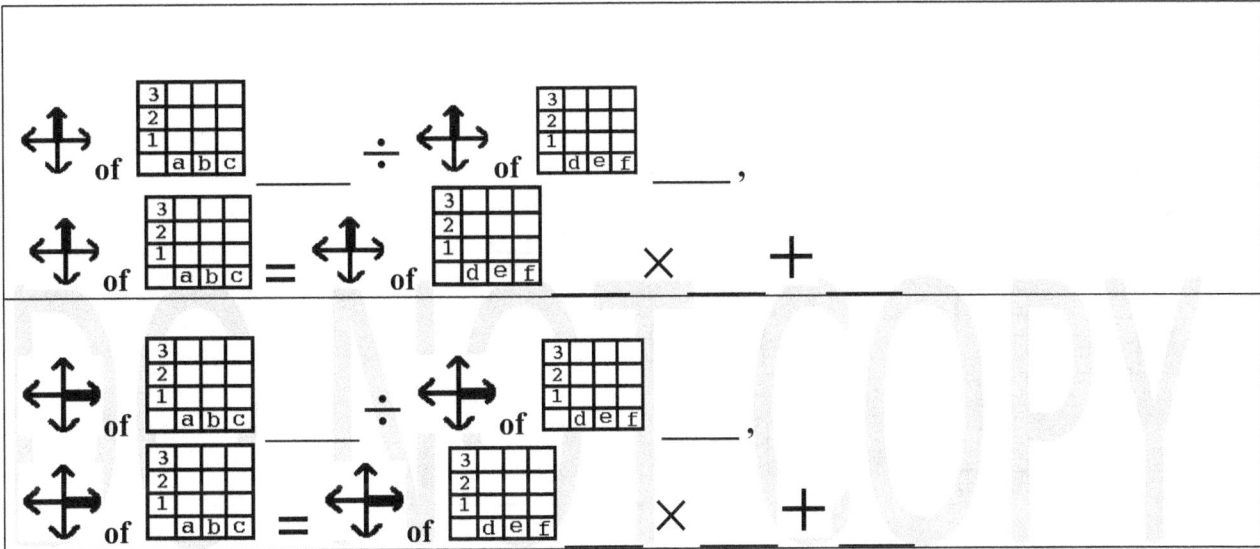

Mom! I Learn Division Using Math-Chess-Puzzles Connection

Division and remainder

3	9	72	18
2	54	81	27
1	36	45	63
	a	b	c

You are at b2 = ☐.

3	1	2	3
2	4	9	6
1	7	8	5
	d	e	f

You are at e2 = ☐.

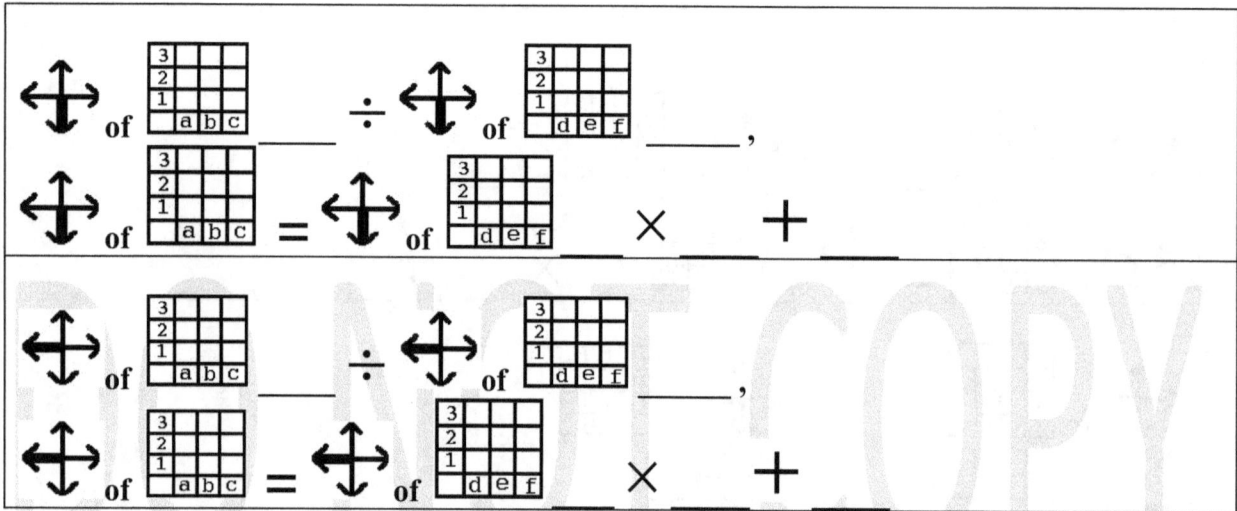

Mom! I Learn Division Using Math-Chess-Puzzles Connection

Ho Math Chess　何数棋谜　妈!我会棋谜式除法啦!

Frank Ho, Amanda Ho © 2004 − 2020, all rights reserved.

Student's Name _____   Date _____

Division and remainder

3	9	72	18
2	54	81	27
1	36	45	63
	a	b	c

You are at b2 = ☐.

3	1	2	3
2	4	9	6
1	7	8	5
	d	e	f

You are at e2 = ☐.

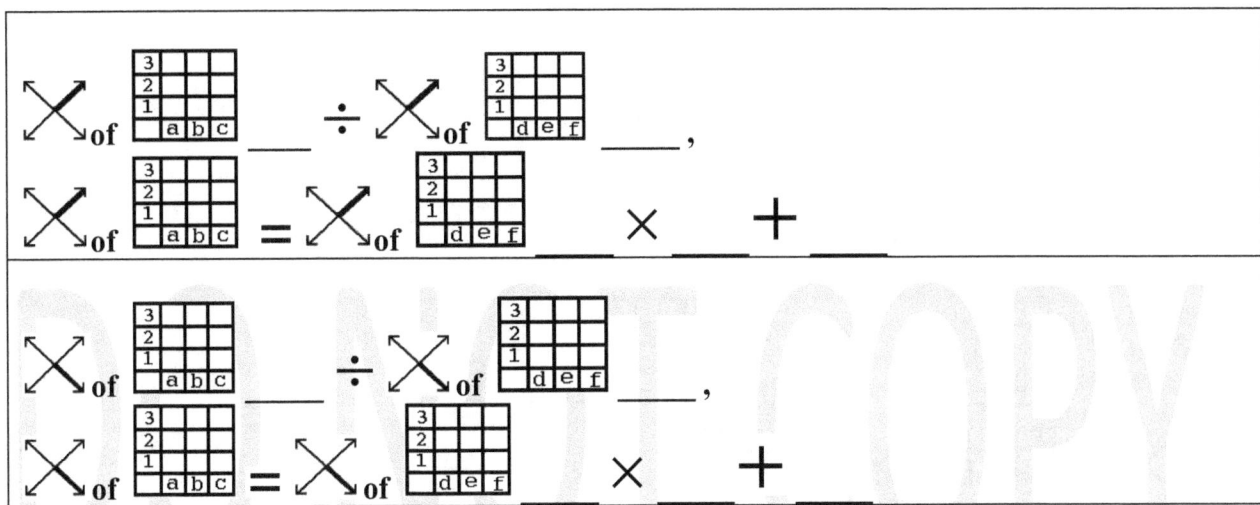

Mom! I Learn Division Using Math-Chess-Puzzles Connection

Ho Math Chess 何数棋谜 妈!我会棋谜式除法啦!

Frank Ho, Amanda Ho © 2004 – 2020, all rights reserved.

Student's Name _____ Date _____

Division and remainder

3	9	72	18
2	54	81	27
1	36	45	63
	a	b	c

You are at b2 = ☐.

3	1	2	3
2	4	9	6
1	7	8	5
	d	e	f

You are at e2 = ☐.

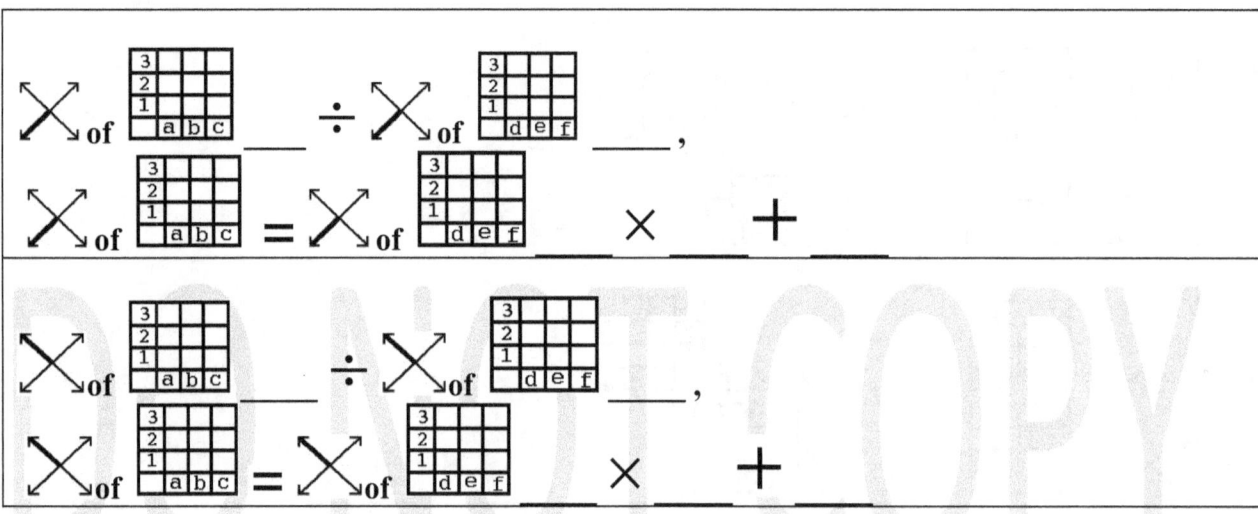

Mom! I Learn Division Using Math-Chess-Puzzles Connection

Division and remainder

3	8	32	16
2	20	4	24
1	12	28	36
	a	b	c

You are at b2 = ☐.

3	1	2	3
2	5	4	6
1	7	8	9
	d	e	f

You are at e2 = ☐.

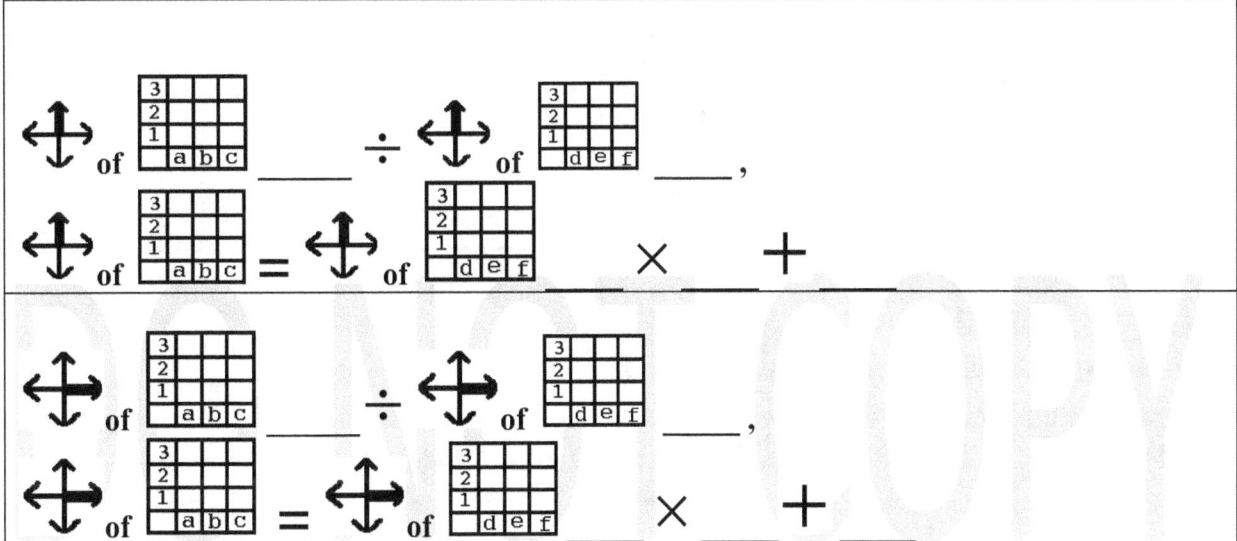

Mom! I Learn Division Using Math-Chess-Puzzles Connection

Ho Math Chess 何数棋谜 妈!我会棋谜式除法啦!

Frank Ho, Amanda Ho © 2004 − 2020, all rights reserved.

Student's Name _____ Date _____

Division and remainder

3	8	32	16
2	20	4	24
1	12	28	36
	a	b	c

You are at b2 = ☐.

3	1	2	3
2	5	4	6
1	7	8	9
	d	e	f

You are at e2 = ☐.

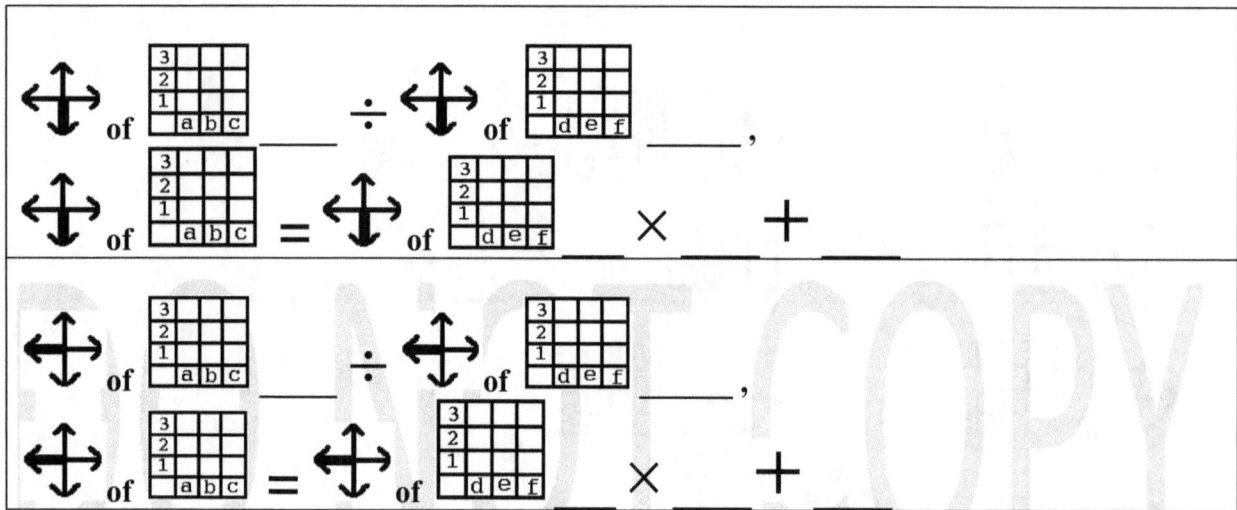

Page 104

Mom! I Learn Division Using Math-Chess-Puzzles Connection

Ho Math Chess 何数棋谜 妈!我会棋谜式除法啦!

Frank Ho, Amanda Ho © 2004 − 2020, all rights reserved.

Student's Name _____ Date _____

Division and remainder

3	8	32	16
2	20	4	24
1	12	28	36
	a	b	c

You are at b2 = ☐.

3	1	2	3
2	5	4	6
1	7	8	9
	d	e	f

You are at e2 = ☐.

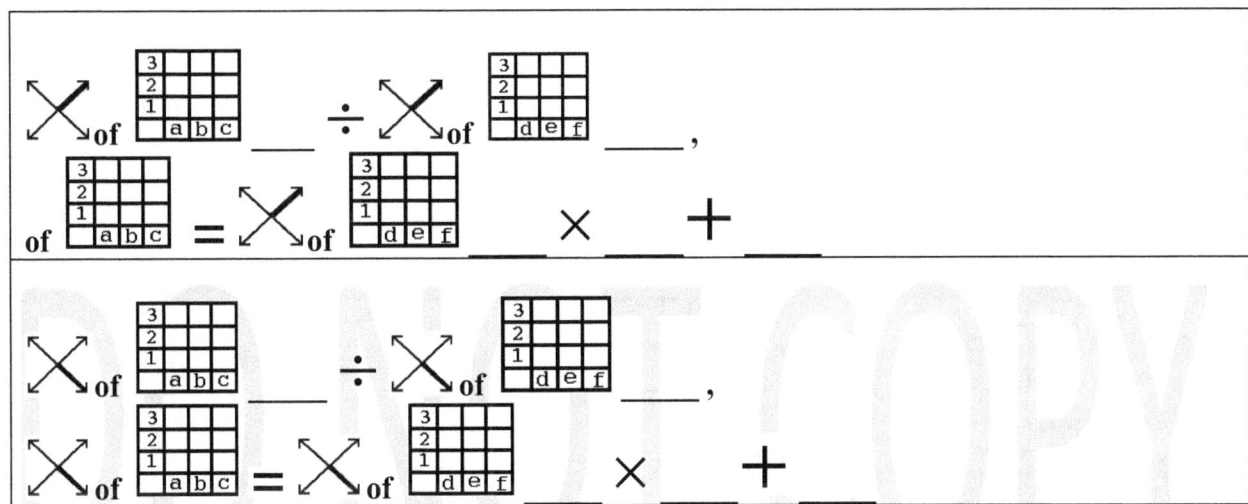

Page 105

Mom! I Learn Division Using Math-Chess-Puzzles Connection

Ho Math Chess 何数棋谜 妈!我会棋谜式除法啦!

Frank Ho, Amanda Ho © 2004 – 2020, all rights reserved.

Student's Name _____ Date _____

Division and remainder

3	8	32	16
2	20	4	24
1	12	28	36
	a	b	c

You are at b2 = ☐.

3	1	2	3
2	5	4	6
1	7	8	9
	d	e	f

You are at e2 = ☐.

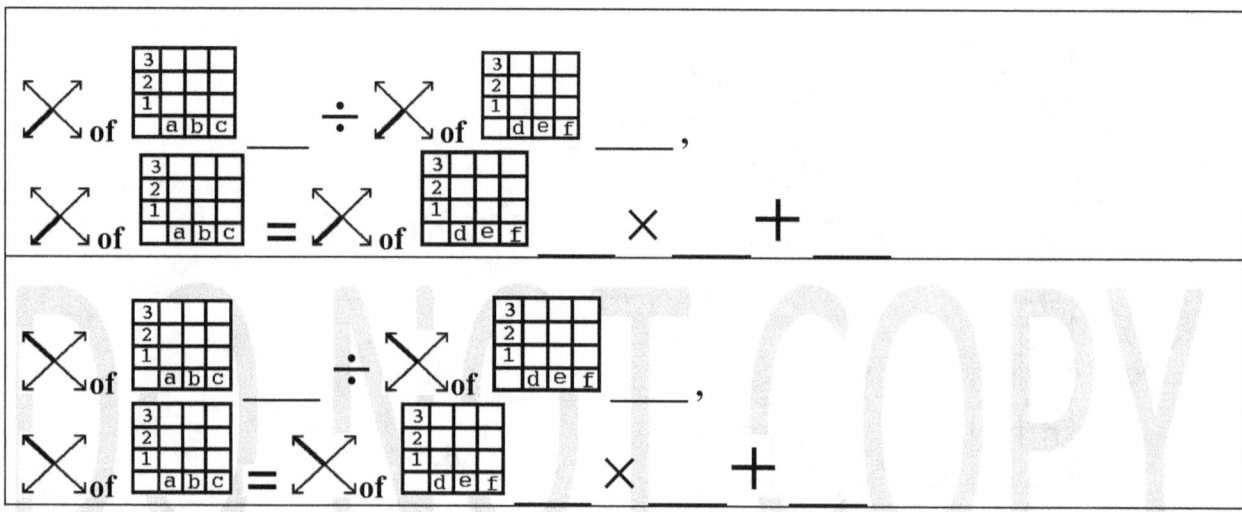

Page 106

Mom! I Learn Division Using Math-Chess-Puzzles Connection

Ho Math Chess 何数棋谜 妈!我会棋谜式除法啦!

Frank Ho, Amanda Ho © 2004 − 2020, all rights reserved.

Student's Name _____ Date _____

Division and remainder

3	6	12	15
2	18	3	21
1	27	24	9
	a	b	c

You are at b2 = ☐.

3	1	2	5
2	4	3	6
1	7	8	9
	d	e	f

You are at e2 = ☐.

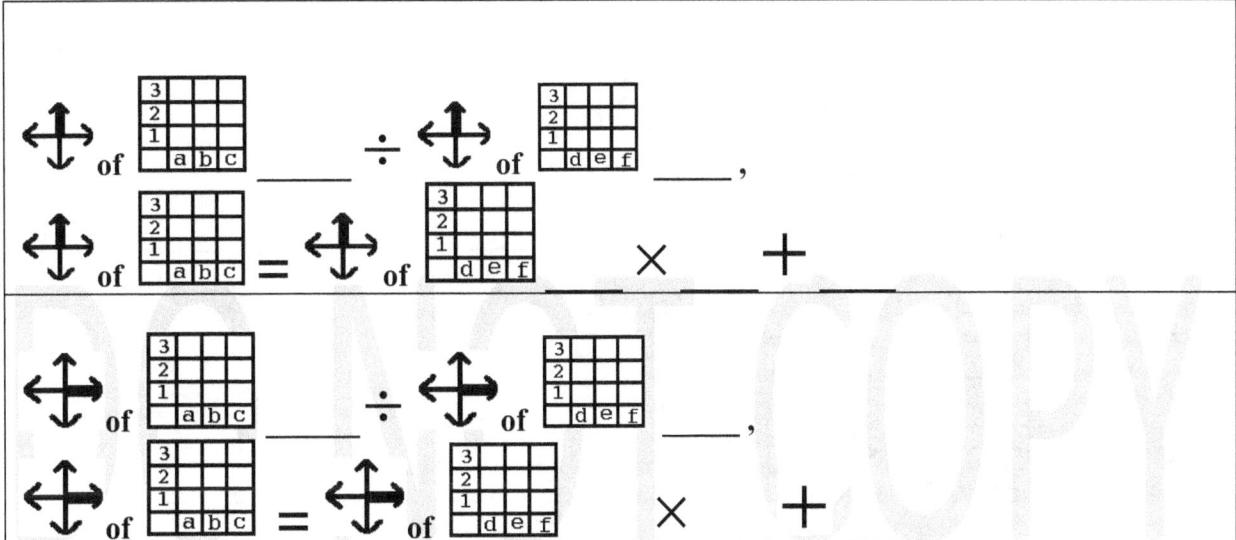

Page 107

Mom! I Learn Division Using Math-Chess-Puzzles Connection

Division and remainder

3	6	12	15
2	18	3	21
1	27	24	9
	a	b	c

You are at b2 = ☐.

3	1	2	5
2	4	3	6
1	7	8	9
	d	e	f

You are at e2 = ☐.

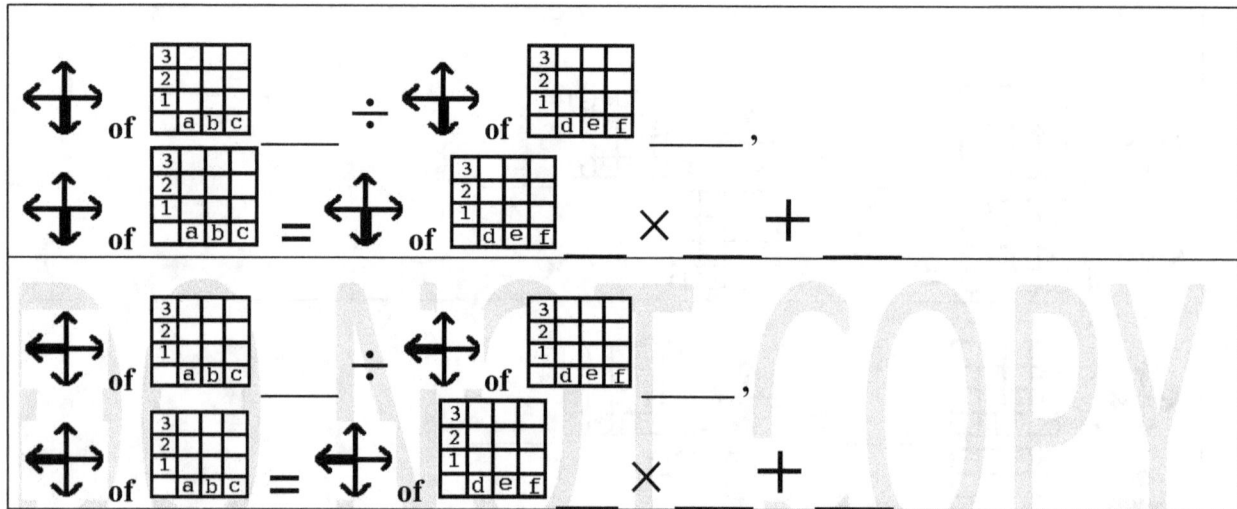

Mom! I Learn Division Using Math-Chess-Puzzles Connection

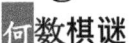 Math Chess　　何数棋谜　妈!我会棋谜式除法啦!

Frank Ho, Amanda Ho © 2004 – 2020, all rights reserved.

Student's Name _____　　Date _____

Division and remainder

3	6	12	15
2	18	3	21
1	27	24	9
	a	b	c

You are at b2 = ☐.

3	1	2	5
2	4	3	6
1	7	8	9
	d	e	f

You are at e2 = ☐.

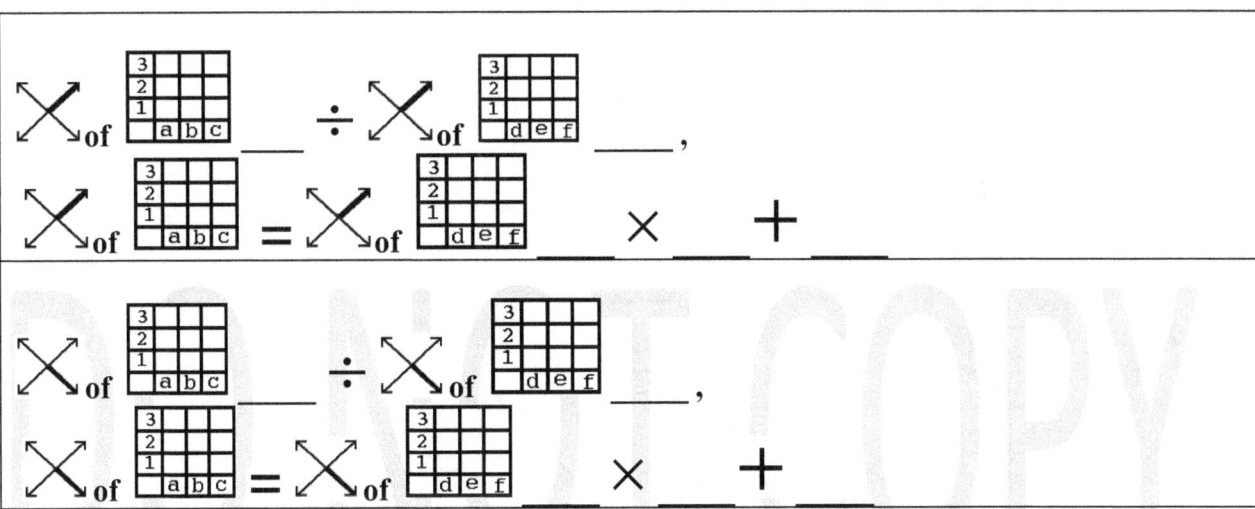

Mom! I Learn Division Using Math-Chess-Puzzles Connection

Ho Math Chess 何数棋谜 妈!我会棋谜式除法啦!

Frank Ho, Amanda Ho © 2004 – 2020, all rights reserved.

Student's Name _____ Date _____

Division and remainder

3	6	12	15
2	18	3	21
1	27	24	9
	a	b	c

You are at b2 = ☐.

3	1	2	5
2	4	3	6
1	7	8	9
	d	e	f

You are at e2 = ☐.

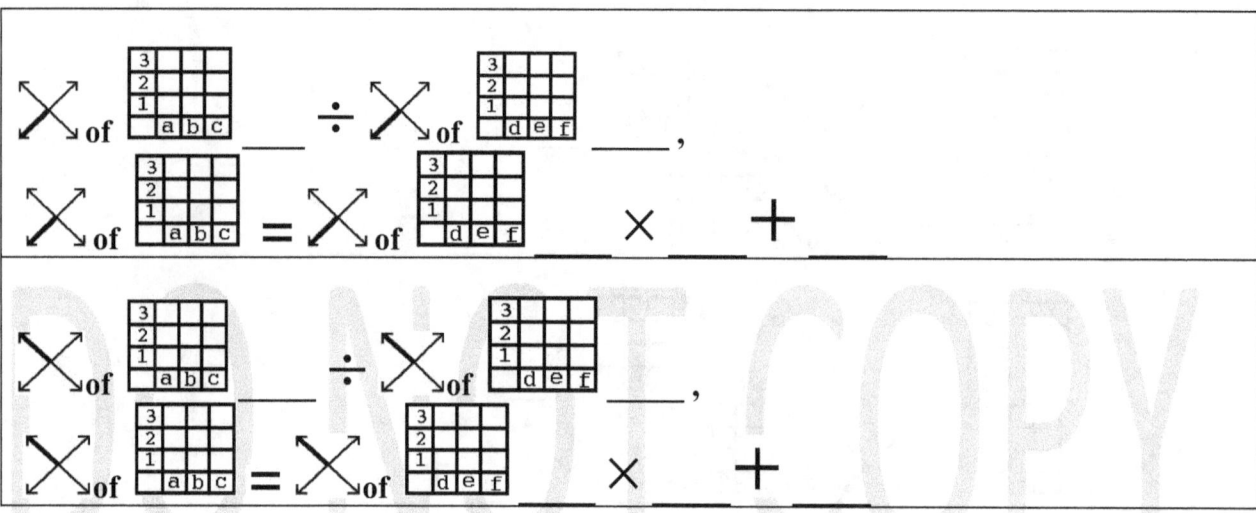

Page 110

Mom! I Learn Division Using Math-Chess-Puzzles Connection

Ho Math Chess 何数棋谜 妈!我会棋谜式除法啦!

Frank Ho, Amanda Ho © 2004 − 2020, all rights reserved.

Student's Name _____ Date _____

Division with minimum quotient and no remainder

3	1	2	3
2	4	5	6
1	7	8	9
	a	b	c

3	19	15	13
2	12	11	18
1	14	16	12
	d	e	f

d3 ÷ a3 = $\underline{19}$ ÷ $\underline{3}$ ($\underline{19}$ − $\underline{1}$) ÷ $\underline{3}$ = $\underline{18}$ ÷ $\underline{3}$ = $\underline{6}$ with no remainder.

e3 ÷ b3 = ___ ÷ ___ (___ − ___) ÷ ___ = ___ ÷ ___ = ___ with no remainder.

f3 ÷ c3 = ___ ÷ ___ (___ − ___) ÷ ___ = ___ ÷ ___ = ___ with no remainder.

d2 ÷ a2 = ___ ÷ ___ (___ − ___) ÷ ___ = ___ ÷ ___ = ___ with no remainder.

d2 ÷ a2 = ___ ÷ ___ (___ − ___) ÷ ___ = ___ ÷ ___ = ___ with no remainder.

e2 ÷ b2 = ___ ÷ ___ (___ − ___) ÷ ___ = ___ ÷ ___ = ___ with no remainder.

f2 ÷ c2 = ___ ÷ ___ (___ − ___) ÷ ___ = ___ ÷ ___ = ___ with no remainder.

d1 ÷ a1 = ___ ÷ ___ (___ − ___) ÷ ___ = ___ ÷ ___ = ___ with no remainder.

e1 ÷ b1 = ___ ÷ ___ (___ − ___) ÷ ___ = ___ ÷ ___ = ___ with no remainder.

f1 ÷ c1 = ___ ÷ ___ (___ − ___) ÷ ___ = ___ ÷ ___ = ___ with no remainder.

Mom! I Learn Division Using Math-Chess-Puzzles Connection

Ho Math Chess 何数棋谜   妈!我会棋谜式除法啦!

Frank Ho, Amanda Ho © 2004 − 2020, all rights reserved.

Student's Name _____   Date _____

Division with minimum quotient and no remainder

3	1	2	3
2	4	5	6
1	7	8	9
	a	B	c

3	14	19	17
2	15	11	13
1	18	12	16
	d	e	f

$d3 \div a3$ = __14__ ÷ __1__ (__14__ − __13__) ÷ __1__ = __1__ ÷ __1__ = __1__ with no remainder.

$e3 \div b3$ = __19__ ÷ __2__ (__19__ − __17__) ÷ __2__ = __2__ ÷ __2__ = __1__ with no remainder.

$f3 \div c3$ = __17__ ÷ __3__ (__17__ − __14__) ÷ __3__ = __3__ ÷ __3__ = __1__ with no remainder.

Mom! I Learn Division Using Math-Chess-Puzzles Connection

Division and remainder

Reduce the following fractions.

1. $\frac{\cancel{2}^1}{\cancel{4}_2} = \frac{1}{2}$	2. $\frac{8}{10} = $ ___	3. $\frac{2}{6} = $ ___
4. $\frac{4}{14} = $ ___	5. $\frac{6}{16} = $ ___	6. $\frac{8}{18} = $ ___
7. $\frac{12}{14} = $ ___	8. $\frac{14}{16} = $ ___	9. $\frac{16}{18} = $ ___
10. $\frac{22}{24} = $ ___	11. $\frac{18}{20} = $ ___	12. $\frac{8}{22} = $ ___
13. $\frac{24}{34} = $ ___	14. $\frac{26}{36} = $ ___	15. $\frac{28}{38} = $ ___
16. $\frac{16}{46} = $ ___	17. $\frac{14}{44} = $ ___	18. $\frac{24}{46} = $ ___
19. $\frac{10}{52} = $ ___	20. $\frac{16}{82} = $ ___	21. $\frac{18}{76} = $ ___

Mom! I Learn Division Using Math-Chess-Puzzles Connection

Ho Math Chess 何数棋谜 妈!我会棋谜式除法啦!

Frank Ho, Amanda Ho © 2004 − 2020, all rights reserved.

Student's Name _____ Date _____

Reduce the following fractions.

1. $\dfrac{3}{9} =$ ___		2. $\dfrac{12}{15} =$ ___		3. $\dfrac{9}{12} =$ ___	
4. $\dfrac{6}{15} =$ ___		5. $\dfrac{12}{21} =$ ___		6. $\dfrac{15}{24} =$ ___	
7. $\dfrac{18}{33} =$ ___		8. $\dfrac{15}{36} =$ ___		9. $\dfrac{15}{42} =$ ___	
10. $\dfrac{27}{30} =$ ___		11. $\dfrac{18}{57} =$ ___		12. $\dfrac{21}{63} =$ ___	
13. $\dfrac{36}{63} =$ ___		14. $\dfrac{24}{51} =$ ___		15. $\dfrac{24}{45} =$ ___	
16. $\dfrac{27}{57} =$ ___		17. $\dfrac{39}{81} =$ ___		18. $\dfrac{63}{78} =$ ___	

Mom! I Learn Division Using Math-Chess-Puzzles Connection

Ho Math Chess　何数棋谜　妈!我会棋谜式除法啦!

Frank Ho, Amanda Ho © 2004 – 2020, all rights reserved.

Student's Name _____	Date _____

Reduce the following fractions.

1. $\dfrac{5}{25} = $ _____

2. $\dfrac{10}{35} = $ _____

3. $\dfrac{15}{25} = $ _____

4. $\dfrac{15}{40} = $ _____

5. $\dfrac{25}{55} = $ _____

6. $\dfrac{10}{25} = $ _____

7. $\dfrac{25}{60} = $ _____

8. $\dfrac{30}{65} = $ _____

9. $\dfrac{30}{35} = $ _____

10. $\dfrac{15}{50} = $ _____

11. $\dfrac{20}{45} = $ _____

12. $\dfrac{35}{100} = $ _____

13. $\dfrac{30}{85} = $ _____

14. $\dfrac{35}{75} = $ _____

15. $\dfrac{50}{95} = $ _____

16. $\dfrac{40}{85} = $ _____

17. $\dfrac{55}{75} = $ _____

18. $\dfrac{60}{85} = $ _____

Mom! I Learn Division Using Math-Chess-Puzzles Connection

Ho Math Chess 何数棋谜 妈!我会棋谜式除法啦!

Frank Ho, Amanda Ho © 2004 – 2020, all rights reserved.

Student's Name _____ Date _____

Reduce the following fractions.

1. $\dfrac{7}{77} = $ _____

2. $\dfrac{21}{35} = $ _____

3. $\dfrac{21}{49} = $ _____

4. $\dfrac{14}{63} = $ _____

5. $\dfrac{14}{77} = $ _____

6. $\dfrac{28}{49} = $ _____

7. $\dfrac{56}{77} = $ _____

8. $\dfrac{35}{63} = $ _____

9. $\dfrac{28}{77} = $ _____

10. $\dfrac{42}{91} = $ _____

11. $\dfrac{49}{84} = $ _____

12. $\dfrac{77}{84} = $ _____

13. $\dfrac{35}{98} = $ _____

14. $\dfrac{42}{91} = $ _____

15. $\dfrac{35}{84} = $ _____

16. $\dfrac{63}{77} = $ _____

17. $\dfrac{63}{98} = $ _____

18. $\dfrac{49}{84} = $ _____

Reduce the following fractions.

1. $\dfrac{10}{100} = $ _____

2. $\dfrac{20}{50} = $ _____

3. $\dfrac{30}{40} = $ _____

4. $\dfrac{70}{200} = $ _____

5. $\dfrac{40}{150} = $ _____

6. $\dfrac{50}{160} = $ _____

7. $\dfrac{20}{230} = $ _____

8. $\dfrac{120}{350} = $ _____

9. $\dfrac{100}{1000} = $ _____

10. $\dfrac{80}{130} = $ _____

11. $\dfrac{60}{700} = $ _____

12. $\dfrac{160}{900} = $ _____

13. $\dfrac{200}{900} = $ _____

14. $\dfrac{300}{800} = $ _____

15. $\dfrac{400}{700} = $ _____

16. $\dfrac{600}{1100} = $ _____

17. $\dfrac{700}{1000} = $ _____

18. $\dfrac{400}{9000} = $ _____

Mom! I Learn Division Using Math-Chess-Puzzles Connection

Ho Math Chess 何数棋谜 妈!我会棋谜式除法啦!

Frank Ho, Amanda Ho © 2004 − 2020, all rights reserved.

Student's Name _____ Date _____

Reduce the following fractions.

1. $\dfrac{6}{15} = $ _____
2. $\dfrac{8}{14} = $ _____
3. $\dfrac{12}{21} = $ _____

4. $\dfrac{16}{22} = $ _____
5. $\dfrac{12}{22} = $ _____
6. $\dfrac{8}{26} = $ _____

7. $\dfrac{6}{28} = $ _____
8. $\dfrac{12}{15} = $ _____
9. $\dfrac{4}{18} = $ _____

10. $\dfrac{12}{21} = $ _____
11. $\dfrac{15}{24} = $ _____
12. $\dfrac{8}{26} = $ _____

13. $\dfrac{18}{57} = $ _____
14. $\dfrac{14}{36} = $ _____
15. $\dfrac{1}{26} = $ _____

16. $\dfrac{18}{39} = $ _____
17. $\dfrac{15}{36} = $ _____
18. $\dfrac{24}{51} = $ _____

Mom! I Learn Division Using Math-Chess-Puzzles Connection

Ho Math Chess 何数棋谜 妈!我会棋谜式除法啦!

Frank Ho, Amanda Ho © 2004 − 2020, all rights reserved.

Student's Name _____ Date _____

Reduce the following fractions.

1. $\dfrac{6}{9} = $ _____

2. $\dfrac{10}{25} = $ _____

3. $\dfrac{12}{45} = $ _____

4. $\dfrac{15}{25} = $ _____

5. $\dfrac{12}{15} = $ _____

6. $\dfrac{15}{25} = $ _____

7. $\dfrac{10}{15} = $ _____

8. $\dfrac{15}{35} = $ _____

9. $\dfrac{15}{36} = $ _____

10. $\dfrac{30}{39} = $ _____

11. $\dfrac{30}{55} = $ _____

12. $\dfrac{9}{15} = $ _____

13. $\dfrac{20}{45} = $ _____

14. $\dfrac{21}{45} = $ _____

15. $\dfrac{42}{45} = $ _____

16. $\dfrac{45}{50} = $ _____

17. $\dfrac{45}{66} = $ _____

18. $\dfrac{25}{30} = $ _____

Mom! I Learn Division Using Math-Chess-Puzzles Connection

Ho Math Chess 何数棋谜 妈!我会棋谜式除法啦!

Frank Ho, Amanda Ho © 2004 – 2020, all rights reserved.

Student's Name _____ Date _____

Reduce the following fractions.

1. $\dfrac{35}{42} = $ _____

2. $\dfrac{49}{70} = $ _____

3. $\dfrac{25}{35} = $ _____

4. $\dfrac{15}{40} = $ _____

5. $\dfrac{28}{63} = $ _____

6. $\dfrac{35}{55} = $ _____

7. $\dfrac{70}{85} = $ _____

8. $\dfrac{56}{91} = $ _____

9. $\dfrac{30}{65} = $ _____

10. $\dfrac{35}{84} = $ _____

11. $\dfrac{30}{55} = $ _____

12. $\dfrac{45}{85} = $ _____

13. $\dfrac{40}{85} = $ _____

14. $\dfrac{65}{80} = $ _____

15. $\dfrac{84}{91} = $ _____

16. $\dfrac{63}{84} = $ _____

17. $\dfrac{63}{91} = $ _____

18. $\dfrac{70}{84} = $ _____

Mom! I Learn Division Using Math-Chess-Puzzles Connection

Ho Math Chess　何数棋谜　妈!我会棋谜式除法啦!

Frank Ho, Amanda Ho © 2004 – 2020, all rights reserved.

Student's Name _____ Date _____

Reduce the following fractions.

1. $\dfrac{15}{27}$ = _____

2. $\dfrac{20}{30}$ = _____

3. $\dfrac{24}{42}$ = _____

4. $\dfrac{20}{50}$ = _____

5. $\dfrac{45}{84}$ = _____

6. $\dfrac{10}{40}$ = _____

7. $\dfrac{36}{45}$ = _____

8. $\dfrac{30}{70}$ = _____

9. $\dfrac{39}{60}$ = _____

10. $\dfrac{50}{70}$ = _____

11. $\dfrac{60}{93}$ = _____

12. $\dfrac{40}{70}$ = _____

13. $\dfrac{48}{87}$ = _____

14. $\dfrac{30}{40}$ = _____

15. $\dfrac{20}{70}$ = _____

16. $\dfrac{27}{42}$ = _____

17. $\dfrac{30}{50}$ = _____

18. $\dfrac{30}{93}$ = _____

Mom! I Learn Division Using Math-Chess-Puzzles Connection

Ho Math Chess 何数棋谜 妈!我会棋谜式除法啦!

Frank Ho, Amanda Ho © 2004 – 2020, all rights reserved.

Student's Name _____ Date _____

dd divided by dd

3	17	19	14
2	18	23	12
1	13	15	11
	a	b	c

The original square is at b2.

	Long division	Dividend = ?	Division in fraction form
b2 ÷ ⤢ = 23 ÷ 14	$14\overline{)23}$ gives 1, remainder 9 $\begin{array}{r}1\\14\overline{)23}\\ \underline{14}\\ 9\end{array}$	b2 (23) = ⤢ (14) × _1_ + _9_	$\dfrac{b2}{⤢} = \dfrac{㉓}{⑭} = ① \dfrac{⑨}{⑭}$
b2 ÷ ⤢	$\overline{)}$	b2 (_) = ⤢ (_) × _ + _	$\dfrac{b2}{⤢} = \dfrac{○}{○} = ○ \dfrac{○}{○}$

No part of this publication can be copied, duplicated, or reproduced.

Mom! I Learn Division Using Math-Chess-Puzzles Connection

Ho Math Chess　何数棋谜　妈!我会棋谜式除法啦!

Frank Ho, Amanda Ho © 2004 – 2020, all rights reserved.

Student's Name _____ Date _____

dd divided by dd

3	17	19	14
2	18	32	12
1	13	15	11
	a	b	c

The original square is at b2.

	Long division	Dividend = ?	Division in fractional form
b2 ÷ ✥	⌐	b2 (__) = ✥ (__) × __ + __	$\frac{b2}{✥} = \frac{○}{○} = ○\frac{○}{○}$
b2 ÷ ✥	⌐	b2 (__) = ✥ (__) × __ + __	$\frac{b2}{✥} = \frac{○}{○} = ○\frac{○}{○}$

Mom! I Learn Division Using Math-Chess-Puzzles Connection

Ho Math Chess 何数棋谜 妈!我会棋谜式除法啦!

Frank Ho, Amanda Ho © 2004 – 2020, all rights reserved.

Student's Name _____ Date _____

dd divided by dd

3	17	19	14
2	18	32	12
1	13	15	11
	a	b	c

The original square is at b2.

	Long division	Dividend = ?	Division in fraction form
b2 ÷ ✕	⌐	b2 (__) = ✕ (__) ✕__ + __	$\dfrac{b2}{✕} = \dfrac{\bigcirc}{\bigcirc} = \bigcirc \dfrac{\bigcirc}{\bigcirc}$
b2 ÷ ✕	⌐	b2 (__) = ✕ (__) ✕__ + __	$\dfrac{b2}{✕} = \dfrac{\bigcirc}{\bigcirc} = \bigcirc \dfrac{\bigcirc}{\bigcirc}$

Page 124

Mom! I Learn Division Using Math-Chess-Puzzles Connection

Ho Math Chess   何数棋谜   妈!我会棋谜式除法啦!

Frank Ho, Amanda Ho © 2004 – 2020, all rights reserved.

Student's Name _____   Date _____

dd divided by dd

3	17	19	14
2	18	47	12
1	13	15	11
	A	b	c

The original square is at b2.

	Long division	Dividend = ?	Division in fractional form
b2 ÷ ✥	⌐	b2(__) = ✥ (__) × __ + __	$\frac{b2}{✥} = \frac{O}{O} = O\frac{O}{O}$
b2 ÷ ✥	⌐	b2(__) = ✥ (__) × __ + __	$\frac{b2}{✥} = \frac{O}{O} = O\frac{O}{O}$

Mom! I Learn Division Using Math-Chess-Puzzles Connection

Ho Math Chess 何数棋谜 妈!我会棋谜式除法啦!

Frank Ho, Amanda Ho © 2004 – 2020, all rights reserved.

Student's Name _____ Date _____

dd divided by dd

3	17	19	14
2	18	47	12
1	13	15	11
	a	b	C

The original square is at b2.

	Long division	Dividend = ?	Division in fraction form
b2 ÷ ✕	⟌	b2 (__) = ✕ (__) ✕ __ + __	$\dfrac{b2}{✕} = \dfrac{\bigcirc}{\bigcirc} = \bigcirc \dfrac{\bigcirc}{\bigcirc}$
b2 ÷ ✕	⟌	b2 (__) = ✕ (__) ✕ __ + __	$\dfrac{b2}{✕} = \dfrac{\bigcirc}{\bigcirc} = \bigcirc \dfrac{\bigcirc}{\bigcirc}$

Mom! I Learn Division Using Math-Chess-Puzzles Connection

Ho Math Chess 何数棋谜 妈!我会棋谜式除法啦!

Frank Ho, Amanda Ho © 2004 – 2020, all rights reserved.

Student's Name _____ Date _____

dd divided by dd

3	17	19	14
2	18	45	12
1	13	15	11
	a	b	c

The original square is at b2.

	Long division	Dividend = ?	Division in fractional form
b2 ÷ ⬌	⎯⎯⎯⎯	b2 (__) = ⬌ (__) × __ + __	$\frac{b2}{⬌} = \frac{○}{○} = ○\frac{○}{○}$
b2 ÷ ⬌	⎯⎯⎯⎯	b2 (__) = ⬌ (__) × __ + __	$\frac{b2}{⬌} = \frac{○}{○} = ○\frac{○}{○}$

Mom! I Learn Division Using Math-Chess-Puzzles Connection

Ho Math Chess 何数棋谜 妈!我会棋谜式除法啦!

Frank Ho, Amanda Ho © 2004 – 2020, all rights reserved.

Student's Name _____ Date _____

dd divided by dd

3	17	19	14
2	18	45	12
1	13	15	11
	a	b	c

The original square is at b2.

	Long division	Dividend = ?	Division in fraction form
b2 ÷ ⤢	⟌	b2 (__) = ⤢ (__) × __ + __	$\frac{b2}{⤢} = \frac{○}{○} = ○\frac{○}{○}$
b2 ÷ ⤢	⟌	b2 (__) = ⤢ (__) × __ + __	$\frac{b2}{⤢} = \frac{○}{○} = ○\frac{○}{○}$

Mom! I Learn Division Using Math-Chess-Puzzles Connection

Ho Math Chess 何数棋谜 妈!我会棋谜式除法啦!

Frank Ho, Amanda Ho © 2004 − 2020, all rights reserved.

Student's Name _____ Date _____

dd divided by dd

3	17	19	14
2	18	51	12
1	13	15	11
	A	b	C

The original square is at b2.

	Long division	Dividend = ?	Division in fractional form
b2 ÷ ✥	⌐	b2 (__) = ✥ (__) × __ + __	$\frac{b2}{✥} = \frac{O}{O} = O\frac{O}{O}$
b2 ÷ ✥	⌐	b2 (__) = ✥ (__) × __ + __	$\frac{b2}{✥} = \frac{O}{O} = O\frac{O}{O}$

Mom! I Learn Division Using Math-Chess-Puzzles Connection

Ho Math Chess　　何数棋谜　　妈!我会棋谜式除法啦!

Frank Ho, Amanda Ho © 2004 – 2020, all rights reserved.

Student's Name _____ Date _____

dd divided by dd

3	17	19	14
2	18	53	12
1	13	15	11
	a	B	C

The original square is at b2.

	Long division	Dividend = ?	Division in fraction form
b2 ÷ ✗	⟌	b2 (__) = ✗ (__)　　✗ __ + __	$\dfrac{b2}{✗} = \dfrac{\bigcirc}{\bigcirc} = \bigcirc \dfrac{\bigcirc}{\bigcirc}$
b2 ÷ ✗	⟌	b2 (__) = ✗ (__)　　✗ __ + __	$\dfrac{b2}{✗} = \dfrac{\bigcirc}{\bigcirc} = \bigcirc \dfrac{\bigcirc}{\bigcirc}$

Mom! I Learn Division Using Math-Chess-Puzzles Connection

Ho Math Chess 何数棋谜 妈!我会棋谜式除法啦!

Frank Ho, Amanda Ho © 2004 – 2020, all rights reserved.

Student's Name _____ Date _____

dd divided by dd

3	17	19	14
2	18	62	12
1	13	15	11
	a	b	c

The original square is at b2.

	Long division	Dividend = ?	Division in fractional form
b2 ÷ ✥	⌐	b2 (__) = ✥ (__) × __ + __	$\frac{b2}{✥} = \frac{○}{○} = ○\frac{○}{○}$
b2 ÷ ✥	⌐	b2 (__) = ✥ (__) × __ + __	$\frac{b2}{✥} = \frac{○}{○} = ○\frac{○}{○}$

No part of this publication can be copied, duplicated, or reproduced.

Mom! I Learn Division Using Math-Chess-Puzzles Connection

Ho Math Chess 何数棋谜 妈!我会棋谜式除法啦!

Frank Ho, Amanda Ho © 2004 – 2020, all rights reserved.

Student's Name _____ Date _____

dd divided by dd

3	17	19	14
2	18	67	12
1	13	15	11
	a	b	C

The original square is at b2.

	Long division	Dividend = ?	Division in fraction form
b2 ÷ ✗		b2 (__) = ✗ (__) ✗ __ + __	$\dfrac{b2}{✗} = \dfrac{○}{○} = ○\dfrac{○}{○}$
b2 ÷ ✗		b2 (__) = ✗ (__) ✗ __ + __	$\dfrac{b2}{✗} = \dfrac{○}{○} = ○\dfrac{○}{○}$

Page 132

Mom! I Learn Division Using Math-Chess-Puzzles Connection

Ho Math Chess　何数棋谜　妈!我会棋谜式除法啦!

Frank Ho, Amanda Ho © 2004 – 2020, all rights reserved.

Student's Name _____　Date _____

dd divided by dd

3	17	19	14
2	18	75	12
1	13	15	11
	A	b	c

The original square is at b2.

	Long division	Dividend = ?	Division in fractional form
b2 ÷ ↔	⌐	b2 (__) = ↕ (__) × __ + __	$\frac{b2}{↔} = \frac{○}{○} = ○\frac{○}{○}$
b2 ÷ ↔	⌐	b2 (__) = ↕ (__) × __ + __	$\frac{b2}{↔} = \frac{○}{○} = ○\frac{○}{○}$

Mom! I Learn Division Using Math-Chess-Puzzles Connection

Ho Math Chess　何数棋谜　妈!我会棋谜式除法啦!

Frank Ho, Amanda Ho © 2004 – 2020, all rights reserved.

Student's Name _____   Date _____

dd divided by dd

3	17	19	14
2	18	75	12
1	13	15	11
	a	B	c

The original square is at b2.

b2 ÷ ✗	Long division	Dividend = ?	Division in fraction form
b2 ÷ ✗		b2 (__) = ✗ (__) ✗ __ + __	$\dfrac{b2}{✗} = \dfrac{○}{○} = ○\dfrac{○}{○}$
b2 ÷ ✗		b2 (__) = ✗ (__) ✗ __ + __	$\dfrac{b2}{✗} = \dfrac{○}{○} = ○\dfrac{○}{○}$

Mom! I Learn Division Using Math-Chess-Puzzles Connection

Ho Math Chess 何数棋谜 妈!我会棋谜式除法啦!

Frank Ho, Amanda Ho © 2004 – 2020, all rights reserved.

Student's Name _____ Date _____

dd divided by dd

3	17	19	14
2	18	78	12
1	13	15	11
	A	B	c

The original square is at b2.

	Long division	Dividend = ?	Division in fractional form
b2 ÷ ✥	⌐	b2 (__) = ✥ (__) × __ + __	$\frac{b2}{✥} = \frac{○}{○} = ○\frac{○}{○}$
b2 ÷ ✥	⌐	b2 (__) = ✥ (__) × __ + __	$\frac{b2}{✥} = \frac{○}{○} = ○\frac{○}{○}$

Mom! I Learn Division Using Math-Chess-Puzzles Connection

Ho Math Chess 何数棋谜 妈!我会棋谜式除法啦!

Frank Ho, Amanda Ho © 2004 − 2020, all rights reserved.

Student's Name _____ Date _____

dd divided by dd

3	17	19	14
2	18	78	12
1	13	15	11
	a	b	c

The original square is at b2.

	Long division	Dividend = ?	Division in fraction form
b2 ÷ ✕	⌐‾‾‾‾‾	b2 (__) = ✕ (__) ✕ __ + __	$\frac{b2}{✕} = \frac{○}{○} = ○\frac{○}{○}$
b2 ÷ ✕	⌐‾‾‾‾‾	b2 (__) = ✕ (__) ✕ __ + __	$\frac{b2}{✕} = \frac{○}{○} = ○\frac{○}{○}$

Mom! I Learn Division Using Math-Chess-Puzzles Connection

Ho Math Chess 何数棋谜 妈!我会棋谜式除法啦!

Frank Ho, Amanda Ho © 2004 – 2020, all rights reserved.

Student's Name _____ Date _____

dd divided by dd

3	17	19	14
2	18	86	12
1	13	15	11
	a	b	c

The original square is at b2.

	Long division	Dividend = ?	Division in fractional form
b2 ÷ ✥	⌐	b2 (__) = ✥ (__) × __ + __	$\frac{b2}{✥} = \frac{○}{○} = ○\frac{○}{○}$
b2 ÷ ✥	⌐	b2 (__) = ✥ (__) × __ + __	$\frac{b2}{✥} = \frac{○}{○} = ○\frac{○}{○}$

Mom! I Learn Division Using Math-Chess-Puzzles Connection

Ho Math Chess　何数棋谜　妈!我会棋谜式除法啦!

Frank Ho, Amanda Ho © 2004 − 2020, all rights reserved.

Student's Name _____ Date _____

dd divided by dd

3	17	19	14
2	18	89	12
1	13	15	11
	a	b	c

The original square is at b2.

	Long division	Dividend = ?	Division in fraction form
b2 ÷ ✗	⟌	b2 (__) = ✗ (__) ✗ __ + __	$\dfrac{b2}{\times} = \dfrac{\bigcirc}{\bigcirc} = \bigcirc \dfrac{\bigcirc}{\bigcirc}$
b2 ÷ ✗	⟌	b2 (__) = ✗ (__) ✗ __ + __	$\dfrac{b2}{\times} = \dfrac{\bigcirc}{\bigcirc} = \bigcirc \dfrac{\bigcirc}{\bigcirc}$

Mom! I Learn Division Using Math-Chess-Puzzles Connection

Ho Math Chess 何数棋谜 妈!我会棋谜式除法啦!

Frank Ho, Amanda Ho © 2004 − 2020, all rights reserved.

Student's Name _____ Date _____

dd divided by dd

3	17	19	14
2	18	93	12
1	13	15	11
	a	b	c

The original square is at b2.

	Long division	Dividend = ?	Division in fractional form
b2 ÷ ✥	⌐	b2 (__) = ✥ (__) × __ + __	$\frac{b2}{✥} = \frac{O}{O} = O\frac{O}{O}$
b2 ÷ ✥	⌐	b2 (__) = ✥ (__) × __ + __	$\frac{b2}{✥} = \frac{O}{O} = O\frac{O}{O}$

Mom! I Learn Division Using Math-Chess-Puzzles Connection

Ho Math Chess 何数棋谜 妈!我会棋谜式除法啦!

Frank Ho, Amanda Ho © 2004 – 2020, all rights reserved.

Student's Name _____ Date _____

dd divided by dd

3	17	19	14
2	18	97	12
1	13	15	11
	a	b	c

The original square is at b2.

	Long division	Dividend = ?	Division in fraction form
b2 ÷ ✕	⟌	b2 (__) = ✕ (__) ✕ __ + __	$\frac{b2}{✕} = \frac{○}{○} = ○\frac{○}{○}$
b2 ÷ ✕	⟌	b2 (__) = ✕ (__) ✕ __ + __	$\frac{b2}{✕} = \frac{○}{○} = ○\frac{○}{○}$

Mom! I Learn Division Using Math-Chess-Puzzles Connection

Ho Math Chess 何数棋谜 妈!我会棋谜式除法啦!

Frank Ho, Amanda Ho © 2004 – 2020, all rights reserved.

Student's Name _____ Date _____

ddd divided by dd

3	17	19	14
2	18	123	12
1	13	15	11
	a	b	c

The original square is at b2.

	Long division	Dividend = ?	Division in fractional form
b2 ÷ ✦	⌐	b2(__) = ✦(__) × __ + __	$\frac{b2}{✦} = \frac{○}{○} = ○\frac{○}{○}$
b2 ÷ ✦	⌐	b2(__) = ✦(__) × __ + __	$\frac{b2}{✦} = \frac{○}{○} = ○\frac{○}{○}$

Mom! I Learn Division Using Math-Chess-Puzzles Connection

Ho Math Chess　何数棋谜　妈!我会棋谜式除法啦!

Frank Ho, Amanda Ho © 2004 − 2020, all rights reserved.

Student's Name _____ Date _____

ddd divided by dd

3	17	19	14
2	18	123	12
1	13	15	11
	a	b	c

The original square is at b2.

	Long division	Dividend = ?	Division in fraction form
b2 ÷ ↗	⟌	b2 (__) = ↗ (__) ×__ +__	$\frac{b2}{↗} = \frac{\bigcirc}{\bigcirc} = \bigcirc \frac{\bigcirc}{\bigcirc}$
b2 ÷ ↘	⟌	b2 (__) = ↘ (__) ×__ +__	$\frac{b2}{↘} = \frac{\bigcirc}{\bigcirc} = \bigcirc \frac{\bigcirc}{\bigcirc}$

Mom! I Learn Division Using Math-Chess-Puzzles Connection

Ho Math Chess　何数棋谜　妈!我会棋谜式除法啦!

Frank Ho, Amanda Ho © 2004 – 2020, all rights reserved.

Student's Name _____　Date _____

ddd divided by dd

3	17	19	14
2	18	223	12
1	13	15	11
	a	b	c

The original square is at b2.

	Long division	Dividend = ?	Division in fractional form
b2 ÷ ✥	⌐	b2(__) = ✥(__) × __ + __	$\frac{b2}{✥} = \frac{○}{○} = ○\frac{○}{○}$
b2 ÷ ✥	⌐	b2(__) = ✥(__) × __ + __	$\frac{b2}{✥} = \frac{○}{○} = ○\frac{○}{○}$

Mom! I Learn Division Using Math-Chess-Puzzles Connection

Ho Math Chess 何数棋谜 妈!我会棋谜式除法啦!

Frank Ho, Amanda Ho © 2004 – 2020, all rights reserved.

Student's Name _____ Date _____

ddd divided by dd

3	17	19	14
2	18	475	12
1	13	15	11
	a	b	c

The original square is at b2.

475

Mom! I Learn Division Using Math-Chess-Puzzles Connection

Ho Math Chess 何数棋谜 妈!我会棋谜式除法啦!

Frank Ho, Amanda Ho © 2004 – 2020, all rights reserved.

Student's Name _____ Date _____

***** Part 2 Multiplication Review *****

Many students only mastered the 1 digit multiplying 1 digit times table and have difficulties in doing 2-digit multiplying 2-digit or 3-digit multiplying 2-digit multiplication, so when they learn division they equally have problems doing a number divided by 2-digit. Because of this reason, this section has a specially designed multiplication format to train students to get familiar with the multi-digit multiplication procedures.

Mom! I Learn Division Using Math-Chess-Puzzles Connection

Ho Math Chess 何数棋谜 妈!我会棋谜式除法啦!

Frank Ho, Amanda Ho © 2004 – 2020, all rights reserved.

Student's Name _____ Date _____

dd × dd multiplication concepts

Horizontal multiplication

$23 \times 24 = 23 \times (4 + 20) = 23 \times 4 + 23 \times 20 = 92 + 460 = 552$

Vertical multiplication

It is extremely important for the teacher to explain the concepts of why and how multiplication is done. Repeated drills without explanations only add prolong learning curve which could have been reduced if concepts such as the following had been explained.

1. Why line up ones multiplication at the rightmost position? Because it is ones place.
2. Why a 0 is placed in the ones place when doing tens place multiplication? Because tens place multiplication always has a 0 at ones place such as 20 in the example, the ones place value is 0.
3. How is the horizontal multiplication related to the vertical multiplication? The vertical multiplication is using the concept of distributive law to do the work but written in a vertical way. The following is an example.

```
       27
    ×  36
    ─────
       42
      120
       21
    + 600
    ─────
      972
```

Mom! I Learn Division Using Math-Chess-Puzzles Connection

Ho Math Chess　何数棋谜　妈!我会棋谜式除法啦!

Frank Ho, Amanda Ho © 2004 − 2020, all rights reserved.

Student's Name _____ Date _____

Step 1	Step 2
2 3 × 　 4 ────── 　　9 2	2 3 × 　2 0 ────── 　4 6 0

Step 3: The answer is 92 + 460 = 552

$25 \times 24 = 25 \times (4 + 20) = 25 \times 4 + 25 \times 20 =$

$24 \times 25 = 24 \times (5 + 20) = 24 \times 5 + 24 \times 20 =$

$25 \times 36 = 25 \times (6 + 30) = 25 \times 6 + 25 \times 30 =$

$36 \times 25 = 36 \times (5 + 20) = 36 \times 5 + 36 \times 20 =$

$27 \times 28 = 27 \times (8 + 20) = 27 \times 8 + 27 \times 20 =$

$28 \times 27 = 28 \times (7 + 20) = 28 \times 7 + 28 \times 20 =$

Mom! I Learn Division Using Math-Chess-Puzzles Connection

Ho Math Chess 何数棋谜 妈!我会棋谜式除法啦!

Frank Ho, Amanda Ho © 2004 – 2020, all rights reserved.

Student's Name _____ Date _____

dd × dd with carrying

```
      2
     1 3          1 4          1 5          1 6
   x 8 8        x 8 8        x 8 8        x 8 8
   1 0 4        ☐☐☐         ☐☐☐          ☐☐☐
 +1 0 4       +☐☐☐        +☐☐☐         +☐☐☐
   ─────        ─────        ─────         ─────
   ☐☐☐☐        ☐☐☐☐        ☐☐☐☐         ☐☐☐☐


     1 7          1 8          1 9           1 2
   x 8 8        x 8 8        x 8 8         x 9 9
   ☐☐☐         ☐☐☐          ☐☐☐           ☐☐☐
 +☐☐☐        +☐☐☐         +☐☐☐          +☐☐☐
   ─────        ─────        ─────         ─────
   ☐☐☐☐        ☐☐☐☐        ☐☐☐☐          ☐☐☐☐


     1 2          1 3          1 4           1 5
   x 9 9        x 9 9        x 9 9         x 9 9
   ☐☐☐         ☐☐☐          ☐☐☐           ☐☐☐
 +☐☐☐        +☐☐☐         +☐☐☐          +☐☐☐
   ─────        ─────        ─────         ─────
   ☐☐☐☐        ☐☐☐☐        ☐☐☐☐          ☐☐☐☐


     1 6          1 7          1 8           1 9
   x 9 9        x 9 9        x 9 9         x 9 9
   ☐☐☐         ☐☐☐          ☐☐☐           ☐☐☐
 +☐☐☐        +☐☐☐         +☐☐☐          +☐☐☐
   ─────        ─────        ─────         ─────
   ☐☐☐☐        ☐☐☐☐        ☐☐☐☐          ☐☐☐☐
```

dd × dd with carrying

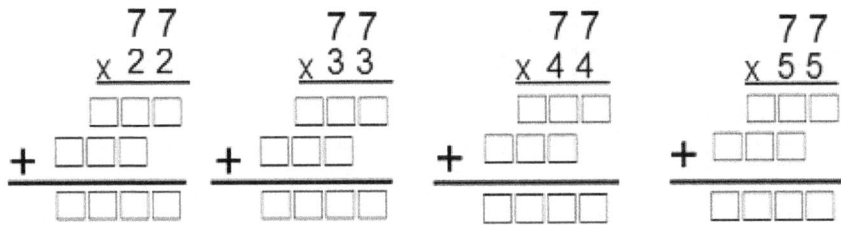

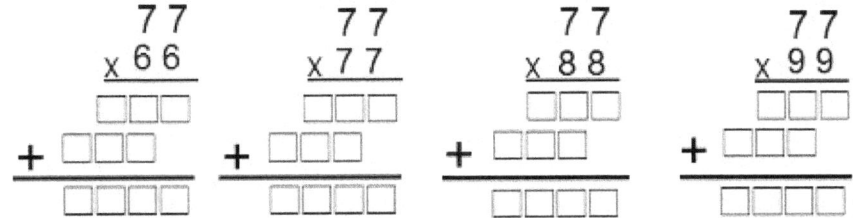

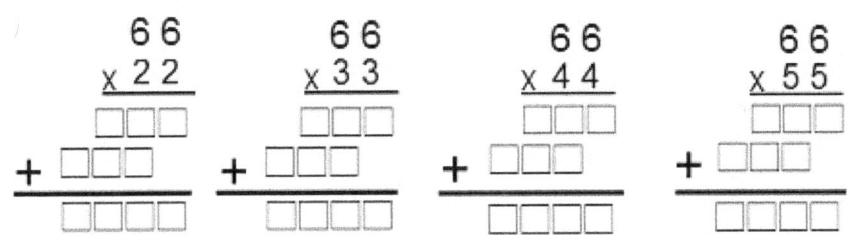

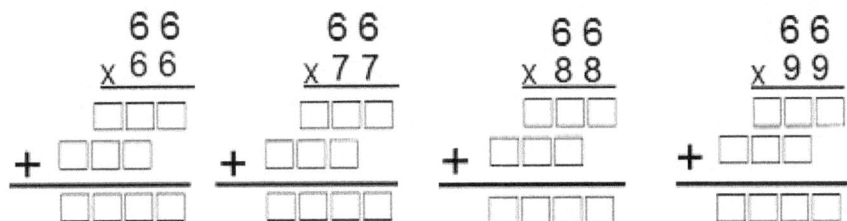

dd × dd without carrying

```
   47        32        23        38
 x 11      x 22      x 33      x 11


   42        32        29        37
 x 22      x 22      x 11      x 11


   27        33        37        14
 x 11      x 22      x 11      x 22
```

Mom! I Learn Division Using Math-Chess-Puzzles Connection

Ho Math Chess   何数棋谜   妈!我会棋谜式除法啦!

Frank Ho, Amanda Ho © 2004 − 2020, all rights reserved.

Student's Name _____   Date _____

dd × dd with carrying

```
   45        36        27        38
 × 25      × 46      × 57      × 48
 □□□      □□□      □□□      □□□
□□□       □□□       □□□       □□□
```

```
   33        22        24        44
 × 22      × 33      × 22      × 22
```

Mom! I Learn Division Using Math-Chess-Puzzles Connection

dd × dd with carrying

```
    27        36        37        18
  × 27      × 56      × 67      × 78
```

```
    59        26        27        88
  × 29      × 46      × 37      × 68
```

```
    17        26        25        48
  × 21      × 42      × 56      × 36
```

dd × dd with carrying

```
  45      12      29      37
x 19    x 47    x 55    x 23


  27      11      57      14
x 11    x 56    x 26    x 52


  32      23      24      24
x 21    x 42    x 32    x 13
```

Mom! I Learn Division Using Math-Chess-Puzzles Connection

Ho Math Chess 何数棋谜 妈!我会棋谜式除法啦!

Frank Ho, Amanda Ho © 2004 – 2020, all rights reserved.

Student's Name _____ Date _____

dd × dd with carrying

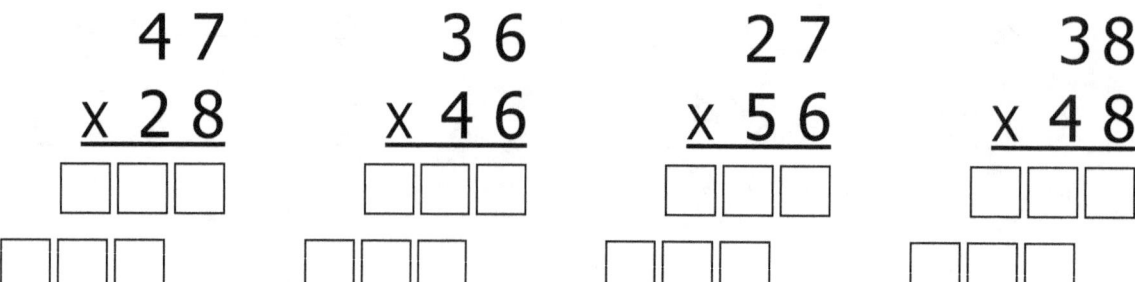

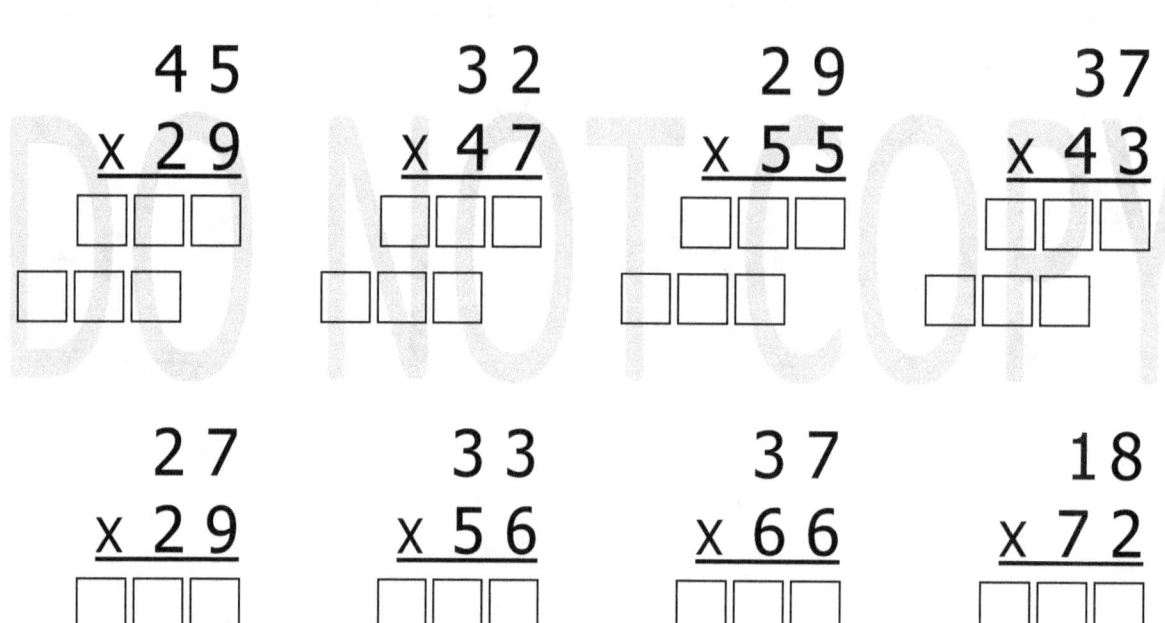

dd × dd with carrying

```
  57      26      27      88
x 29    x 46    x 36    x 66
```

```
  51      36      29      68
x 28    x 42    x 31    x 62
```

```
  63      78      84      74
x 84    x 46    x 25    x 68
```

Mom! I Learn Division Using Math-Chess-Puzzles Connection

dd × dd with carrying

```
   47        36        27        38
  x28       x46       x56       x46
  ___       ___       ___       ___
 ___       ___       ___       ___


   45        32        29        37
  x29       x47       x55       x43


   27        33        37        18
  x29       x56       x66       x72
```

Mom! I Learn Division Using Math-Chess-Puzzles Connection

dd × dd with carrying

12 X 28 =		32 X 27 =		52 X 35 =

33 X 45 = 1485		52 X 25 =		63 X 21 =

32 X 27 =		54 X 18 =		17 X 48 =

27 X 83 =		62 X 24 =		72 X 32 =

Mom! I Learn Division Using Math-Chess-Puzzles Connection

Ho Math Chess 何数棋谜 妈!我会棋谜式除法啦!

Frank Ho, Amanda Ho © 2004 – 2020, all rights reserved.

Student's Name _____ Date _____

dd × dd with carrying

42 X 38 =   35 X 25 =   52 X 25 =

38 X 45 =   48 X 25 =   69 X 21 =

76 X 27 =   36 X 41 =   95 X 28 =

62 X 73 =   53 X 26 =   74 X 36 =

Mom! I Learn Division Using Math-Chess-Puzzles Connection

Ho Math Chess 何数棋谜 妈!我会棋谜式除法啦!

Frank Ho, Amanda Ho © 2004 – 2020, all rights reserved.

Student's Name _____ Date _____

dd ✕ dd with carrying

54 X 23 =   62 X 23 =   71 X 85 =

53 X 45 =   82 X 75 =   63 X 48 =

81 X 37 =   76 X 52 =   49 X 68 =

77 X 84 =   93 X 54 =   82 X 39 =

ddd × dd with carrying

125 × 16

126 × 17

127 × 15

234 × 56

235 × 57

236 × 58

Mom! I Learn Division Using Math-Chess-Puzzles Connection

ddd × dd with carrying

```
   345          345          345
x   65       x   67       x   68
 ☐☐☐          ☐☐☐          ☐☐☐
☐☐☐☐         ☐☐☐☐         ☐☐☐☐
─────         ─────        ─────
☐☐☐☐☐       ☐☐☐☐☐        ☐☐☐☐☐


   666          777          888
x   66       x   77       x   88
 ☐☐☐          ☐☐☐          ☐☐☐
☐☐☐☐         ☐☐☐☐         ☐☐☐☐
─────        ─────         ─────
☐☐☐☐☐       ☐☐☐☐☐         ☐☐☐☐☐
```

Mom! I Learn Division Using Math-Chess-Puzzles Connection

ddd × dd with carrying

```
   345          345          345
x   77       x   88       x   99
 □□□□         □□□□         □□□□
□□□□         □□□□         □□□□
□□□□□       □□□□□       □□□□□


   999          999          999
x   77       x   88       x   99
 □□□□         □□□□         □□□□
□□□□         □□□□         □□□□
□□□□□       □□□□□       □□□□□
```

Mom! I Learn Division Using Math-Chess-Puzzles Connection

Ho Math Chess 何数棋谜 妈!我会棋谜式除法啦!

Frank Ho, Amanda Ho © 2004 − 2020, all rights reserved.

Student's Name _____ Date _____

ddd × dd with carrying

```
   567          765          675
 ×  77        ×  88        ×  99
 ☐☐☐☐        ☐☐☐☐         ☐☐☐☐
☐☐☐☐         ☐☐☐☐         ☐☐☐☐
─────        ─────         ─────
☐☐☐☐☐       ☐☐☐☐☐        ☐☐☐☐☐


   678          876          786
 ×  77        ×  88        ×  99
 ☐☐☐☐        ☐☐☐☐         ☐☐☐☐
☐☐☐☐         ☐☐☐☐         ☐☐☐☐
─────        ─────         ─────
☐☐☐☐☐       ☐☐☐☐☐        ☐☐☐☐☐
```

No part of this publication can be copied, duplicated, or reproduced.

Mom! I Learn Division Using Math-Chess-Puzzles Connection

Ho Math Chess 何数棋谜 妈!我会棋谜式除法啦!

Frank Ho, Amanda Ho © 2004 – 2020, all rights reserved.

Student's Name _____ Date _____

ddd × dd without carrying

```
  472        425        432        384
x  11      x  22      x  33      x  11
```

```
  323        421        224        352
x  22      x  22      x  11      x  11
```

```
  286        412        374        243
x  11      x  22      x  11      x  22
```

Mom! I Learn Division Using Math-Chess-Puzzles Connection

Ho Math Chess 何数棋谜 妈!我会棋谜式除法啦!

Frank Ho, Amanda Ho © 2004 – 2020, all rights reserved.

Student's Name _____ Date _____

ddd × dd with carrying

```
  474        316        237        589
x  15      x  36      x  28      x  31
```

```
  457        628        275        874
x  52      x  27      x  61      x  39
```

```
  577        368        779        147
x  61      x  42      x  43      x  29
```

Mom! I Learn Division Using Math-Chess-Puzzles Connection

Ho Math Chess 何数棋谜 妈!我会棋谜式除法啦!

Frank Ho, Amanda Ho © 2004 – 2020, all rights reserved.

Student's Name _____ Date _____

ddd × dd with carrying

159 X 64 =   357 X 24 =   684 X 86 =

268 X 57 =   842 X 17 =   368 X 43 =

251 X 74 =   961 X 19 =   254 X 24 =

741 X 27 =   217 X 14 =   364 X 43 =

Mom! I Learn Division Using Math-Chess-Puzzles Connection

Ho Math Chess 何数棋谜 妈!我会棋谜式除法啦!

Frank Ho, Amanda Ho © 2004 – 2020, all rights reserved.

Student's Name _____ Date _____

ddd × dd with carrying

148 X 24 =   572 X 47 =   351 X 34 =

381 X 56 =   729 X 72 =   349 X 764 =

941 X 48 =   149 X 24 =   324 X 27 =

327 X 34 =   243 X 63 =   751 X 82 =

Mom! I Learn Division Using Math-Chess-Puzzles Connection

d0d × dd

305 X 47 =   507 X 55 =   805 X 51 =

609 X 34 =   709 X 78 =   501 X 39 =

207 X 49 =   608 X 56 =   901 X 27 =

206 X 91 =   604 X 28 =   908 X 62 =

Mom! I Learn Division Using Math-Chess-Puzzles Connection

Ho Math Chess 何数棋谜 妈!我会棋谜式除法啦!

Frank Ho, Amanda Ho © 2004 – 2020, all rights reserved.

Student's Name _____   Date _____

dd X d0d

The 0s in the middle of a factor do not change the sum, so no product needs to be done.

Long form

```
    1 2 3
x   1 0 1
   ☐ ☐ ☐
  ☐ ☐ ☐
 ☐ ☐
  ─────
 ☐ ☐ ☐ ☐ ☐
```

Short form

```
    1 2 3
x   1 0 1
   ☐ ☐ ☐
(Do not multiply 0)
  ☐ ☐ ☐
  ─────
 ☐ ☐ ☐ ☐ ☐
```

```
    2 1          2 1          1 9          1 9
x 2 0 1      x 3 0 1      x 4 0 1      x 5 0 1
   ☐ ☐          ☐ ☐          ☐ ☐          ☐ ☐
  ☐ ☐          ☐ ☐          ☐ ☐          ☐ ☐
  ─────        ─────        ─────        ─────
 ☐ ☐ ☐ ☐      ☐ ☐ ☐ ☐      ☐ ☐ ☐ ☐      ☐ ☐ ☐ ☐
```

***** Part 3 Traditional worksheets *****

This part contains more of traditional worksheets.

Mom! I Learn Division Using Math-Chess-Puzzles Connection

Ho Math Chess　何数棋谜　妈!我会棋谜式除法啦!

Frank Ho, Amanda Ho © 2004 − 2020, all rights reserved.

Student's Name _____　Date _____

Less than or equal $\leq$

The whole numbers $\leq$ 5 are 0, 1, 2, 3, 4, 5.
Fill in ☐ with the greatest factor such that the inequality exists.

Greatest factor

☐ × 2 ≤ 6
☐ × 2 ≤ 7
☐ × 2 ≤ 8
☐ × 2 ≤ ♛
☐ × 2 ≤ 10
☐ × 2 ≤ 11
☐ × 4 ≤ 33
☐ × 4 ≤ 37
☐ × 5 ≤ 31
☐ × 6 ≤ 19
☐ × 7 ≤ 11
☐ × 7 ≤ 20
☐ × 8 ≤ 26
☐ × 9 ≤ 29

Greatest factor

☐ × ♝ ≤ 9
☐ × 3 ≤ 10
☐ × ♝ ≤ 11
☐ × 3 ≤ 12
☐ × 3 ≤ 13
☐ × ♞ ≤ 14
☐ × 4 ≤ 37
☐ × 4 ≤ 38
☐ × ♜ ≤ 17
☐ × 6 ≤ 26
☐ × 7 ≤ 15
☐ × 7 ≤ 25
☐ × 8 ≤ 41
☐ × ♛ ≤ 44

Mom! I Learn Division Using Math-Chess-Puzzles Connection

Division notations

Symbols	Verbal expressions	Comments	Concept
8 ÷ 2	8 divided by 2 is (equals) 4.	Dividend ÷ divisor = quotient	♙♙♙♙ ♙♙♙♙ There are 8 pawns. $8 = 2 \times 4$ 1. If eight pawns are divided evenly into two group, how many pawns does each group get? 2. How many groups of 4 pawns are there?
8 / 2	The quotient of 8 and 2 is (equals) 4.		
$\frac{8}{2}$	The quotient of 8 divided 2 is (is equal) 4.		
2)‾8	2 divides 8 is 4.		
2)8	2 goes into 8 is 4.		

Mom! I Learn Division Using Math-Chess-Puzzles Connection

Ho Math Chess　何数棋谜　妈!我会棋谜式除法啦!

Frank Ho, Amanda Ho © 2004 − 2020, all rights reserved.

Student's Name _____ Date _____

Divisible by 2

Circle those numbers which can be divided by 2 with no remainder.

Observe the results and write the observation _____

♗	2	♞	4	♖	6	7	8	♕	10
11	12	13	14	15	16	17	18	19	20
21	22	23	24	25	26	27	28	29	30
31	32	33	34	35	36	37	38	39	40
41	42	43	44	45	46	47	48	49	50
51	52	53	54	55	56	57	58	59	60
61	62	63	64	65	66	67	68	69	70
71	72	73	74	75	76	77	78	79	80
81	82	83	84	85	86	87	88	89	90
91	92	93	94	95	96	97	98	99	100

Mom! I Learn Division Using Math-Chess-Puzzles Connection

Ho Math Chess 何数棋谜 妈!我会棋谜式除法啦!

Frank Ho, Amanda Ho © 2004 – 2020, all rights reserved.

Student's Name _____ Date _____

Divisible by 3

Circle those numbers which can be divided by 3 with no remainder.

Observe the results and write the observation _____

♗	2	♘	4	♖	6	7	8	♕	10
11	12	13	14	15	16	17	18	19	20
21	22	23	24	25	26	27	28	29	30
31	32	33	34	35	36	37	38	39	40
41	42	43	44	45	46	47	48	49	50
51	52	53	54	55	56	57	58	59	60
61	62	63	64	65	66	67	68	69	70
71	72	73	74	75	76	77	78	79	80
81	82	83	84	85	86	87	88	89	90
91	92	93	94	95	96	97	98	99	100

Mom! I Learn Division Using Math-Chess-Puzzles Connection

Ho Math Chess 何数棋谜 妈!我会棋谜式除法啦!

Frank Ho, Amanda Ho © 2004 – 2020, all rights reserved.

Student's Name _____ Date _____

Divisible by 4

Circle those numbers which can be divided by 4 with no remainder.

Observe the results and write the observation _____

♗	2	♘	4	♖	6	7	8	♕	10
11	12	13	14	15	16	17	18	19	20
21	22	23	24	25	26	27	28	29	30
31	32	33	34	35	36	37	38	39	40
41	42	43	44	45	46	47	48	49	50
51	52	53	54	55	56	57	58	59	60
61	62	63	64	65	66	67	68	69	70
71	72	73	74	75	76	77	78	79	80
81	82	83	84	85	86	87	88	89	90
91	92	93	94	95	96	97	98	99	100

Mom! I Learn Division Using Math-Chess-Puzzles Connection

Ho Math Chess 何数棋谜 妈!我会棋谜式除法啦!

Frank Ho, Amanda Ho © 2004 − 2020, all rights reserved.

Student's Name _____ Date _____

Divisible by 5

Circle those numbers which can be divided by 5 with no remainder.

Observe the results and write the observation _____

♗	2	♘	4	♖	6	7	8	♕	10
11	12	13	14	15	16	17	18	19	20
21	22	23	24	25	26	27	28	29	30
31	32	33	34	35	36	37	38	39	40
41	42	43	44	45	46	47	48	49	50
51	52	53	54	55	56	57	58	59	60
61	62	63	64	65	66	67	68	69	70
71	72	73	74	75	76	77	78	79	80
81	82	83	84	85	86	87	88	89	90
91	92	93	94	95	96	97	98	99	100

Mom! I Learn Division Using Math-Chess-Puzzles Connection

Ho Math Chess 何数棋谜 妈!我会棋谜式除法啦!

Frank Ho, Amanda Ho © 2004 – 2020, all rights reserved.

Student's Name _____ Date _____

Divisible by 6

Circle those numbers which can be divided by 6 with no remainder.

Observe the results and write the observation _____

♗	2	♘	4	♖	6	7	8	♕	10
11	12	13	14	15	16	17	18	19	20
21	22	23	24	25	26	27	28	29	30
31	32	33	34	35	36	37	38	39	40
41	42	43	44	45	46	47	48	49	50
51	52	53	54	55	56	57	58	59	60
61	62	63	64	65	66	67	68	69	70
71	72	73	74	75	76	77	78	79	80
81	82	83	84	85	86	87	88	89	90
91	92	93	94	95	96	97	98	99	100

Mom! I Learn Division Using Math-Chess-Puzzles Connection

Divisible by 9

Circle those numbers which can be divided by 9 with no remainder.

Observe the results and write the observation _____

♗	2	♞	4	♖	6	7	8	♕	10
11	12	13	14	15	16	17	18	19	20
21	22	23	24	25	26	27	28	29	30
31	32	33	34	35	36	37	38	39	40
41	42	43	44	45	46	47	48	49	50
51	52	53	54	55	56	57	58	59	60
61	62	63	64	65	66	67	68	69	70
71	72	73	74	75	76	77	78	79	80
81	82	83	84	85	86	87	88	89	90
91	92	93	94	95	96	97	98	99	100

Mom! I Learn Division Using Math-Chess-Puzzles Connection

Ho Math Chess   何数棋谜   妈!我会棋谜式除法啦!

Frank Ho, Amanda Ho © 2004 – 2020, all rights reserved.

Student's Name _____ Date _____

Divisible by 10

Circle those numbers which can be divided by 10 with no remainder.

Observe the results and write the observation _____

♙	2	♘	4	♖	6	7	8	♕	10
11	12	13	14	15	16	17	18	19	20
21	22	23	24	25	26	27	28	29	30
31	32	33	34	35	36	37	38	39	40
41	42	43	44	45	46	47	48	49	50
51	52	53	54	55	56	57	58	59	60
61	62	63	64	65	66	67	68	69	70
71	72	73	74	75	76	77	78	79	80
81	82	83	84	85	86	87	88	89	90
91	92	93	94	95	96	97	98	99	100

No part of this publication can be copied, duplicated, or reproduced.

Mom! I Learn Division Using Math-Chess-Puzzles Connection

Ho Math Chess 何数棋谜 妈!我会棋谜式除法啦!

Frank Ho, Amanda Ho © 2004 − 2020, all rights reserved.

Student's Name _____ Date _____

Forward slash (/) those numbers that are divisible by 2 and backslash (\) those numbers that are divisible by 4.

Observe the results and write the observation _____

♙	2	♘	4	♖	6	7	8	♕	10
11	12	13	14	15	16	17	18	19	20
21	22	23	24	25	26	27	28	29	30
31	32	33	34	35	36	37	38	39	40
41	42	43	44	45	46	47	48	49	50
51	52	53	54	55	56	57	58	59	60
61	62	63	64	65	66	67	68	69	70
71	72	73	74	75	76	77	78	79	80
81	82	83	84	85	86	87	88	89	90
91	92	93	94	95	96	97	98	99	100

No part of this publication can be copied, duplicated, or reproduced.

Mom! I Learn Division Using Math-Chess-Puzzles Connection

Ho Math Chess   何数棋谜   妈!我会棋谜式除法啦!

Frank Ho, Amanda Ho © 2004 – 2020, all rights reserved.

Student's Name _____ Date _____

Forward slash (/) those numbers that are divisible by 3 and backslash (\) those numbers that are divisible by 9.

Observe the results and write the observation _____

♙	2	♗	4	♖	6	7	8	♕	10
11	12	13	14	15	16	17	18	19	20
21	22	23	24	25	26	27	28	29	30
31	32	33	34	35	36	37	38	39	40
41	42	43	44	45	46	47	48	49	50
51	52	53	54	55	56	57	58	59	60
61	62	63	64	65	66	67	68	69	70
71	72	73	74	75	76	77	78	79	80
81	82	83	84	85	86	87	88	89	90
91	92	93	94	95	96	97	98	99	100

Mom! I Learn Division Using Math-Chess-Puzzles Connection

Ho Math Chess 何数棋谜 妈!我会棋谜式除法啦!

Frank Ho, Amanda Ho © 2004 − 2020, all rights reserved.

Student's Name _____ Date _____

Forward slash (/) those numbers that are divisible by 5 and backslash (\) those numbers that are divisible by 10.

Observe the results and write the observation _____

♙	2	♗	4	♖	6	7	8	♕	10
11	12	13	14	15	16	17	18	19	20
21	22	23	24	25	26	27	28	29	30
31	32	33	34	35	36	37	38	39	40
41	42	43	44	45	46	47	48	49	50
51	52	53	54	55	56	57	58	59	60
61	62	63	64	65	66	67	68	69	70
71	72	73	74	75	76	77	78	79	80
81	82	83	84	85	86	87	88	89	90
91	92	93	94	95	96	97	98	99	100

Mom! I Learn Division Using Math-Chess-Puzzles Connection

Ho Math Chess 何数棋谜 妈!我会棋谜式除法啦!

Frank Ho, Amanda Ho © 2004 − 2020, all rights reserved.

Student's Name _____ Date _____

Dividing by relating

⌐÷ 2 ÷ ⌐	⌐÷ 4 ÷ ⌐	⌐÷ 8 ÷ ⌐
♙ ÷ 2	2 ÷ 4	4 ÷ 4
□ ♙ □	□ 2 □	□ 8 □
÷ ♙	÷ ♙	÷ ♙
□	□	□

⌐÷ 16 ÷ ⌐	⌐÷ 30 ÷ ⌐	⌐÷ 42 ÷ ⌐
4 ÷ 8	♖ ÷ 6	6 ÷ 7
□ 4 □	□ ♖ □	□ 6 □
÷ 1	÷ 1	÷ ♙
□	□	□

⌐÷ 56 ÷ ⌐	⌐÷ 72 ÷ ⌐	⌐÷ 28 ÷ ⌐
7 ÷ 8	8 ÷ ♕	4 ÷ 7
□ 7 □	□ 8 □	□ 4 □
÷ ♙	÷ 1	÷ ♙
□	□	□

Mom! I Learn Division Using Math-Chess-Puzzles Connection

Dividing by relating

♘ ÷ 24 ÷ ↴	♘ ÷ 60 ÷ ↴	♗ ÷ 12 ÷ ↴
♘ ÷ 4	♘ ÷ 5	♗ ÷ 4
☐ ♘ ☐	☐ 4 ☐	☐ ♗ ☐
÷ ♙ ☐	÷ ♙ ☐	÷ ♙ ☐

÷ 35 ÷	÷ 15 ÷	÷ 18 ÷
5 × 7	♘ ÷ ♖	♘ ÷ ♘
☐ ♖ ☐	☐ 3 ☐	☐ 6 ☐
÷ 1 ☐	÷ 1 ☐	÷ ♙ ☐

÷ 18 ÷	÷ 21 ÷	÷ 24 ÷
♘ ÷ ♘	♘ ÷ ♘	♘ ÷ ♘
☐ 6 ☐	☐ 7 ☐	☐ 8 ☐
÷ ♙ ☐	÷ 1 ☐	÷ ♙ ☐

Mom! I Learn Division Using Math-Chess-Puzzles Connection

Ho Math Chess 何数棋谜 妈!我会棋谜式除法啦!

Frank Ho, Amanda Ho © 2004 − 2020, all rights reserved.

Student's Name _____ Date _____

From multiplication to division procedure

In this workbook, the division procedure is based on the reverse procedure of multiplication, For example, $\square \times 2 = 6$, the division procedure is to find out what is the greatest factor of $\square$ such that $\square \times 2 \leq 6$ with the following division notation

$$2\overline{)6}$$

There are a few restrictions to follow such as the divisor must be a whole number and the remainder must be less than the divisor and divide the dividends one digit at a time. The reason of dividing the dividend digit one at a time is it automatically takes care of the zeros at the beginning, in the middle, and at the end. The divisor must be the whole number would make the decimal division easier.

A simple problem could be used to demonstrate the above concept. For example, $25 is to be divided equally among 5 children. The divisor is 5 children so it must be the whole number, but the $ amount could be decimals. If we would write the division as $25 ÷ 5 = \frac{\$25}{5}$ then

$$\frac{\$25}{5} = \frac{2\$10 + 1\$5}{5} = 2\$2 + \$1 = \$5$$

If we follow the above procedure for the division, it would be very tedious, so we convert 2 $10 to 20 of $1 and add $5 to be 5 of $1. So, the division procedure will be

$$5\overline{)25}$$

. This is the reason that quotient 5 must be placed rightmost to show we actually divide 25 of 1$ by 5 children.

For decimal division, the division flowchart included in this workbook can also be used. Bring down 0 until the desired decimal places are found. If the dividend has a decimal point, line up a decimal point in the quotient and just carry out the division as it is whole number division. If the dividend is a whole number, place a decimal point at the place after the dividend digit has been all used and before 0 needs to be brought down.

Mom! I Learn Division Using Math-Chess-Puzzles Connection

Ho Math Chess　何数棋谜　妈!我会棋谜式除法啦!

Frank Ho, Amanda Ho © 2004 − 2020, all rights reserved.

Student's Name _____ Date _____

From multiplication to division (d ÷ d)

Multiplication	Division
Factor × factor ≤ product	$\text{divisor}\overline{\smash{)}\text{dividend}}^{\text{quotinet}}$
☐ × 2 ≤ 6	× ☐ ← step 1: What times 2 is ≤ 6. 2) 6 − ☐ ← step 2: 6 − 6 = 0 0 ← Remainder = 0
☐ × 2 ≤ 8	× ☐ ← step 1: What times 2 is ≤ 8. 2) 8 − ☐ ← step 2: 8 − 8 = 0 0 ← Remainder = 0
☐ × 3 ≤ ♛	× ☐ ← step 1: What times 3 is ≤ 9. 3) 9 − ☐ ← step 2: 9 − 9 = 0 0 ← Remainder = 0

Mom! I Learn Division Using Math-Chess-Puzzles Connection

Ho Math Chess 何数棋谜 妈!我会棋谜式除法啦!

Frank Ho, Amanda Ho © 2004 − 2020, all rights reserved.

Student's Name _____ Date _____

From multiplication to division (d ÷ d)

□ × 2 ≤ 8	8 = □ × 2	×□ ← step 1: What times 2 is ≤ 8. 2)‾8 − □ ← step 2: 8 − 8 = 0 0 ← Remainder = 0
□ × 3 ≤ 0	0 = □ × ♗	×□ ← step 1: What times 3 is ≤ 0. 3)‾0 − □ ← step 2: 0 − 0 = 0 0 ← Remainder = 0
□ × 6 ≤ 6	6 = □ × 6	×□ ← step 1: What times 6 is ≤ 6. 6)‾6 − □ ← step 2: 6 − 6 = 0 0 ← Remainder = 0

Mom! I Learn Division Using Math-Chess-Puzzles Connection

Ho Math Chess 何数棋谜 妈!我会棋谜式除法啦!

Frank Ho, Amanda Ho © 2004 − 2020, all rights reserved.

Student's Name _____ Date _____

dd ÷ d with 1-digit quotient and no remainder

☐ × 6 = 42	42 = ☐ × 7	Step 1: Do ☐ × 6 ≤ 42 (4 is too small, use 42) **Place the quotient in the rightmost position** × ☐ ← step 2: 7 × 6 = 42 6)42 −☐☐ ← step 3: 42 − 42 = 0 0 ← Remainder = 0
☐ × 2 = 18	18 = ☐ × ♛	Step 1: Do ☐ × 2 ≤ 18 (1 is too small, use 18) **Place the quotient in the rightmost position** × ☐ ← step 2: 9 × 2 = 18 2)18 −☐☐ ← step 3: 18 − 18 = 0 0 ← Remainder = 0
☐ × ♛ = 81	81 = ☐ × 9	Step 1: Do ☐ × 9 ≤ 81 (8 is too small, use 81) **Place the quotient in the rightmost position** × ☐ ← step 2: 9 × 9 = 81 9)81 −☐☐ ← step 3: 81 − 81 = 0 0 ← Remainder = 0

Mom! I Learn Division Using Math-Chess-Puzzles Connection

Ho Math Chess 何数棋谜 妈!我会棋谜式除法啦!

Frank Ho, Amanda Ho © 2004 − 2020, all rights reserved.

Student's Name _____ Date _____

dd ÷ d with 1-digit quotients and no remainder

Step 1: Do ☐ × 3 ≤ 15 (1 is too small, use 15)

× ☐ ← step 2: Do multiplication, 5 × 3 =

3) 15

− ☐☐ ← step 3: Do subtraction, 15 − 15 = 0

0 ← Remainder = 0

Step 1: Do ☐ × 3 ≤ 18 (3 is too small, use 18)

× ☐ ← step 2: Do multiplication, 6 × 3 =

3) 18

− ☐☐ ← step 3: Do subtraction, 18 − 18 = 0

0 ← Remainder = 0

Step 1: Do ☐ × 5 ≤ 25 (2 is too small, use 25)

× ☐ ← step 2: Do multiplication

5) 25

− ☐☐ ← step 3: Do subtraction

0 ← Remainder = 0

Step 1: Do ☐ × 4 ≤ 28 (2 is too small, use 28)

× ☐ ← step 2: Do multiplication

4) 28

− ☐☐ ← step 3: Do subtraction

0 ← Remainder = 0

Step 1: Do ☐ × 4 ≤ 32 (3 is too small, use 32)

× ☐ ← step 2: Do multiplication

4) 32

− ☐☐ ← step 3: Do subtraction

0 ← Remainder = 0

Step 1: Do ☐ × 2 ≤ 16 (1 is too small, use 16)

× ☐ ← step 2: Do multiplication

2) 16

− ☐☐ ← step 3: Do subtraction

0 ← Remainder = 0

Mom! I Learn Division Using Math-Chess-Puzzles Connection

From multiplication to division

☐ × 2 ≤ 12 ☐ × 6 ≤ 12	6)12̄ with ×☐ above and ☐☐ below	2)12̄ with ×☐ above and ☐☐ below	12 ÷ 2 = ☐ 12 ÷ 6 = ☐
☐ × 3 ≤ 18 ☐ × 6 ≤ 18	6)18̄ with ×☐ above and ☐☐ below	3)18̄ with ×☐ above and ☐☐ below	18 ÷ ♞ = ☐ 18 ÷ 6 = ☐
☐ × 4 ≤ 12 ☐ × 3 ≤ 12	4)12̄ with ×☐ above and ☐☐ below	3)12̄ with ×☐ above and ☐☐ below	12 ÷ 4 = ☐ 12 ÷ ♗ = ☐

Mom! I Learn Division Using Math-Chess-Puzzles Connection

Ho Math Chess 何数棋谜 妈!我会棋谜式除法啦!

Frank Ho, Amanda Ho © 2004 − 2020, all rights reserved.

Student's Name _____ Date _____

From multiplication to division

□ × 5 ≤ 15 □ × 3 ≤ 15	5)¯15¯ with ×□ on top and □□ below	3)¯15¯ with ×□ on top and □□ below	15 ÷ ♗ = □ 15 ÷ ♖ = □
□ × ♖ ≤ 30 □ × 6 ≤ 30	6)¯30¯ with ×□ on top and □□ below	5)¯30¯ with ×□ on top and □□ below	30 ÷ 5 = □ 30 ÷ 6 = □
□ × 5 ≤ 40 □ × 8 ≤ 40	5)¯40¯ with ×□ on top and □□ below	8)¯40¯ with ×□ on top and □□ below	40 ÷ 5 = □ 40 ÷ 8 = □

Mom! I Learn Division Using Math-Chess-Puzzles Connection

Ho Math Chess 何数棋谜 妈!我会棋谜式除法啦!

Frank Ho, Amanda Ho © 2004 – 2020, all rights reserved.

Student's Name _____ Date _____

From multiplication to division

□ × 5 ≤ 45 □ × 9 ≤ 45	5)45 with ×□ above and □□ below	9)45 with ×□ above and □□ below	45 ÷ 9 = □ 45 ÷ ♜ = □
□ × ♜ ≤ 10 □ × 2 ≤ 10	2)10 with ×□ above and □□ below	5)10 with ×□ above and □□ below	10 ÷ 5 = □ 10 ÷ 2 = □
□ × 5 ≤ 25 □ × ♜ ≤ 25	5)25 with ×□ above and □□ below	5)25 with ×□ above and □□ below	25 ÷ 5 = □ 25 ÷ 5 = □

Mom! I Learn Division Using Math-Chess-Puzzles Connection

From multiplication to division

□ × 4 ≤ 20 □ × 5 ≤ 20	5)‾20 with ×□ on top and □□ below	4)‾20 with ×□ on top and □□ below	20 ÷ 4 = □ 20 ÷ ♖ = □
□ × ♖ ≤ 35 □ × 7 ≤ 35	7)‾35 with ×□ on top and □□ below	5)‾35 with ×□ on top and □□ below	35 ÷ 5 = □ 35 ÷ 7 = □
□ × 8 ≤ 40 □ × ♖ ≤ 40	5)‾40 with ×□ on top and □□ below	8)‾40 with ×□ on top and □□ below	40 ÷ ♖ = □ 40 ÷ 8 = □

Mom! I Learn Division Using Math-Chess-Puzzles Connection

Ho Math Chess 何数棋谜 妈!我会棋谜式除法啦!

Frank Ho, Amanda Ho © 2004 − 2020, all rights reserved.

Student's Name _____ Date _____

From multiplication to division (d ÷ d)

□ × 4 ≤ 24 □ × 6 ≤ 24	$4\overline{)24}$ ×□ □□	$6\overline{)24}$ ×□ □□	24 ÷ 4 = □ 24 ÷ 6 = □
□ × 6 ≤ 42 □ × 7 ≤ 42	$7\overline{)42}$ ×□ □□	$6\overline{)42}$ ×□ □□	42 ÷ 6 = □ 42 ÷ 7 = □
□ × 6 ≤ 36 □ × 6 ≤ 36	$6\overline{)36}$ ×□ □□	$6\overline{)36}$ ×□ □□	36 ÷ 6 = □ 36 ÷ 6 = □

Mom! I Learn Division Using Math-Chess-Puzzles Connection

Ho Math Chess　何数棋谜　妈!我会棋谜式除法啦!

Frank Ho, Amanda Ho © 2004 − 2020, all rights reserved.

Student's Name _____ Date _____

dd ÷ d with 1-digit quotient and no remainder

□ × 5 ≤ 30 □ × ♖ ≤ 30	×□ 6)30 □□	×□ 5)30 □□	30 ÷ 5 = □ 30 ÷ 6 = □
□ × 6 ≤ 24 □ × 4 ≤ 24	×□ 4)24 □□	×□ 6)24 □□	24 ÷ 6 = □ 24 ÷ 4 = □
□ × ♗ ≤ 18 □ × 6 ≤ 18	×□ 6)18 □□	×□ 3)18 □□	18 ÷ 6 = □ 18 ÷ ♗ = □

Page 195

Mom! I Learn Division Using Math-Chess-Puzzles Connection

dd ÷ d with 1-digit quotient and no remainder

□ × 5 ≤ 45 □ × ♛ ≤ 45	5)45	9)45	45 ÷ 5 = □ 45 ÷ ♛ = □
□ × ♜ ≤ 40 □ × 8 ≤ 40	5)40	8)40	40 ÷ 5 = □ 40 ÷ 8 = □
□ × 6 ≤ 30 □ × 5 ≤ 30	6)30	5)30	30 ÷ 6 = □ 30 ÷ ♜ = □

Page 196

Mom! I Learn Division Using Math-Chess-Puzzles Connection

Ho Math Chess 何数棋谜 妈!我会棋谜式除法啦!

Frank Ho, Amanda Ho © 2004 – 2020, all rights reserved.

Student's Name _____ Date _____

dd ÷ d with 1-digit quotient and no remainder

□ × ♖ ≤ 35 □ × 7 ≤ 35	$5\overline{)35}$ with ×□ on top and □□ below	$7\overline{)35}$ with ×□ on top and □□ below	35 ÷ ♖ = □ 35 ÷ 7 = □
□ × 5 ≤ 30 □ × 6 ≤ 30	$5\overline{)30}$ with ×□ on top and □□ below	$6\overline{)30}$ with ×□ on top and □□ below	30 ÷ ♖ = □ 30 ÷ 6 = □
□ × 4 ≤ 20 □ × ♖ ≤ 20	$5\overline{)20}$ with ×□ on top and □□ below	$4\overline{)20}$ with ×□ on top and □□ below	20 ÷ 4 = □ 20 ÷ ♖ = □

Mom! I Learn Division Using Math-Chess-Puzzles Connection

Ho Math Chess 何数棋谜 妈!我会棋谜式除法啦!

Frank Ho, Amanda Ho © 2004 − 2020, all rights reserved.

Student's Name _____ Date _____

dd ÷ d with remainder vs. no remainder

$35 \div 7 = \square$	$5\overline{)35}$	$5\overline{)36}$
$20 \div ♖ = \square$	$4\overline{)20}$	$4\overline{)22}$
$56 \div 8 = \square$	$7\overline{)56}$	$7\overline{)59}$
$81 \div ♕ = \square$	$9\overline{)81}$	$9\overline{)85}$

Mom! I Learn Division Using Math-Chess-Puzzles Connection

Ho Math Chess   何数棋谜   妈!我会棋谜式除法啦!

Frank Ho, Amanda Ho © 2004 – 2020, all rights reserved.

Student's Name _____   Date _____

dd ÷ d with remainder vs. no remainder

21 ÷ ♞ = ☐	7)21 ×☐ ☐☐	7)25 ×☐ ☐☐ ☐
42 ÷ 6 = ☐	7)42 ×☐ ☐☐	7)45 ×☐ ☐☐ ☐
32 ÷ 4 = ☐	8)32 ×☐ ☐☐	8)38 ×☐ ☐☐ ☐
30 ÷ 6 = ☐	5)30 ×☐ ☐☐	5)33 ×☐ ☐☐ ☐

Mom! I Learn Division Using Math-Chess-Puzzles Connection

Ho Math Chess　何数棋谜　妈!我会棋谜式除法啦!

Frank Ho, Amanda Ho © 2004 − 2020, all rights reserved.

Student's Name _____ Date_____

dd ÷ d with remainder vs. no remainder

$18 \div ♕ = \Box$	$2 \overline{) 18}$ with $\times \Box$ above and $\Box\Box$ below	$2 \overline{) 19}$ with $\times \Box$ above and $\Box\Box$ below, $\Box$
$12 \div 6 = \Box$	$2 \overline{) 12}$ with $\times \Box$ above and $\Box\Box$ below	$2 \overline{) 13}$ with $\times \Box$ above and $\Box\Box$ below, $\Box$
$14 \div 7 = \Box$	$2 \overline{) 14}$ with $\times \Box$ above and $\Box\Box$ below	$2 \overline{) 15}$ with $\times \Box$ above and $\Box\Box$ below, $\Box$
$28 \div 4 = \Box$	$7 \overline{) 28}$ with $\times \Box$ above and $\Box\Box$ below	$7 \overline{) 33}$ with $\times \Box$ above and $\Box\Box$ below, $\Box$

Mom! I Learn Division Using Math-Chess-Puzzles Connection

Ho Math Chess   何数棋谜   妈!我会棋谜式除法啦!

Frank Ho, Amanda Ho © 2004 − 2020, all rights reserved.

Student's Name _____   Date _____

dd ÷ d with remainder vs. no remainder

$15 \div \text{♖} = \square$	$3\overline{)15}$ with $\times\square$ above and $\square\square$ below	$3\overline{)16}$ with $\times\square$ above, $\square\square$ and $\square$ below
$18 \div 6 = \square$	$3\overline{)18}$	$3\overline{)19}$
$24 \div 8 = \square$	$3\overline{)24}$	$3\overline{)26}$
$27 \div \text{♕} = \square$	$3\overline{)27}$	$3\overline{)29}$

Page 201

Mom! I Learn Division Using Math-Chess-Puzzles Connection

Ho Math Chess 何数棋谜 妈!我会棋谜式除法啦!

Frank Ho, Amanda Ho © 2004 – 2020, all rights reserved.

Student's Name _____ Date _____

dd ÷ d with remainder vs. no remainder

12 ÷ ♝ = ☐	4)12	4)13
16 ÷ 4 = ☐	4)16	4)18
20 ÷ ♜ = ☐	4)20	4)23
24 ÷ 6 = ☐	4)24	4)27

Page 202

Mom! I Learn Division Using Math-Chess-Puzzles Connection

Ho Math Chess 何数棋谜 妈!我会棋谜式除法啦!

Frank Ho, Amanda Ho © 2004 – 2020, all rights reserved.

Student's Name _____ Date _____

dd ÷ d with remainder vs. no remainder

$10 \div 2 = \square$	$5 \overline{)10}$ with ×□ on top, □□ below	$5 \overline{)14}$ with ×□ on top, □□ and □ below
$20 \div 4 = \square$	$5 \overline{)20}$ with ×□ on top, □□ below	$5 \overline{)24}$ with ×□ on top, □□ and □ below
$25 \div ♖ = \square$	$5 \overline{)25}$ with ×□ on top, □□ below	$5 \overline{)24}$ with ×□ on top, □□ and □ below
$40 \div 8 = \square$	$5 \overline{)40}$ with ×□ on top, □□ below	$5 \overline{)44}$ with ×□ on top, □□ and □ below

Mom! I Learn Division Using Math-Chess-Puzzles Connection

Ho Math Chess   何数棋谜   妈!我会棋谜式除法啦!

Frank Ho, Amanda Ho © 2004 − 2020, all rights reserved.

Student's Name _____   Date _____

From multiplication to division

Fill in the following ☐ with a number.

$\begin{array}{r} 2 \\ \times\ \underline{♛} \\ \square \div 9 = \square\ \ 18,2 \end{array}$	$\begin{array}{r} 9 \\ \times\ \underline{2} \\ \square \div 2 = \square \end{array}$
$\begin{array}{r} 3 \\ \times\ \underline{♛} \\ \square \div ♛ = \square \end{array}$	$\begin{array}{r} ♛ \\ \times\ \underline{3} \\ \square \div 3 = \square \end{array}$
$\begin{array}{r} 4 \\ \times\ \underline{9} \\ \square \div ♛ = \square \end{array}$	$\begin{array}{r} 9 \\ \times\ \underline{4} \\ \square \div 4 = \square \end{array}$
$\begin{array}{r} 5 \\ \times\ \underline{♛} \\ \square \div 9 = \square \end{array}$	$\begin{array}{r} 9 \\ \times\ \underline{5} \\ \square \div 5 = \square \end{array}$
$\begin{array}{r} 6 \\ \times\ \underline{9} \\ \square \div ♛ = \square \end{array}$	$\begin{array}{r} ♛ \\ \times\ \underline{6} \\ \square \div 6 = \square \end{array}$
$\begin{array}{r} 7 \\ \times\ \underline{9} \\ \square \div 9 = \square \end{array}$	$\begin{array}{r} ♛ \\ \times\ \underline{7} \\ \square \div 7 = \square \end{array}$

Mom! I Learn Division Using Math-Chess-Puzzles Connection

Ho Math Chess 何数棋谜 妈!我会棋谜式除法啦!

Frank Ho, Amanda Ho © 2004 – 2020, all rights reserved.

Student's Name _____ Date _____

From multiplication to division

Fill in the following ☐ with a number.

2 × 8 ☐ ÷ 2 = ☐	6 × 2 ☐ ÷ 2 = ☐
♘ × 7 ☐ ÷ 3 = ☐	♖ × 3 ☐ ÷ 3 = ☐
4 × 6 ☐ ÷ 6 = ☐	4 × 4 ☐ ÷ 4 = ☐
♖ × 5 ☐ ÷ 5 = ☐	7 × 5 ☐ ÷ ♖ = ☐
6 × 4 ☐ ÷ 4 = ☐	8 × 6 ☐ ÷ 8 = ☐
7 × 8 ☐ ÷ 7 = ☐	6 × 7 ☐ ÷ 6 = ☐

Mom! I Learn Division Using Math-Chess-Puzzles Connection

Ho Math Chess　何数棋谜　妈!我会棋谜式除法啦!

Frank Ho, Amanda Ho © 2004 − 2020, all rights reserved.

Student's Name_____ Date_____

From multiplication to division

Fill in the following ☐ with a number.

2 × 8 ☐ ÷ 2 = ☐	8 × 2 ☐ ÷ 8 = ☐
4 × 9 ☐ ÷ ♕ = ☐	4 × 3 ☐ ÷ ♘ = ☐
4 × 6 ☐ ÷ 4 = ☐	8 × 4 ☐ ÷ 4 = ☐
5 × 7 ☐ ÷ 7 = ☐	4 × 5 ☐ ÷ 4 = ☐
6 × 8 ☐ ÷ 6 = ☐	6 × 6 ☐ ÷ 6 = ☐
7 × ♘ ☐ ÷ 3 = ☐	4 × 7 ☐ ÷ 7 = ☐

Mom! I Learn Division Using Math-Chess-Puzzles Connection

Ho Math Chess   何数棋谜   妈!我会棋谜式除法啦!

Frank Ho, Amanda Ho © 2004 − 2020, all rights reserved.

Student's Name _____ Date _____

From multiplication to division

Fill in the following ☐ with a number.

☐ ☐ ___ ÷ 3 × 3 9 ♛	☐ ☐ ___ ÷ 5 × ♜ 6 6
☐ ☐ ___ ÷ 5 × 5 ♛ 9	☐ ☐ ___ ÷ 7 × 7 6 6
☐ ☐ ___ ÷ ♜ × 5 7 7	☐ ☐ ___ ÷ 8 × 8 9 ♛

Mom! I Learn Division Using Math-Chess-Puzzles Connection

From multiplication to division

Fill in the following ☐ with a number.

☐ ÷ ♖♕ = (× 5, 9)

☐ ÷ 8 / 6 = (× 8, 6)

☐ ÷ ♖ / 8 = (× 5, 8)

☐ ÷ 4 / 6 = (× 4, 6)

☐ ÷ 6 / 7 = (× 6, 7)

☐ ÷ 8 / 3 = (× 8, ♗)

Mom! I Learn Division Using Math-Chess-Puzzles Connection

Ho Math Chess   何数棋谜   妈!我会棋谜式除法啦!

Frank Ho, Amanda Ho © 2004 – 2020, all rights reserved.

Student's Name _____   Date _____

From multiplication to division

Fill in the following ☐ with a number.

☐ × ♖ = 4, ☐ ÷ 5 = 4

☐ × 8 = ♕, ☐ ÷ 8 = ♕

☐ × 5 = 8, ☐ ÷ ♖ = 8

☐ × 4 = 8, ☐ ÷ 4 = 8

☐ × 7 = 7, ☐ ÷ 7 = 7

☐ × 6 = 3, ☐ ÷ 6 = ♗

Page 209

Mom! I Learn Division Using Math-Chess-Puzzles Connection

From multiplication to division

Fill in the following ☐ with a number.

☐   ☐
___ ÷ _5_
× ♖   3
  3

☐   ☐
___ ÷ _♘_
× 3   9
 ♕

☐   ☐
___ ÷ _6_
× 6   ♘
 ♘

☐   ☐
___ ÷ _8_
× 3   3
  8

☐   ☐
___ ÷ _3_
× 7   7
  3

☐   ☐
___ ÷ _4_
× 4   3
 ♗

Mom! I Learn Division Using Math-Chess-Puzzles Connection

Ho Math Chess 何数棋谜 妈!我会棋谜式除法啦!

Frank Ho, Amanda Ho © 2004 − 2020, all rights reserved.

Student's Name _____ Date _____

From multiplication to division

Fill in the following ☐ with a number.

☐ ☐
___ ÷ ♖
× 5   6
  6
	☐ ☐
	___ ÷ 6
	× 6 ♕
	  9

☐ ☐
___ ÷ 6
× 6   8
  8
	☐ ☐
	___ ÷ 7
	× 7 8
	  8

☐ ☐
___ ÷ 7
× 6   6
  7
	☐ ☐
	___ ÷ 6
	× 6 4
	  4

Mom! I Learn Division Using Math-Chess-Puzzles Connection

Ho Math Chess 何数棋谜 妈!我会棋谜式除法啦!

Frank Ho, Amanda Ho © 2004 – 2020, all rights reserved.

Student's Name _____ Date _____

Multiplication and division facts

Use 2, 7, 14 to write the following multiplication and division facts.

| □ × □ = □ | □ × □ = □ |
| □ ÷ □ = □ | □ ÷ □ = □ |

Use 3, 8, 24 to write the following multiplication and division facts.

| □ × □ = □ | □ × □ = □ |
| □ ÷ □ = □ | □ ÷ □ = □ |

Use 4, 9, 36 to write the following multiplication and division facts.

| □ × □ = □ | □ × □ = □ |
| □ ÷ □ = □ | □ ÷ □ = □ |

Mom! I Learn Division Using Math-Chess-Puzzles Connection

Ho Math Chess 何数棋谜　妈!我会棋谜式除法啦!

Frank Ho, Amanda Ho © 2004 – 2020, all rights reserved.

Student's Name _____ Date _____

Use 5, 7, 35 to write the following multiplication and division facts.

□ × □ = □	□ × □ = □
□ ÷ □ = □	□ ÷ □ = □

Use 6, 8, 48 to write the following multiplication and division facts.

□ × □ = □	□ × □ = □
□ ÷ □ = □	□ ÷ □ = □

Use 7, 9, 63 to write the following multiplication and division facts.

□ × □ = □	□ × □ = □
□ ÷ □ = □	□ ÷ □ = □

Mom! I Learn Division Using Math-Chess-Puzzles Connection

Ho Math Chess 何数棋谜 妈!我会棋谜式除法啦!

Frank Ho, Amanda Ho © 2004 − 2020, all rights reserved.

Student's Name _____ Date _____

Use the following array

● ● ● ● ● ●
● ● ● ● ● ●

to write the following multiplication and division facts.

| □ × □ = □ | □ × □ = □ |
| □ ÷ □ = □ | □ ÷ □ = □ |

Use the following array

● ● ● ● ● ●
● ● ● ● ● ●
● ● ● ● ● ●

to write the following multiplication and division facts.

| □ × □ = □ | □ × □ = □ |
| □ ÷ □ = □ | □ ÷ □ = □ |

Mom! I Learn Division Using Math-Chess-Puzzles Connection

Ho Math Chess 何数棋谜 妈!我会棋谜式除法啦!

Frank Ho, Amanda Ho © 2004 − 2020, all rights reserved.

Student's Name_____ Date_____

Use the following array

• • • • • • •
• • • • • • •
• • • • • • •
• • • • • • •

to write the following multiplication and division facts.

□ × □ = □	□ × □ = □
□ ÷ □ = □	□ ÷ □ = □

Use the following array

• • • • • • • • •
• • • • • • • • •
• • • • • • • • •

to write the following multiplication and division facts.

□ × □ = □	□ × □ = □
□ ÷ □ = □	□ ÷ □ = □

Mom! I Learn Division Using Math-Chess-Puzzles Connection

Division math minutes

18 ÷ 6 =	15 ÷ ♗ =	12 ÷ 4 =	8 ÷ 2 =
14 ÷ 2 =	16 ÷ 8 =	27 ÷ 9 =	81 ÷ 9 =
32 ÷ 4 =	45 ÷ 5 =	21 ÷ ♗ =	28 ÷ 7 =
25 ÷ ♖ =	35 ÷ 7 =	48 ÷ 4 =	58 ÷ 2 = 29
64 ÷ 8 =	76 ÷ 4 =	87 ÷ ♗ =	99 ÷ ♕ =
82 ÷ 2 =	75 ÷ ♖ =	63 ÷ 3 =	64 ÷ 8 =
58 ÷ 2 =	45 ÷ 9 =	32 ÷ 4 =	28 ÷ 2 =
16 ÷ 8 =	24 ÷ 8 =	33 ÷ ♘ =	45 ÷ 9 =
55 ÷ 5 =	65 ÷ 5 =	72 ÷ 4 =	68 ÷ 4 =
98 ÷ 2 =	15 ÷ 5 =	42 ÷ 2 =	44 ÷ 4 =
54 ÷ ♗ =	66 ÷ 6 =	76 ÷ 4 =	84 ÷ 4 =
96 ÷ 8 =	45 ÷ ♕ =	32 ÷ 8 =	35 ÷ 7 =
24 ÷ 6 =	55 ÷ 5 =	42 ÷ 6 =	68 ÷ 2 =
75 ÷ 3 =	46 ÷ 2 =	27 ÷ 3 =	81 ÷ ♗ =
32 ÷ 8 =	45 ÷ 9 =	21 ÷ 7 =	28 ÷ 4 =
18 ÷ ♘ =	15 ÷ 3 =	12 ÷ ♘ =	8 ÷ 4 =
14 ÷ 7 =	16 ÷ 2 =	27 ÷ 3 =	72 ÷ 9 =
32 ÷ 8 =	45 ÷ 9 =	21 ÷ 7 =	32 ÷ 4 =

Mom! I Learn Division Using Math-Chess-Puzzles Connection

Ho Math Chess   何数棋谜   妈!我会棋谜式除法啦!

Frank Ho, Amanda Ho © 2004 − 2020, all rights reserved.

Student's Name _____   Date _____

Division math minutes

24 ÷ 6 =	45 ÷ 3 =	48 ÷ 4 =	18 ÷ 2 =
38 ÷ 2 =	56 ÷ 8 =	54 ÷ 9 =	72 ÷ 9 =
24 ÷ 4 =	50 ÷ 5 =	24 ÷ ♘ =	56 ÷ 7 =
30 ÷ ♖ =	42 ÷ 7 =	56 ÷ 4 =	72 ÷ 2 =
40 ÷ 8 =	36 ÷ 4 =	72 ÷ 6 =	90 ÷ 9 =
96 ÷ 6 =	65 ÷ 5 =	72 ÷ ♕ =	72 ÷ 8 =
84 ÷ 7 =	54 ÷ ♕ =	36 ÷ 4 =	34 ÷ 2 =
24 ÷ 8 =	32 ÷ 8 =	66 ÷ 3 =	18 ÷ 9 =
65 ÷ 5 =	70 ÷ 5 =	80 ÷ 4 =	96 ÷ 4 =
86 ÷ 2 =	25 ÷ ♖ =	44 ÷ 2 =	60 ÷ ♖ =
57 ÷ ♘ =	72 ÷ 6 =	84 ÷ 7 =	96 ÷ 4 =
64 ÷ 8 =	54 ÷ 9 =	40 ÷ 8 =	42 ÷ 7 =
30 ÷ 6 =	65 ÷ 5 =	48 ÷ 6 =	72 ÷ 2 =
45 ÷ 3 =	98 ÷ 2 =	18 ÷ 3 =	27 ÷ ♕ =
40 ÷ 8 =	54 ÷ ♕ =	28 ÷ 7 =	36 ÷ 4 =
18 ÷ 3 =	48 ÷ 6 =	75 ÷ 5 =	96 ÷ 8 =
21 ÷ 7 =	16 ÷ 2 =	27 ÷ ♘ =	72 ÷ 9 =
45 ÷ ♕ =	54 ÷ 9 =	28 ÷ 7 =	35 ÷ ♖ =

Mom! I Learn Division Using Math-Chess-Puzzles Connection

Ho Math Chess 何数棋谜 妈!我会棋谜式除法啦!

Frank Ho, Amanda Ho © 2004 − 2020, all rights reserved.

Student's Name _____ Date _____

dd ÷ d with 2-digit quotient and no remainder

Step 1: Do ☐ × 2 ≤ 6

× ☐☐ ← step 2: 3 × 2 = 6

2) 66

− ☐ ↓ ← step 3: 6 − 6 = 0

= 3   ☐ ← step 4: bring down 6, 6 ÷ 2

− ☐ ← step 5: 3 × 2 = 6

0 ← Remainder = 0

Step 1: Do ☐ × 3 ≤ 4 [the remainder must be ≤ divisor (the outside number)]

× ☐☐ ← step 2: 1 × 3 = 3

3) 48

− ☐ ↓ ← step 3: 4 − 3 = 1

☐☐ ← step 4: bring down 8, 18 ÷ 3 = 6

− ☐☐ ← step 5: 6 × 3 = 18

0 ← Remainder = 0

Step 1: Do ☐ × 5 ≤ 7

× ☐☐ ← step 2: Do multiplication

5) 75

− ☐ ↓ ← step 3: Do subtraction

☐☐ ← step 4: bring down one more digit

− ☐☐ ← step 5: Do multiplication

0 ← Remainder = 0

Step 1: Do ☐ × 3 ≤ 7 4 [the remainder must be ≤ divisor (the outside number)]

× ☐☐ ← step 2: Do multiplication

3) 75

− ☐ ↓ ← step 3: Do subtraction

☐☐ ← step 4: bring down one more digit

− ☐☐ ← step 5: Do multiplication

0 ← Remainder = 0

Mom! I Learn Division Using Math-Chess-Puzzles Connection

Ho Math Chess   何数棋谜   妈!我会棋谜式除法啦!

Frank Ho, Amanda Ho © 2004 − 2020, all rights reserved.

Student's Name _____   Date _____

dd ÷ d with 2-digit quotient and no remainder

Step 1: Do ☐ × 6 ≤ 6

× ☐☐ ← step 2: 1 × 6 = 6

6) 60

− ☐ ↓ ← step 3: 6 − 6 = 0

☐ ← step 4: bring down 0, 0 ÷ 6 = 0

− ☐ ← step 5: 0 × 6 = 0

0 ← Remainder = 0

Step 1: Do ☐ × 9 ≤ 9

× ☐☐ ← step 2: 1 × 9 = 9

9) 90

− ☐ ↓ ← step 3: 9 − 9 = 0

☐ ← step 4: bring down 0, 0 ÷ 9 = 0

− ☐ ← step 5: 0 × 9 = 0

0 ← Remainder = 0

Step 1: Do ☐ × 5 ≤ 5

× ☐☐ ← step 2: Do multiplication

5) 50

− ☐ ↓ ← Step 3: Do subtraction

☐ ← step 4: bring down one more digit

− ☐ ← step 5: Do multiplication

0 ← Remainder = 0

Step 1: Do ☐ × 3 ≤ 3

× ☐☐ ← step 2: Do multiplication

3) 30

− ☐ ↓ ← Step 3: Do subtraction

☐ ← step 4: bring down one more digit

− ☐ ← step 5: Do multiplication

0 ← Remainder = 0

Mom! I Learn Division Using Math-Chess-Puzzles Connection

Ho Math Chess 何数棋谜 妈!我会棋谜式除法啦!

Frank Ho, Amanda Ho © 2004 – 2020, all rights reserved.

Student's Name _____ Date _____

dd ÷ d with 2-digit quotient and no remainder

□ × 2 ≤ ♗	□ × 2 ≤ 12	2)32
□ × 2 ≤ 3	□ × 2 ≤ 18	2)38
□ × ♗ ≤ 4	□ × 3 ≤ 18	3)48

Mom! I Learn Division Using Math-Chess-Puzzles Connection

Ho Math Chess　何数棋谜　妈!我会棋谜式除法啦!

Frank Ho, Amanda Ho © 2004 − 2020, all rights reserved.

Student's Name_____ Date_____

dd ÷ d with 2-digit quotient and no remainder

□ × 4 ≤ 8	□ × 4 ≤ 4	4)84
□ × 5 ≤ ♛	□ × ♜ ≤ 40	5)90
□ × 6 ≤ 9	□ × 6 ≤ 36	6)96

Page 221

Mom! I Learn Division Using Math-Chess-Puzzles Connection

Ho Math Chess 何数棋谜 妈!我会棋谜式除法啦!

Frank Ho, Amanda Ho © 2004 − 2020, all rights reserved.

Student's Name _____ Date _____

dd ÷ d with 2-digit quotient and no remainder

$3 \overline{)96}$

$2 \overline{)52}$

$4 \overline{)72}$

$4 \overline{)84}$

$4 \overline{)52}$

$2 \overline{)34}$

$4 \overline{)84}$

$4 \overline{)52}$

$4 \overline{)64}$

Mom! I Learn Division Using Math-Chess-Puzzles Connection

Ho Math Chess 何数棋谜 妈!我会棋谜式除法啦!

Frank Ho, Amanda Ho © 2004 − 2020, all rights reserved.

Student's Name _____ Date _____

dd ÷ d with 2-digit quotient and no remainder

$7\overline{)84}$

$6\overline{)72}$

$7\overline{)91}$

$9\overline{)99}$

$8\overline{)88}$

$6\overline{)66}$

$8\overline{)96}$

$6\overline{)78}$

$6\overline{)90}$

Mom! I Learn Division Using Math-Chess-Puzzles Connection

dd ÷ d with 2-digit quotient and remainder

4)69	4)79	4)86
5)69	6)79	8)89
5)99	6)85	3)37

Mom! I Learn Division Using Math-Chess-Puzzles Connection

Ho Math Chess   何数棋谜   妈!我会棋谜式除法啦!

Frank Ho, Amanda Ho © 2004 – 2020, all rights reserved.

Student's Name _____   Date _____

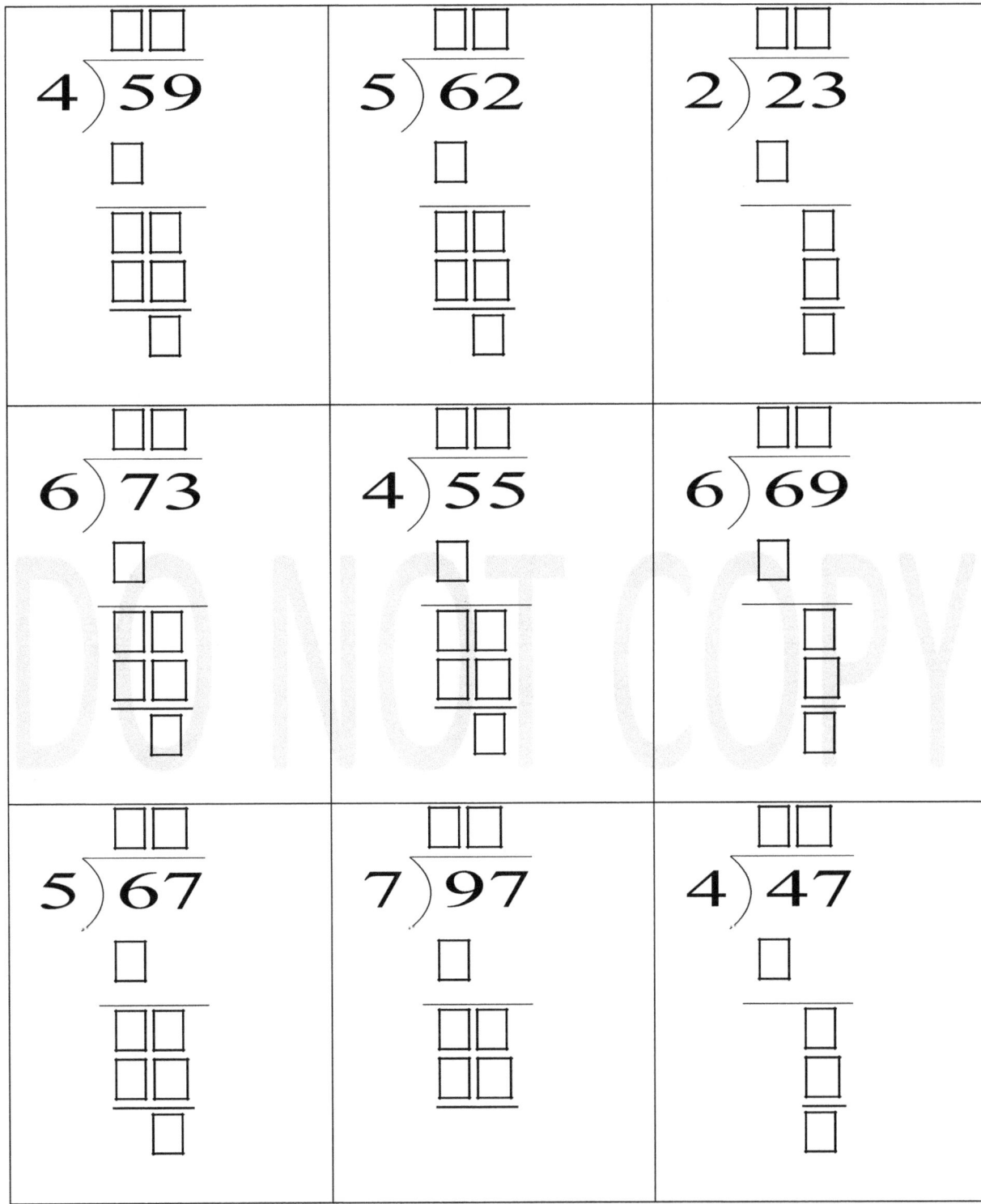

Mom! I Learn Division Using Math-Chess-Puzzles Connection

ddd ÷ d with three-digit quotient and no remainder

☐ × 7 ≤ 8

☐ × 7 ≤ 14

7) 840

☐ × 6 ≤ ♛

☐ × 6 ≤ 36

6) 960

Mom! I Learn Division Using Math-Chess-Puzzles Connection

ddd ÷ d with three-digit quotient and no remainder

605 ÷ ♖ = _____

786 ÷ 6 = _____

987 ÷ 7 = _____

968 ÷ 8 = _____

Mom! I Learn Division Using Math-Chess-Puzzles Connection

Ho Math Chess   何数棋谜   妈!我会棋谜式除法啦!

Frank Ho, Amanda Ho © 2004 − 2020, all rights reserved.

Student's Name _____   Date _____

ddd ÷ d with three-digit quotient and no remainder

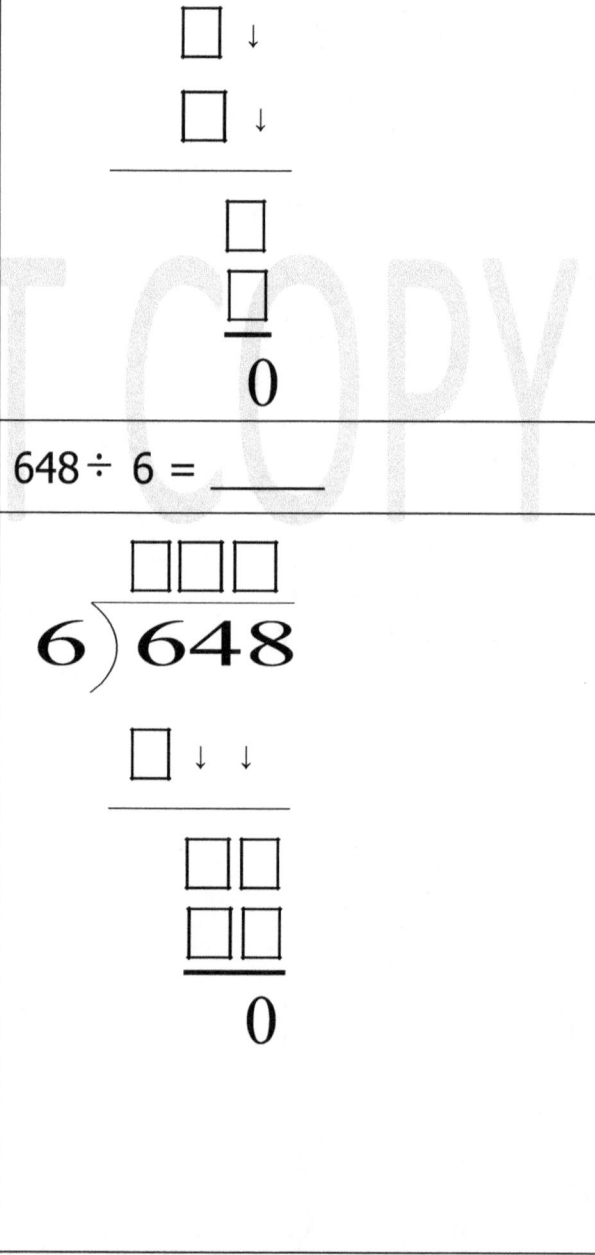

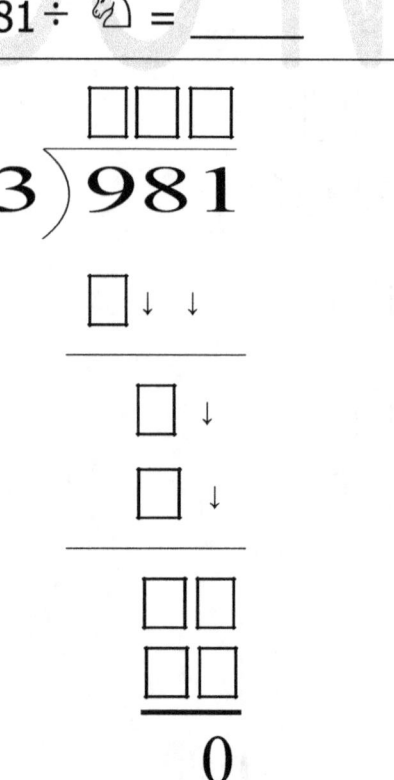

Page 228

Mom! I Learn Division Using Math-Chess-Puzzles Connection

Ho Math Chess   何数棋谜   妈!我会棋谜式除法啦!

Frank Ho, Amanda Ho © 2004 – 2020, all rights reserved.

Student's Name _____   Date _____

ddd ÷ d with three-digit quotient and no remainder

526 ÷ 2 = _____

696 ÷  = _____

981 ÷ ♛ = _____

636 ÷ 6 = _____

Mom! I Learn Division Using Math-Chess-Puzzles Connection

Ho Math Chess 何数棋谜 妈!我会棋谜式除法啦!

Frank Ho, Amanda Ho © 2004 − 2020, all rights reserved.

Student's Name _____ Date _____

ddd ÷ d with three-digit quotient and remainder

982 ÷ ♛ = _____

9)982

967 ÷ ♞ = _____

3)967

929 ÷ ♝ = _____

3)929

637 ÷ 6 = _____

6)637

Page 230

Mom! I Learn Division Using Math-Chess-Puzzles Connection

Ho Math Chess 何数棋谜 妈!我会棋谜式除法啦!

Frank Ho, Amanda Ho © 2004 − 2020, all rights reserved.

Student's Name _____ Date _____

ddd ÷ d with two-digit quotient and remainder

253 ÷ 8 = _____

196 ÷ ♝ = _____

629 ÷ 7 = _____

537 ÷ 6 = _____

Mom! I Learn Division Using Math-Chess-Puzzles Connection

Ho Math Chess 何数棋谜 妈!我会棋谜式除法啦!

Frank Ho, Amanda Ho © 2004 − 2020, all rights reserved.

Student's Name _____ Date _____

dddd ÷ d

1234 ÷ 2 = _____

$$2\overline{)1234}$$

1876 ÷ 2 = _____

$$2\overline{)1876}$$

3612 ÷ 4 = _____

$$4\overline{)3612}$$

41228 ÷ 4 = _____

$$4\overline{)41228}$$

Page 232

Mom! I Learn Division Using Math-Chess-Puzzles Connection

Ho Math Chess 何数棋谜 妈!我会棋谜式除法啦!

Frank Ho, Amanda Ho © 2004 – 2020, all rights reserved.

Student's Name _____ Date _____

Short Division

$\square\square\square$ $2\overline{)123^14}$	$\square\square\square$ $2\overline{)187^16}$
$\square\square\square$ $4\overline{)3612}$	$\square\square\square\square\square$ $4\overline{)41228}$
$4\overline{)2150241}$	$2\overline{)1776}$
$5\overline{)1789}$	$7\overline{)1876}$
$3\overline{)1334}$	$6\overline{)1976}$

Mom! I Learn Division Using Math-Chess-Puzzles Connection

Ho Math Chess 何数棋谜 妈!我会棋谜式除法啦!

Frank Ho, Amanda Ho © 2004 – 2020, all rights reserved.

Student's Name _____ Date _____

Short Division

9)1234	8)1876
4)3713	4)51218
5)2150241	5)1776
6)1789	8)1876
4)1334	8)1976

Mom! I Learn Division Using Math-Chess-Puzzles Connection

Ho Math Chess 何数棋谜 妈!我会棋谜式除法啦!

Frank Ho, Amanda Ho © 2004 – 2020, all rights reserved.

Student's Name _____ Date _____

Rounding whole number (5 up, 4 down)

Rounding is a method of giving an approximate value to a number. The procedure of rounding a whole number is the same as the procedure of rounding a decimal number; only the place value is different. For example, round $29 to the nearest tens, it means to get an estimated number whose value is as close to the tens position of $29 as possible.

When $29 is rounded to the nearest tens position, there will be two answers: $20 or $30.

Is $29 closer to $20 or is $29 closer to $30? $29 is closer to $30, so the nearest tens value will be $30. The rule of rounding is as follows:

Question: Round the following numbers to the nearest tens (underlined)	Step 1: Point to the place value to be rounded by circling it.	Step 2: Look at the digit (single number) to the right of the circled number.	Step 3: **5 up, 4 down** If it is 5 or more the add 1 to the circled number (round up); if it is less than 5 do not add 1 to the circled number (round down).	Step 4: All digits to the right of the circle number should be changed to 0.	Final answer
412̲8	41②8	8	41③8	41③0	4130
2̲9	②9	9	②9	③0	30
2̲5	②5	5	②5	③0	30
2̲4	②4	4	②4	②0	20
3̲5					
3̲9					
3̲4					
35̲5					
41̲2					
40̲0					
55̲0					

No part of this publication can be copied, duplicated, or reproduced.

Mom! I Learn Division Using Math-Chess-Puzzles Connection

Ho Math Chess   何数棋谜   妈!我会棋谜式除法啦!

Frank Ho, Amanda Ho © 2004 – 2020, all rights reserved.

Student's Name _____   Date _____

Rounding whole number

Question: Round the following numbers to the nearest hundreds	Step 1: Point to the place value to be rounded by circling it.	Step 2: Look at the digit (single number) to the right of circled number.	Step 3: If it is 5 or more then add 1 to the circled number; if it is less than 5, do not add 1 to the circled number.	Step 4: All digits to the right of the circle number should be changed to 0.	Final answer
219999					
200099					
200051					
200150					
209951					
209949					
209940					
299999					

Question: Round the following numbers to the nearest thousands	Step 1: Point to the place value to be rounded by circling it.	Step 2: Look at the digit (single number) to the right of circled number.	Step 3: If it is 5 or more the add 1 to the circled number; if it is less than 5 do not add 1 to the circled number.	Step 4: All digits to the right of the circle number should be changed to 0.	Final answer
99999					
88888					
12699					
49999					
43111					
45959					

Mom! I Learn Division Using Math-Chess-Puzzles Connection

Ho Math Chess　何数棋谜　妈!我会棋谜式除法啦!

Frank Ho, Amanda Ho © 2004 − 2020, all rights reserved.

Student's Name _____ Date _____

Round the following numbers to the nearest place values indicated.

Standard form	10000	1000	100	10	Total place value underlined
99999					
55555					
54545					
50	N/A	N/A			

Insert digits in the ☐ so that the following rounding would make sense.

5 ☐ 9 rounds to 600, to the nearest tens place,
_____

99☐ rounds to 1000, to the nearest tens place,
_____

123☐4 rounds to 12300, to the nearest hundreds place,
_____

55☐55 rounds to 56000, to the nearest hundreds place,
_____

49☐99 rounds to 50000, to the nearest tens place,
_____

Mom! I Learn Division Using Math-Chess-Puzzles Connection

Write the place value to which each number has been rounded.

Number rounded	Place value rounded
3590 ⇒ 3600	Hundreds
3590 ⇒ 4000	_____
43995 ⇒ 44000	_____
43995 ⇒ 40000	_____
3590 ⇒ 4000	_____
135910 ⇒ 135900	_____
135910 ⇒ 136000	_____

Mom! I Learn Division Using Math-Chess-Puzzles Connection

Ho Math Chess 何数棋谜 妈!我会棋谜式除法啦!

Frank Ho, Amanda Ho © 2004 − 2020, all rights reserved.

Student's Name _____ Date _____

Trailing zeros in the dividend

$1\overline{)7}$ with □ above and □ below	7 tens ↵ $1\overline{)7\,tens}$ ↑ (Just bring up 0's) <u>7 tens</u>	7 hundreds $1\overline{)7\,hundreds}$ <u>7 hundreds</u>
	□□ above $1\overline{)70}$ <u>□ 0</u>	□□□ above $1\overline{)700}$ <u>□□□</u>
□ above $1\overline{)9}$ <u>□</u>	□□ above $1\overline{)90}$ <u>□□</u>	□□□ above $1\overline{)900}$ <u>□□□</u>

Page 239

Mom! I Learn Division Using Math-Chess-Puzzles Connection

Trailing zeros in the dividend and divisor

Crossing out 1 zero in divisor and dividend.	Crossing out 1 zero in divisor and dividend.	Crossing out 2 zeros in divisor and dividend. (Cross out equal number of 0's in divisor and dividend)
10)60	60)6000	600)600000
20)1200	300)1800	120)240000
3)240	3)2400	30)480000

Page 240

Mom! I Learn Division Using Math-Chess-Puzzles Connection

Ho Math Chess   何数棋谜   妈!我会棋谜式除法啦!

Frank Ho, Amanda Ho © 2004 – 2020, all rights reserved.

Student's Name _____   Date _____

Dividend with trailing 0's (with no remainder)

$8100 \div 81$

$\,\mathbf{1\ 0\ 0} \leftarrow$ (Just bring up the 0's straight up as the quotient)
$81 \overline{)8100} \;\uparrow$
$\underline{8\ 1\ 0\ 0}$

$810 \div 81 =$ ___	$8100 \div 81 =$ _____	$81000 \div 81 =$ _____
$480 \div 6 =$ ___	$4800 \div 60 =$ _____ Think as $480\cancel{0} \div 6\cancel{0} = 480 \div 6$	$48000 \div 6000 =$ _____ Think as $48\cancel{000} \div 6\cancel{000} = 48 \div 6$
$490 \div 7 =$ ___	$49000 \div 70 =$ ___ Think as $4900\cancel{0} \div 7\cancel{0} = 4900 \div 7$	$490000 \div 7000 =$ ___ Think as $490\cancel{000} \div 7\cancel{000} = 490 \div 7$
$640 \div 4 =$ _____	$64000 \div 40 =$ ___	$640000 \div 4000 =$ ___
$250 \div$ ♖ $=$ _____	$25000 \div 500 =$ ___	$250000 \div 5000 =$ ___

Page 241

Mom! I Learn Division Using Math-Chess-Puzzles Connection

Trailing zeros in the dividend and divisor

120 ÷ ♗ = ___	12000 ÷ 300 = ___	120000 ÷ 3000 = ___
240 ÷ ♘ = ___	24000 ÷ 300 = ___	240000 ÷ 3000 = ___
840 ÷ 24 = ___	84000 ÷ 2400 = ___	840000 ÷ 24000 = ___
750 ÷ 25 = ___	75000 ÷ 2500 = ___	750000 ÷ 25000 = ___
240 ÷ 12 = ___	24000 ÷ 1200 = ___	240000 ÷ 12000 = ___
390 ÷ 13 = ___	39000 ÷ 1300 = ___	390000 ÷ 13000 = ___
280 ÷ 14 = ___	28000 ÷ 1400 = ___	14000 ÷ 280 = ___

Mom! I Learn Division Using Math-Chess-Puzzles Connection

Ho Math Chess 何数棋谜 妈!我会棋谜式除法啦!

Frank Ho, Amanda Ho © 2004 − 2020, all rights reserved.

Student's Name _____   Date _____

50 ÷ 25 = _____	50 × 2 = _____ 100 ÷ 25 = _____
200 ÷ 25 = _____	200 × 2 = _____ 400 ÷ 25 = _____
60 ÷ 30 = _____	60 × 2 = _____ 120 ÷ 30 = _____
240 ÷ 30 = _____	240 × 2 = _____ 480 ÷ 30 = _____
600 ÷ 40 = _____	120 ÷ 40 = _____
120 ÷ 20 = _____	120 × 2 = _____ 20 × 2 = _____ 240 ÷ 40 = _____
160 ÷ 40 = _____	320 ÷ 80 = _____
160 ÷ 80 = _____	320 ÷ 160 = _____
240 ÷ 30 = _____	480 ÷ 60 = _____
240 ÷ 60 = _____	240 ÷ 120 = _____

Mom! I Learn Division Using Math-Chess-Puzzles Connection

Ho Math Chess 何数棋谜 妈!我会棋谜式除法啦!

Frank Ho, Amanda Ho © 2004 – 2020, all rights reserved.

Student's Name _____ Date _____

Zeros in the middle of quotient

$$2\overline{)212}$$

$$3\overline{)921}$$

$$4\overline{)424}$$

$$4\overline{)1236}$$

$$5\overline{)153505}$$

$$6\overline{)1236}$$

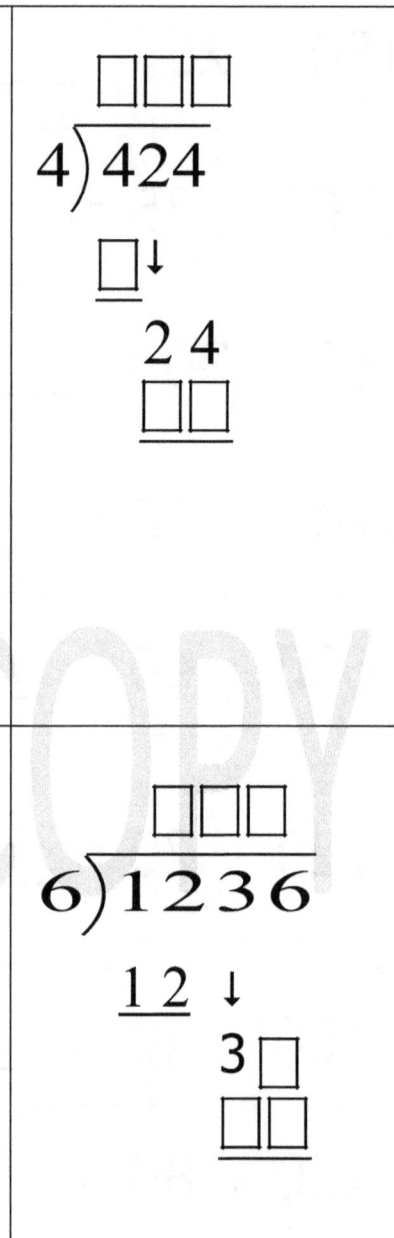

No part of this publication can be copied, duplicated, or reproduced.

Zeros in the middle of quotient

4) 12036

5) 1503505

6) 12036

4) 16032

5) 20035015

6) 120042

Mom! I Learn Division Using Math-Chess-Puzzles Connection

Ho Math Chess　何数棋谜　妈!我会棋谜式除法啦!

Frank Ho, Amanda Ho © 2004 – 2020, all rights reserved.

Student's Name _____ Date _____

Quotient with leading, middle, and training zeros

$4\overline{)36040}$

$3\overline{)70040}$

$5\overline{)140050}$

$4\overline{)130040}$

$6\overline{)17040240}$

$7\overline{)2100490}$

Mom! I Learn Division Using Math-Chess-Puzzles Connection

Ho Math Chess 何数棋谜 妈!我会棋谜式除法啦!

Frank Ho, Amanda Ho © 2004 − 2020, all rights reserved.

Student's Name _____ Date _____

d0...0d. ÷ dd0... with no remainder

$6006 \div ♞ =$ 2002 2002 (Bring up 0's) 3)6006 <u>6006</u>	$60006 \div 3$ = _____	$600006 \div 3$ = _____
$220000 \div 11$ = _____	$220022 \div 11$ = _____	$220000 \div 1100$ = _____
$660066 \div 33$ = _____	$66006600 \div 330$ = _____	$6600066\cancel{00} \div 33\cancel{00} =$ $6600066 \div 33$ = _____
$88880088 \div 44$ = _____	$8888008800 \div 440$ = _____	$88880088000 \div 44000$ = _____
$100000 \div 100$ = _____	$10000000 \div 1000$ = _____	$1000000000000 \div 100000$ = _____

Mom! I Learn Division Using Math-Chess-Puzzles Connection

Ho Math Chess　何数棋谜　妈!我会棋谜式除法啦!

Frank Ho, Amanda Ho © 2004 − 2020, all rights reserved.

Student's Name _____ Date _____

÷ by multiples of 10's (equivalent to × by multiples of 0.1)

$810 \div 10 = 810. \div 10 = 81$ (move the invisible decimal point of the dividend to the left as many as zeros in the divisor, in this case, it is 1 zero in 10.)	$8100 \div 10 = $ _____
$8100 \div 100 = 8100. \div 100 = 81$ (move the invisible decimal point to the left 2 places because there are 2 zeros in 100.)	$8100 \div 100 = $ _____
$10000 \div 10 = $ _____	$120 \div 10 = $ _____
$10000 \div 100 = $ _____	$1200 \div 100 = $ _____
$10000 \div 1000 = $ _____	$12000 \div 1000 = $ _____
$10000 \div 10000 = $ _____	$120000 \div 10000 = $ _____
$100000 \div 10000 = $ _____	$120000 \div 10000 = $ _____

Mom! I Learn Division Using Math-Chess-Puzzles Connection

Ho Math Chess   何数棋谜   妈!我会棋谜式除法啦!

Frank Ho, Amanda Ho © 2004 − 2020, all rights reserved.

Student's Name _____   Date _____

Estimating quotient of ddd ÷ dd

Step1: Round 21 as 20 (multiple of 10), estimate quotient by dividing 64 ÷ 20 = 3.

```
      3
20) 640
     6 0
```

Step 2: Compare 64 > 60, so 3 is the estimated quotient.

Think 64 ÷ 20

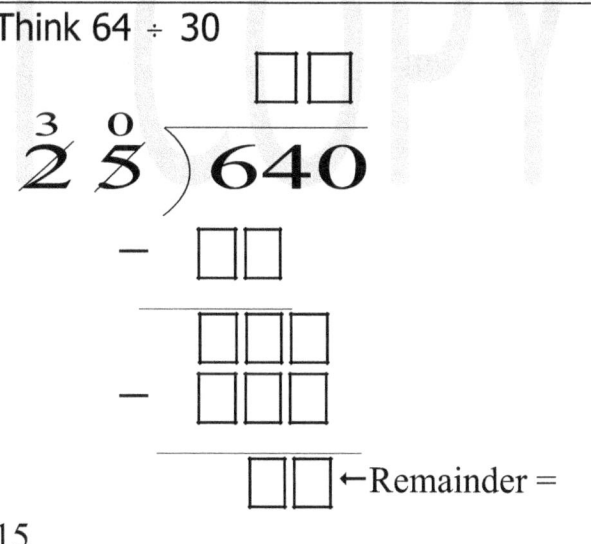

←Remainder = 10

Step1: Round 25 as 30 (multiple of 10), estimate quotient by dividing 64 ÷ 30 = 2.

```
      2
30) 640
     6 0
```

Step 2: Compare 64 > 50, so 2 is the estimated quotient.

```
      4
30) 140
    1 2 0
```

Compare 140 > 120, so 4 is the estimated quotient. Try it, it is too small, so try 5

Think 64 ÷ 30

←Remainder = 15

Mom! I Learn Division Using Math-Chess-Puzzles Connection

Ho Math Chess　何数棋谜　妈!我会棋谜式除法啦!

Frank Ho, Amanda Ho © 2004 − 2020, all rights reserved.

Student's Name _____ Date _____

ddd ÷ dd with 2-digit quotient

□ × 42 ≤ 84

□ × 2 ≤ 84

42) 840

□ × 48 ≤ 96

□ × 2 ≤ 96

48) 960

Page 250

Mom! I Learn Division Using Math-Chess-Puzzles Connection

Ho Math Chess 何数棋谜 妈!我会棋谜式除法啦!

Frank Ho, Amanda Ho © 2004 − 2020, all rights reserved.

Student's Name _____ Date _____

ddd ÷ dd with 2-digit quotient

10)100

10)120

11)132

40)640

51)612

28)896

Mom! I Learn Division Using Math-Chess-Puzzles Connection

Ho Math Chess 何数棋谜 妈!我会棋谜式除法啦!

Frank Ho, Amanda Ho © 2004 – 2020, all rights reserved.

Student's Name _____ Date _____

ddd ÷ dd with 2-digit quotient

$32 \overline{)440}$

$27 \overline{)340}$

$53 \overline{)840}$

$57 \overline{)640}$

$63 \overline{)740}$

$78 \overline{)879}$

ddd ÷ dd with 2-digit quotient

37)440

39)470

52)647

17)245

27)340

68)779

Mom! I Learn Division Using Math-Chess-Puzzles Connection

ddd ÷ dd with 2-digit quotient

57)697

19)278

72)747

29)345

37)451

62)670

Mom! I Learn Division Using Math-Chess-Puzzles Connection

Ho Math Chess 何数棋谜 妈!我会棋谜式除法啦!

Frank Ho, Amanda Ho © 2004 – 2020, all rights reserved.

Student's Name _____ Date _____

ddd ÷ dd with 2-digit quotient

29)349

49)570

35)427

37)447

67)743

57)629

Page 255

Mom! I Learn Division Using Math-Chess-Puzzles Connection

Ho Math Chess 何数棋谜 妈!我会棋谜式除法啦!

Frank Ho, Amanda Ho © 2004 – 2020, all rights reserved.

Student's Name _____ Date _____

ddd ÷ dd with 2-digit quotient

25)775

49)588

35)420

37)481

67)938

57)855

Page 256

Mom! I Learn Division Using Math-Chess-Puzzles Connection

Ho Math Chess 何数棋谜 妈!我会棋谜式除法啦!

Frank Ho, Amanda Ho © 2004 − 2020, all rights reserved.

Student's Name _____ Date _____

ddd ÷ dd with 2-digit quotient

49)588

79)869

37)481

39)546

68)952

67)930

Mom! I Learn Division Using Math-Chess-Puzzles Connection

Ho Math Chess 何数棋谜 妈!我会棋谜式除法啦!

Frank Ho, Amanda Ho © 2004 – 2020, all rights reserved.

Student's Name _____ Date _____

Estimating ddd ÷ dd with 1-digit quotient

Step1: Round 83 as 80 (multiple of 10), estimate quotient by dividing 412 ÷ 80 = 5.

$$80 \overline{)412}$$
$$400$$

Step 2: Try quotient 5. Compare 415 > 412, so 5 is over estimated. Try 4, 332 < 412, so 4 is the right quotient.

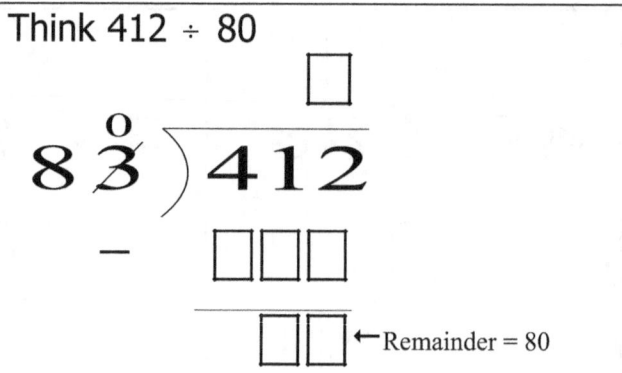

Think 412 ÷ 80

Remainder = 80

Step1: Round 86 as 90 (multiple of 10), estimate quotient by dividing 441 ÷ 90 = 4.

$$90 \overline{)441}$$
$$360$$

Step 2: Compare 441 > 360, so 4 is the estimated quotient. 4 times 86 = 344 < 441. So, the quotient 4 is underestimated. Try 5.

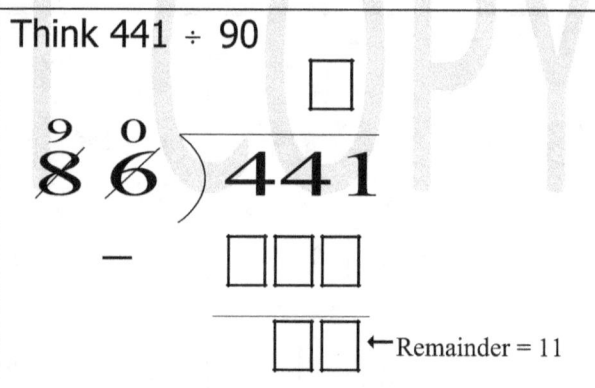

Think 441 ÷ 90

Remainder = 11

Mom! I Learn Division Using Math-Chess-Puzzles Connection

Ho Math Chess 何数棋谜 妈!我会棋谜式除法啦!

Frank Ho, Amanda Ho © 2004 − 2020, all rights reserved.

Student's Name _____ Date _____

ddd ÷ dd with 1-digit quotient

□ × 12 ≤ 108	12) 108	12) 109
□ × 21 ≤ 147	21) 147	21) 157
□ × 33 ≤ 198	32) 192	33) 209

Page 259

Mom! I Learn Division Using Math-Chess-Puzzles Connection

Ho Math Chess 何数棋谜 妈!我会棋谜式除法啦!

Frank Ho, Amanda Ho © 2004 − 2020, all rights reserved.

Student's Name _____ Date _____

ddd ÷ dd with 1-digit quotient

□ × 19 ≤ 152	19)152	19)169
□ × 25 ≤ 147	25)200	25)217
□ × 37 ≤ 222	37)222	37)239

Mom! I Learn Division Using Math-Chess-Puzzles Connection

Ho Math Chess 何数棋谜 妈!我会棋谜式除法啦!

Frank Ho, Amanda Ho © 2004 − 2020, all rights reserved.

Student's Name _____ Date _____

ddd ÷ dd with 1-digit quotient

□ × 42 ≤ 336	42)336	42)349
□ × 53 ≤ 371	53)371	53)387
□ × 67 ≤ 469	67)469	67)512

Mom! I Learn Division Using Math-Chess-Puzzles Connection

ddd ÷ dd with 1-digit quotient

☐ × 83 ≤ 332	83)332	83)353
☐ × 97 ≤ 679	97)679	97)687
☐ × 78 ≤ 624	78)624	78)657

Mom! I Learn Division Using Math-Chess-Puzzles Connection

Ho Math Chess 何数棋谜 妈!我会棋谜式除法啦!

Frank Ho, Amanda Ho © 2004 – 2020, all rights reserved.

Student's Name _____ Date _____

ddd ÷ dd with 1-digit quotient and remainder

□ × 24 ≤ 173	□R□ 24)173 □□□ □□	□R□ 47)299 □□□ □□
□ × 48 ≤ 200	□R□ 48)200 □□□ □□	□□R□ 12)123 □□□ □□
□ × 48 ≤ 348	□R□ 48)348 □□□ □□	□ 78)667 □□□ □□

Page 263

Mom! I Learn Division Using Math-Chess-Puzzles Connection

Ho Math Chess 何数棋谜 妈!我会棋谜式除法啦!

Frank Ho, Amanda Ho © 2004 – 2020, all rights reserved.

Student's Name _____ Date _____

ddd ÷ dd with 1-digit quotient and remainder

☐ × 25 ≤ 213

$25 \overline{)213}$ ☐ R ☐

$37 \overline{)247}$ ☐ R ☐

☐ × 87 ≤ 850

$87 \overline{)850}$

$97 \overline{)887}$

☐ × 58 ≤ 404

$58 \overline{)404}$

$78 \overline{)657}$

Mom! I Learn Division Using Math-Chess-Puzzles Connection

Ho Math Chess　何数棋谜　妈!我会棋谜式除法啦!

Frank Ho, Amanda Ho © 2004 – 2020, all rights reserved.

Student's Name _____ Date _____

ddd ÷ dd with 1-digit quotient and remainder

□ × 83 ≤ 532	83)532	63)253
□ × 37 ≤ 279	37)279	77)687
□ × 68 ≤ 524	68)524	58)557

Mom! I Learn Division Using Math-Chess-Puzzles Connection

ddd ÷ dd with 1-digit quotient and remainder

□ × 43 ≤ 332	43) 332	63) 453
□ × 76 ≤ 679	76) 679	43) 387
□ × 38 ≤ 424	38) 424	48) 557

Mom! I Learn Division Using Math-Chess-Puzzles Connection

Ho Math Chess 何数棋谜 妈!我会棋谜式除法啦!

Frank Ho, Amanda Ho © 2004 − 2020, all rights reserved.

Student's Name _____   Date _____

Estimating of 2-digit(s) quotient by rounding

Step1: Round 53 as 50 (multiple of 10), estimate quotient by dividing 202 ÷ 50 = 4.

```
        4
50 ) 2021
       200
```

Step 2: Try quotient 4. Compare 212 > 202, so 4 is over estimated. Try 3, 159 < 202, so 3 is the right quotient.

Use 431 divided by 50, the estimated quotient is 8.

```
        8
50 ) 431
      400
```

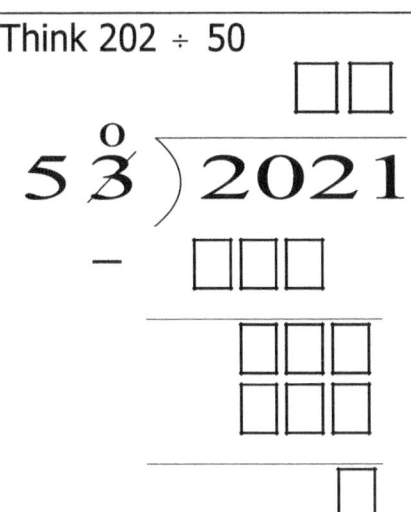

Think 202 ÷ 50

Step1: Round 56 as 60 (multiple of 10), estimate quotient by dividing 202 ÷ 60 = 3.

```
        3
60 ) 2021
       180
```

Step 2: Compare 180 < 202, so 3 is the estimated quotient. 3 times 56 = 198 < 202. So, 3 is the quotient.
Step 3: 341 divided by 60, the estimated quotient is 5.
5 times 56 = 280, 341 − 280 = 61 which is > 56. So, the quotient should be 6.

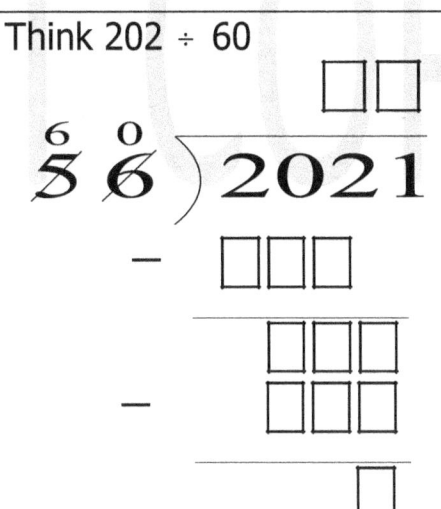

Think 202 ÷ 60

Mom! I Learn Division Using Math-Chess-Puzzles Connection

Ho Math Chess 何数棋谜 妈!我会棋谜式除法啦!

Frank Ho, Amanda Ho © 2004 – 2020, all rights reserved.

Student's Name _____ Date _____

Estimating quotient of 2-digit or more divisors by rounding

30)239	40)325	50)483
60)461	70)365	80)465
(Think 239 ÷ 30) 31)239	(Think 195 ÷ 40) 41)195	(Think 475 ÷ 50) 51)475
(Think 281 ÷ 40) 35)281	(Think 405 ÷ 50) 46)405	(Think 445 ÷ 60) 57)445

Mom! I Learn Division Using Math-Chess-Puzzles Connection

Ho Math Chess　　何数棋谜　　妈!我会棋谜式除法啦!

Frank Ho, Amanda Ho © 2004 – 2020, all rights reserved.

Student's Name _____　　Date _____

Estimating quotient of 2-digit or more divisors by rounding

$40\overline{)239}$	$40\overline{)2391}$	$40\overline{)23911}$
(Think 361 ÷ 70)	(Think 3614 ÷ 70)	(Think 36140 ÷ 70)
$66\overline{)361}$	$66\overline{)3614}$	$66\overline{)36140}$
(Think 239 ÷ 20)	(Think 2391 ÷ 20)	(Think 23913 ÷ 20)
$19\overline{)239}$	$19\overline{)2391}$	$19\overline{)23913}$

Mom! I Learn Division Using Math-Chess-Puzzles Connection

ddd ÷ dd = q with no remainder

105 ÷ 21 = ☐	110 ÷ 22 = ☐	115 ÷ 23 = ☐
126 ÷ 21 = ☐	132 ÷ 22 = ☐	138 ÷ 23 = ☐
144 ÷ 24 = ☐	175 ÷ 25 = ☐	208 ÷ 26 = ☐
200 ÷ 25 = ☐	216 ÷ 36 = ☐	188 ÷ 47 = ☐
156 ÷ 26 = ☐	185 ÷ 37 = ☐	288 ÷ 48 = ☐
243 ÷ 27 = ☐	342 ÷ 38 = ☐	294 ÷ 49 = ☐
224 ÷ 28 = ☐	273 ÷ 39 = ☐	400 ÷ 50 = ☐
203 ÷ 29 = ☐	320 ÷ 40 = ☐	255 ÷ 51 = ☐
150 ÷ 30 = ☐	246 ÷ 41 = ☐	416 ÷ 52 = ☐
186 ÷ 31 = ☐	294 ÷ 42 = ☐	371 ÷ 53 = ☐
224 ÷ 32 = ☐	172 ÷ 43 = ☐	216 ÷ 54 = ☐
264 ÷ 33 = ☐	220 ÷ 44 = ☐	220 ÷ 55 = ☐
306 ÷ 34 = ☐	270 ÷ 45 = ☐	504 ÷ 56 = ☐
315 ÷ 35 = ☐	414 ÷ 46 = ☐	456 ÷ 57 = ☐

Mom! I Learn Division Using Math-Chess-Puzzles Connection

Ho Math Chess　何数棋谜　妈!我会棋谜式除法啦!

Frank Ho, Amanda Ho © 2004 − 2020, all rights reserved.

Student's Name _____　　Date _____

ddd ÷ dd = qq with no remainder

231 ÷ 11 = ☐	792 ÷ 22 = ☐	897 ÷ 23 = ☐
441 ÷ 21 = ☐	990 ÷ 22 = ☐	943 ÷ 23 = ☐
864 ÷ 24 = ☐	850 ÷ 25 = ☐	754 ÷ 26 = ☐

ddd ÷ dd = qq with no remainder

875 ÷ 25 = ☐

828 ÷ 36 = ☐

987 ÷ 47 = ☐

910 ÷ 26 = ☐

592 ÷ 37 = ☐

912 ÷ 48 = ☐

702 ÷ 27 = ☐

874 ÷ 38 = ☐

539 ÷ 49 = ☐

ddd ÷ dd = qq with no remainder

224 ÷ 28 = ☐

273 ÷ 39 = ☐

400 ÷ 50 = ☐

203 ÷ 29 = ☐

320 ÷ 40 = ☐

255 ÷ 51 = ☐

150 ÷ 30 = ☐

246 ÷ 41 = ☐

416 ÷ 52 = ☐

Mom! I Learn Division Using Math-Chess-Puzzles Connection

ddd ÷ dd = qq with no remainder

186 ÷ 31 = ☐	294 ÷ 42 = ☐	371 ÷ 53 = ☐
224 ÷ 32 = ☐	172 ÷ 43 = ☐	216 ÷ 54 = ☐
264 ÷ 33 = ☐	220 ÷ 44 = ☐	265 ÷ 53 = ☐

Mom! I Learn Division Using Math-Chess-Puzzles Connection

Ho Math Chess　何数棋谜　妈!我会棋谜式除法啦!

Frank Ho, Amanda Ho © 2004 – 2020, all rights reserved.

Student's Name _____ Date _____

ddd ÷ dd = qq with no remainder

306 ÷ 34 = ☐	270 ÷ 45 = ☐	504 ÷ 56 = ☐
315 ÷ 35 = ☐	414 ÷ 46 = ☐	456 ÷ 57 = ☐
315 ÷ 35 = ☐	414 ÷ 46 = ☐	456 ÷ 57 = ☐

Mom! I Learn Division Using Math-Chess-Puzzles Connection

Ho Math Chess 何数棋谜 妈!我会棋谜式除法啦!

Frank Ho, Amanda Ho © 2004 – 2020, all rights reserved.

Student's Name _____ Date _____

ddddd ÷ ddd

618)82194	121)72842	533)74620
318)81408	307)49427	256)90624
799)18377	618)82194	596)14304

Page 276

Mom! I Learn Division Using Math-Chess-Puzzles Connection

Ho Math Chess　何数棋谜　妈!我会棋谜式除法啦!

Frank Ho, Amanda Ho © 2004 – 2020, all rights reserved.

Student's Name _____　Date _____

$368\overline{)35328}$	$419\overline{)15503}$	$297\overline{)11583}$
$12\overline{)52872}$	$38\overline{)57988}$	$71\overline{)67734}$
$33\overline{)46563}$	$56\overline{)22848}$	$47\overline{)31396}$

Mom! I Learn Division Using Math-Chess-Puzzles Connection

67)71154	11)17721	31)96627
79)16590	50)40590	92)97888

Mom! I Learn Division Using Math-Chess-Puzzles Connection

Ho Math Chess   何数棋谜   妈!我会棋谜式除法啦!

Frank Ho, Amanda Ho © 2004 − 2020, all rights reserved.

Student's Name _____   Date _____

Addition and subtraction

Fill in 2 circles with 2 consecutive natural numbers having a difference of 1

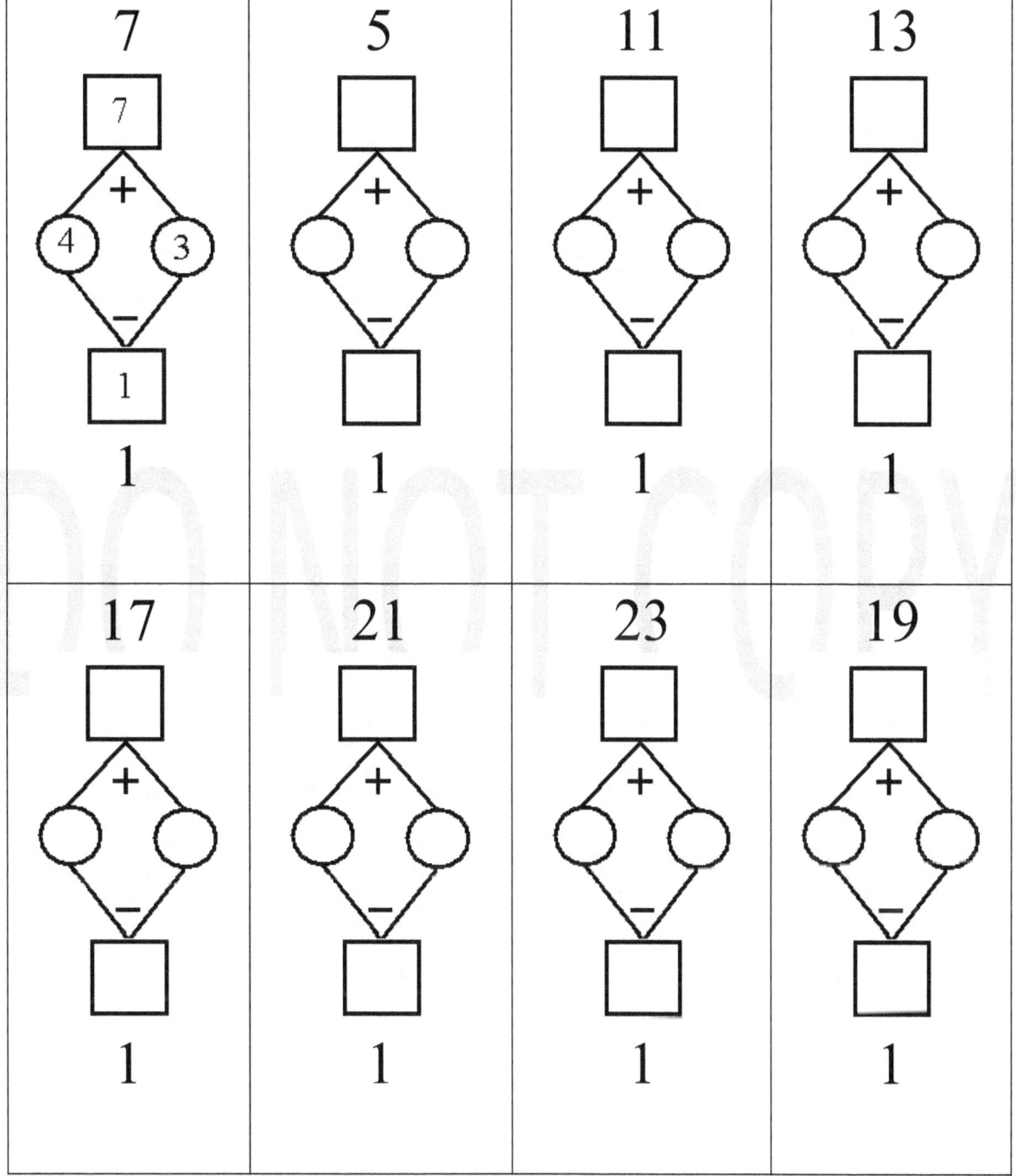

Mom! I Learn Division Using Math-Chess-Puzzles Connection

Addition and subtraction

Fill in 2 circles with 2 consecutive natural numbers having a difference of 1

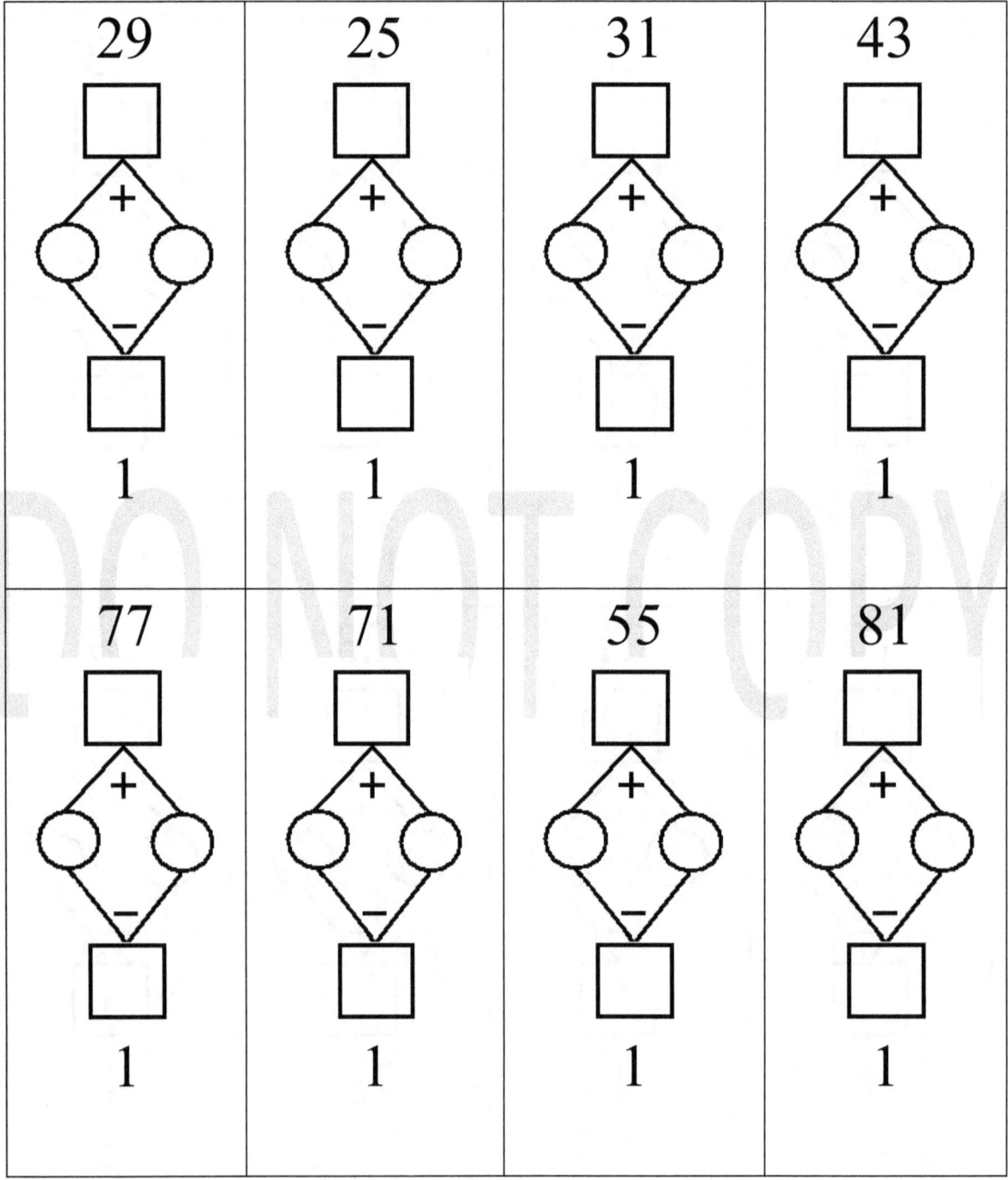

Mom! I Learn Division Using Math-Chess-Puzzles Connection

Ho Math Chess   何数棋谜   妈!我会棋谜式除法啦!

Frank Ho, Amanda Ho © 2004 – 2020, all rights reserved.

Student's Name _____ Date _____

Addition and subtraction

Fill in 2 circles with 2 consecutive natural numbers having a difference of 1

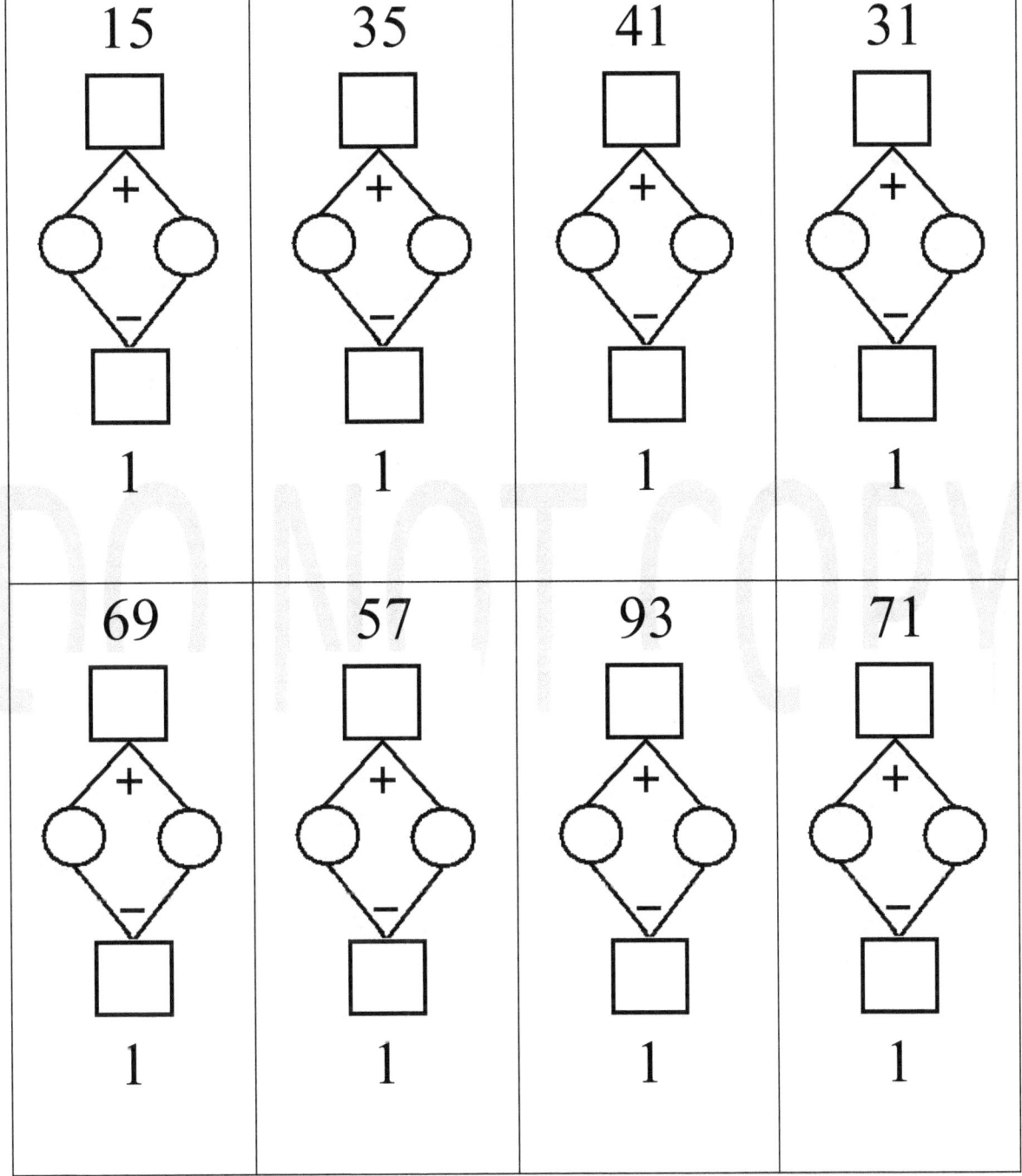

Mom! I Learn Division Using Math-Chess-Puzzles Connection

Ho Math Chess 何数棋谜 妈!我会棋谜式除法啦!

Frank Ho, Amanda Ho © 2004 – 2020, all rights reserved.

Student's Name _____ Date _____

Addition and subtraction

Fill in 2 circles with 2 consecutive natural numbers having a difference of 2

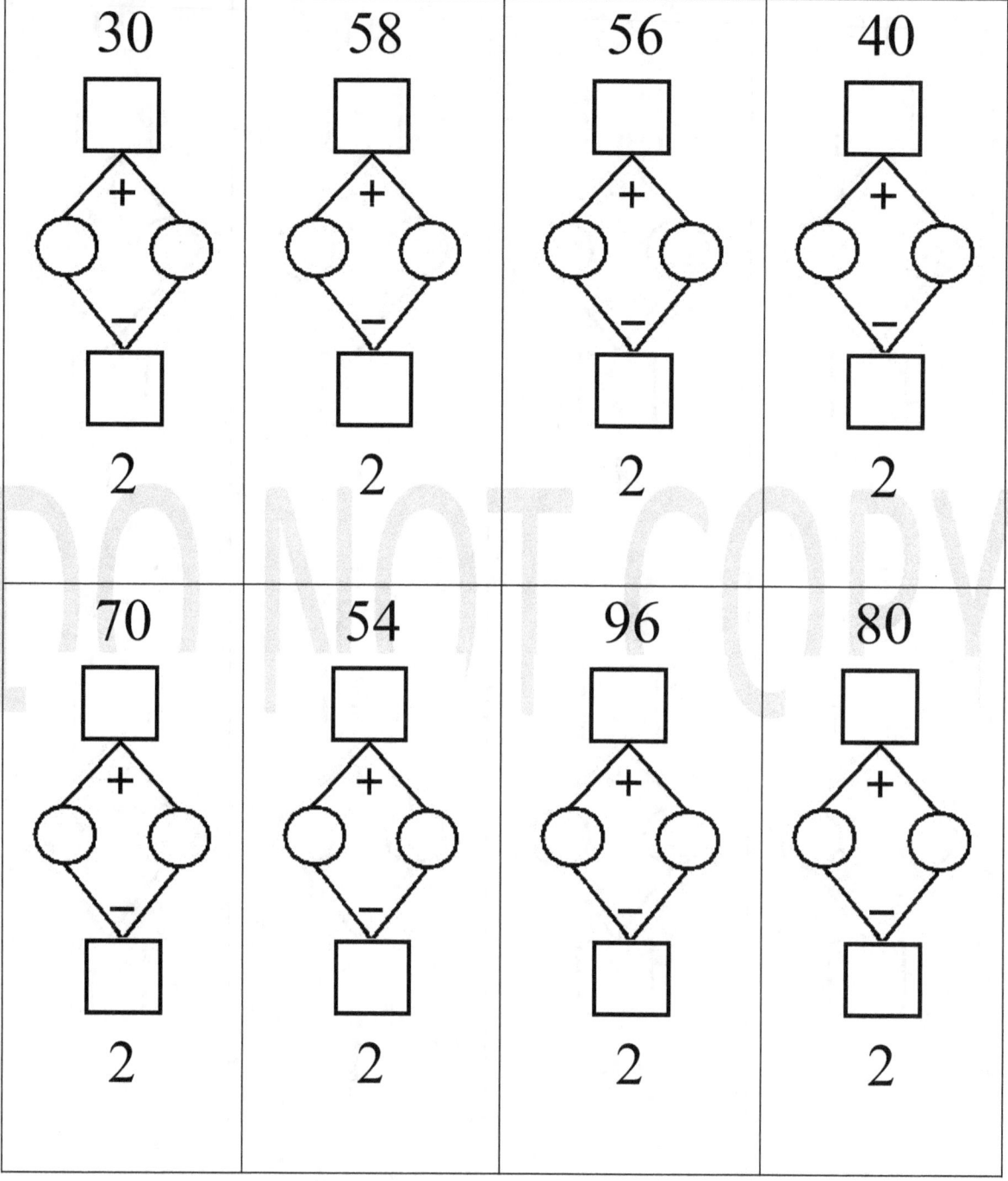

Mom! I Learn Division Using Math-Chess-Puzzles Connection

Ho Math Chess　何数棋谜　妈!我会棋谜式除法啦!

Frank Ho, Amanda Ho © 2004 − 2020, all rights reserved.

Student's Name _____　Date _____

Addition and subtraction

Fill in 2 circles with 2 consecutive natural numbers having a difference of 2

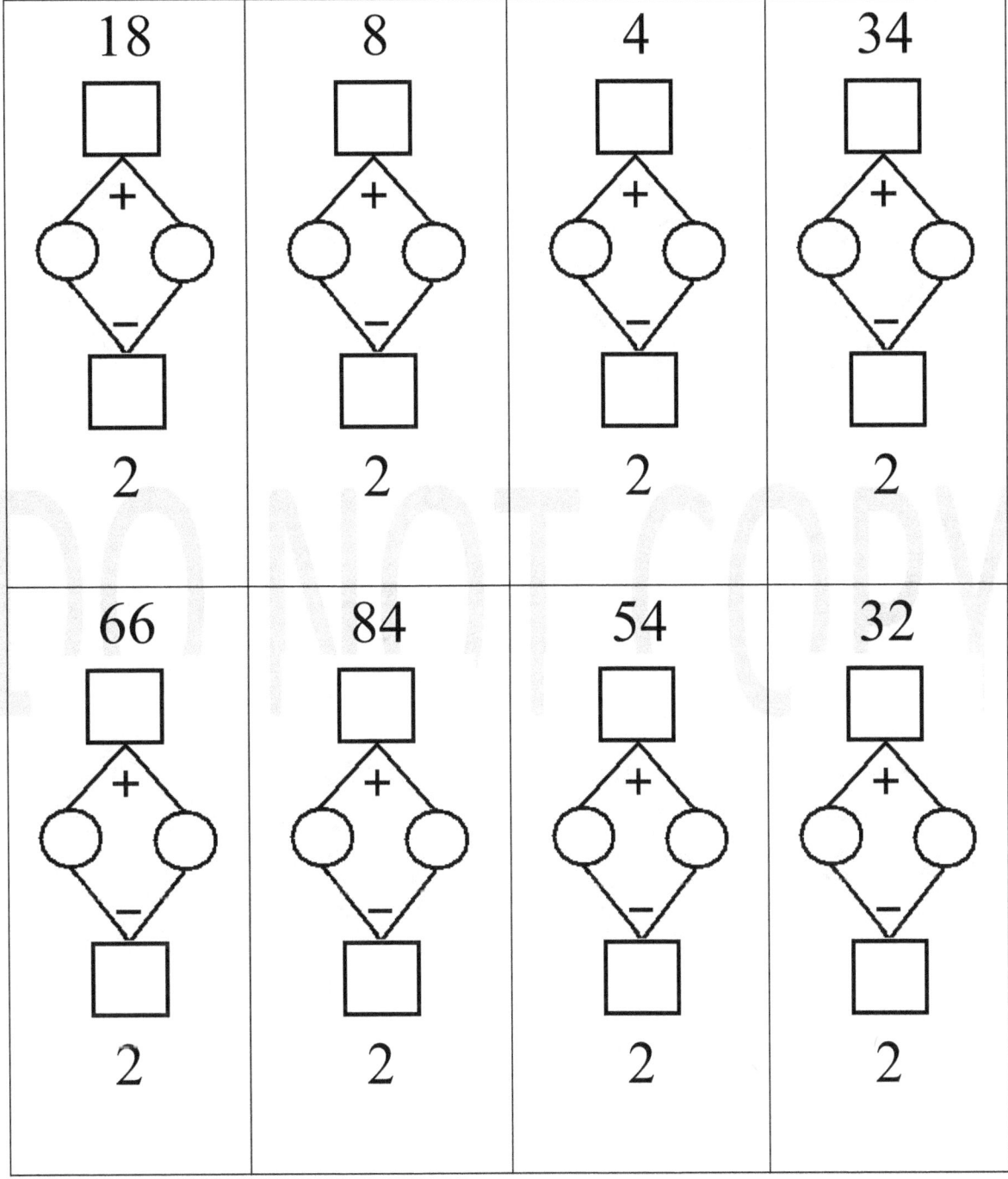

Mom! I Learn Division Using Math-Chess-Puzzles Connection

Ho Math Chess 何数棋谜 妈!我会棋谜式除法啦!

Frank Ho, Amanda Ho © 2004 – 2020, all rights reserved.

Student's Name _____ Date _____

Addition and subtraction

Fill in 2 circles with 2 consecutive natural numbers having a difference of 2

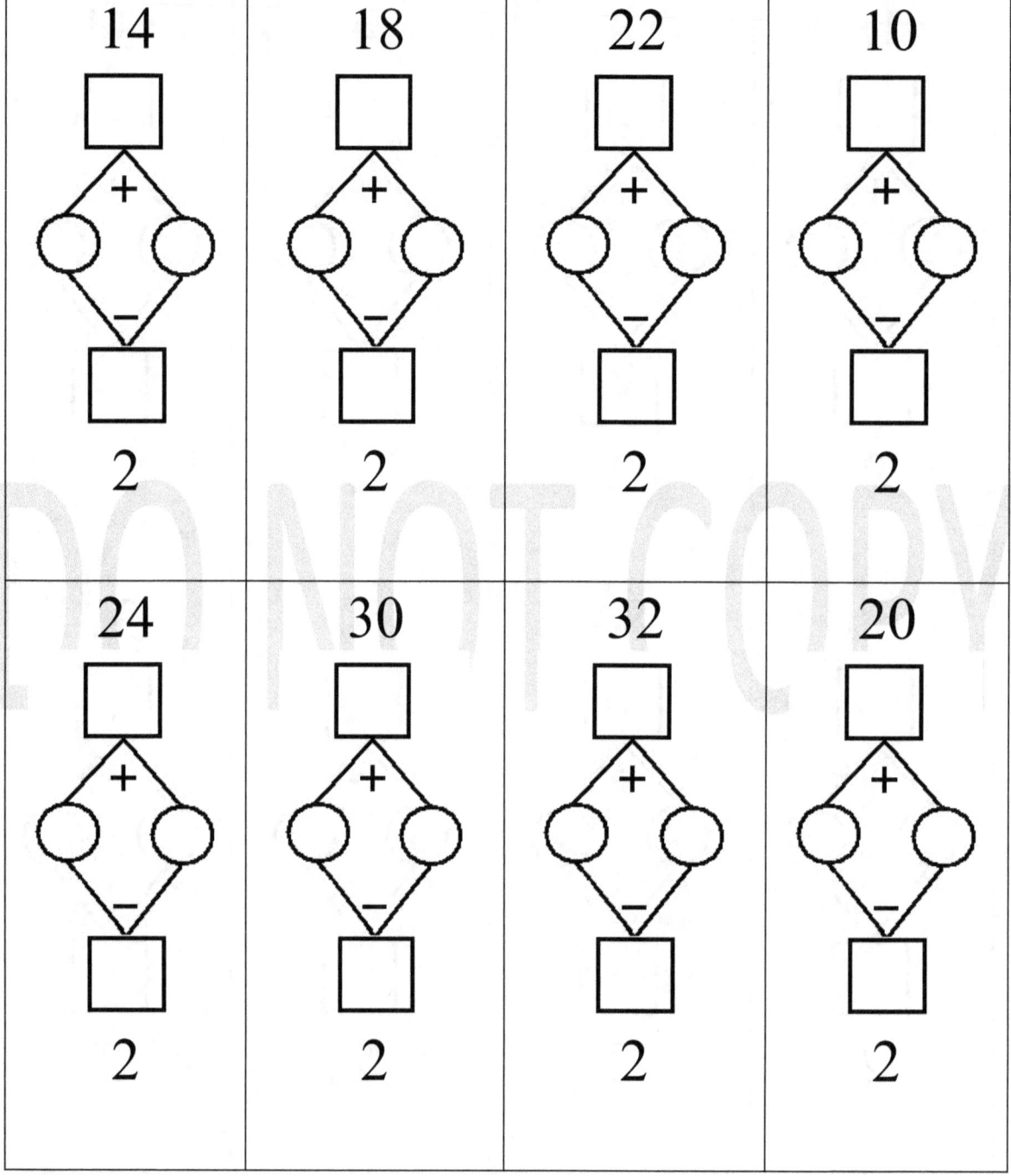

Mom! I Learn Division Using Math-Chess-Puzzles Connection

Ho Math Chess 何数棋谜 妈!我会棋谜式除法啦!

Frank Ho, Amanda Ho © 2004 – 2020, all rights reserved.

Student's Name _____ Date _____

Multiplication and addition

Fill in one natural number in each circle.

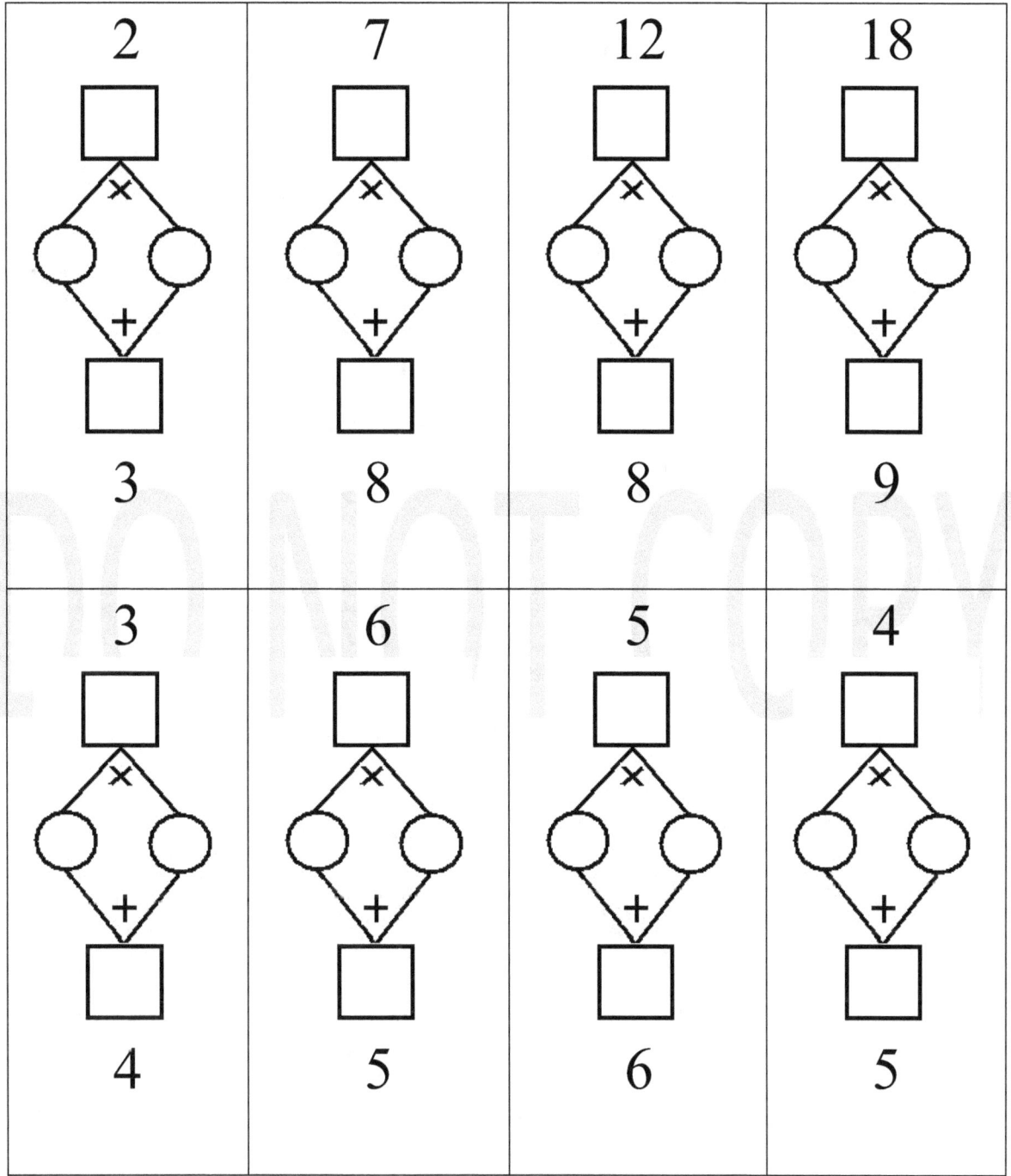

Mom! I Learn Division Using Math-Chess-Puzzles Connection

Multiplication and addition

Fill in one natural number in each circle.

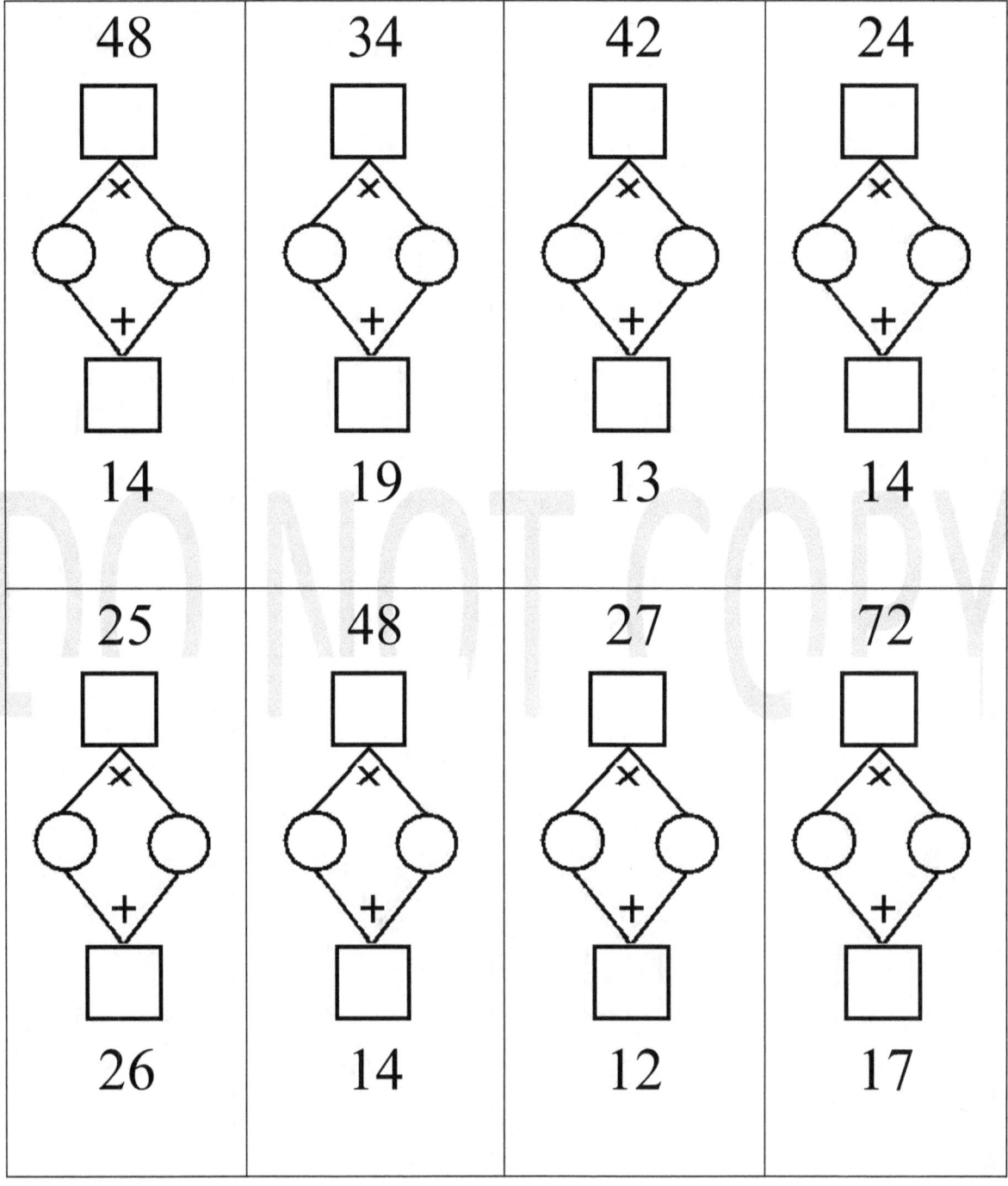

Mom! I Learn Division Using Math-Chess-Puzzles Connection

Ho Math Chess　何数棋谜　妈!我会棋谜式除法啦!

Frank Ho, Amanda Ho © 2004 – 2020, all rights reserved.

Student's Name _____　Date _____

Multiplication and addition

Fill in one natural number in each circle.

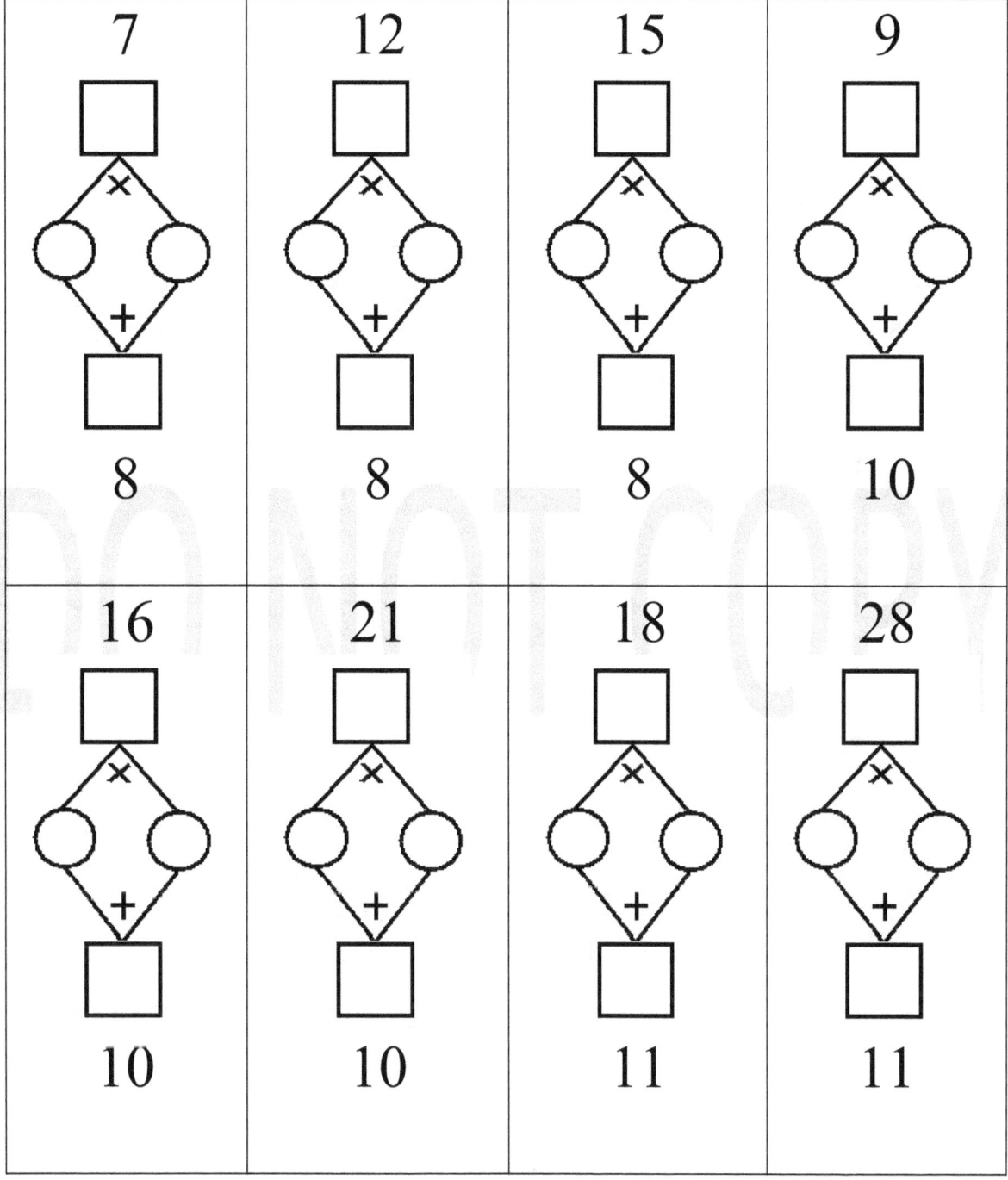

Mom! I Learn Division Using Math-Chess-Puzzles Connection

Ho Math Chess 何数棋谜 妈!我会棋谜式除法啦!

Frank Ho, Amanda Ho © 2004 – 2020, all rights reserved.

Student's Name _____ Date _____

Multiplication and addition

Fill in one natural number in each circle.

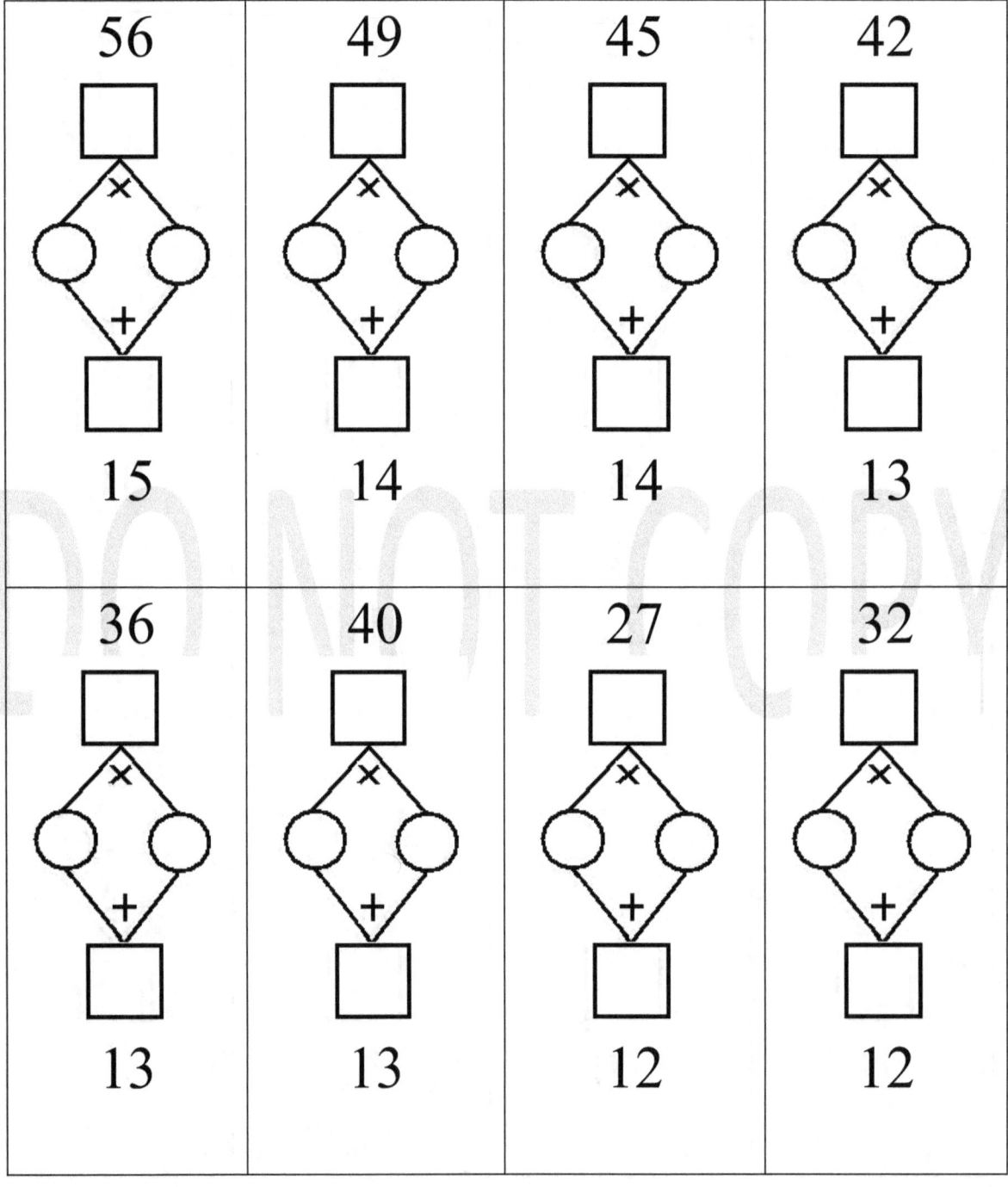

Mom! I Learn Division Using Math-Chess-Puzzles Connection

Ho Math Chess 何数棋谜 妈!我会棋谜式除法啦!

Frank Ho, Amanda Ho © 2004 – 2020, all rights reserved.

Student's Name _____ Date _____

Multiplication and subtraction

Fill in one natural number in each circle.

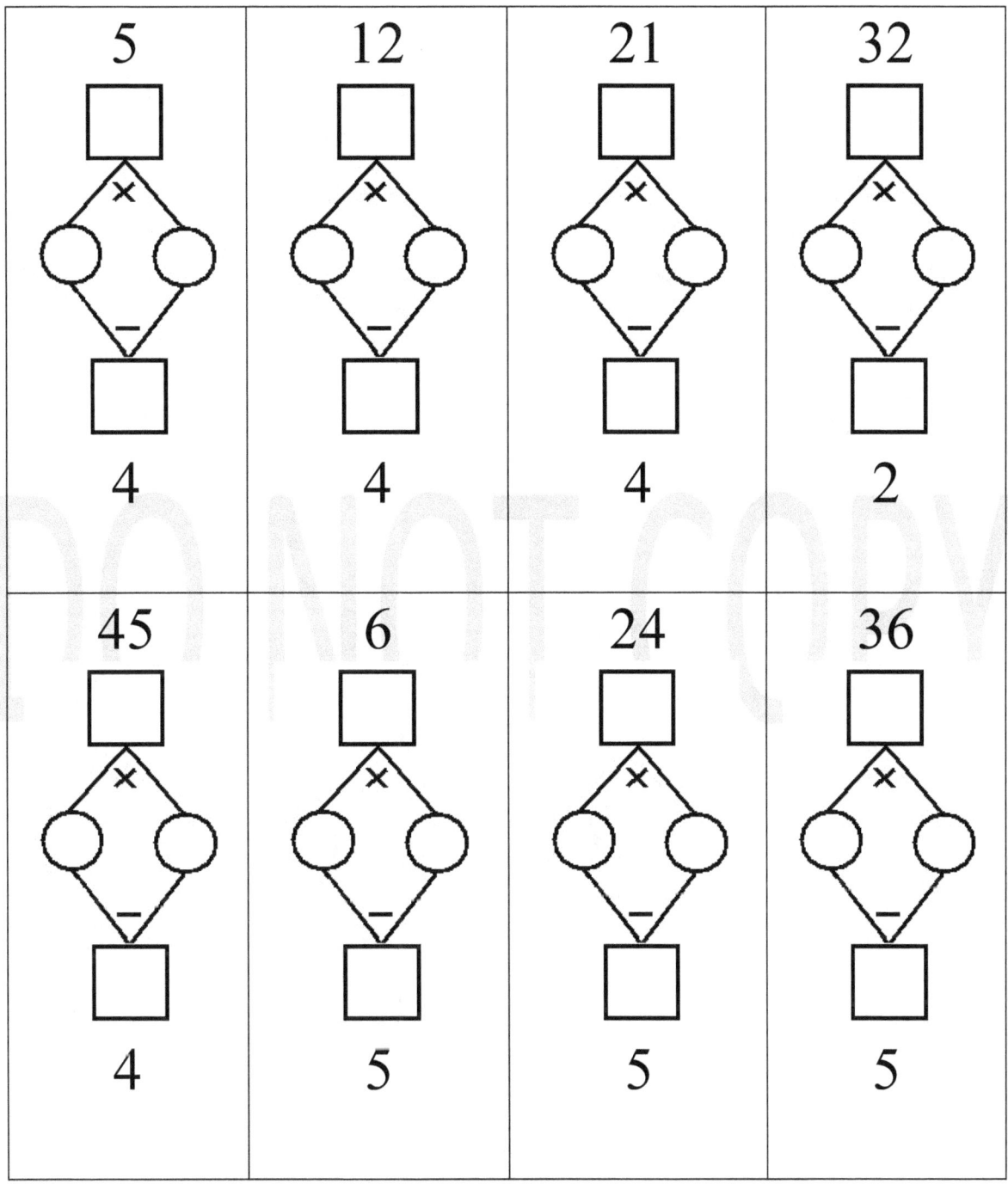

Mom! I Learn Division Using Math-Chess-Puzzles Connection

Multiplication and subtraction

Fill in one natural number in each circle.

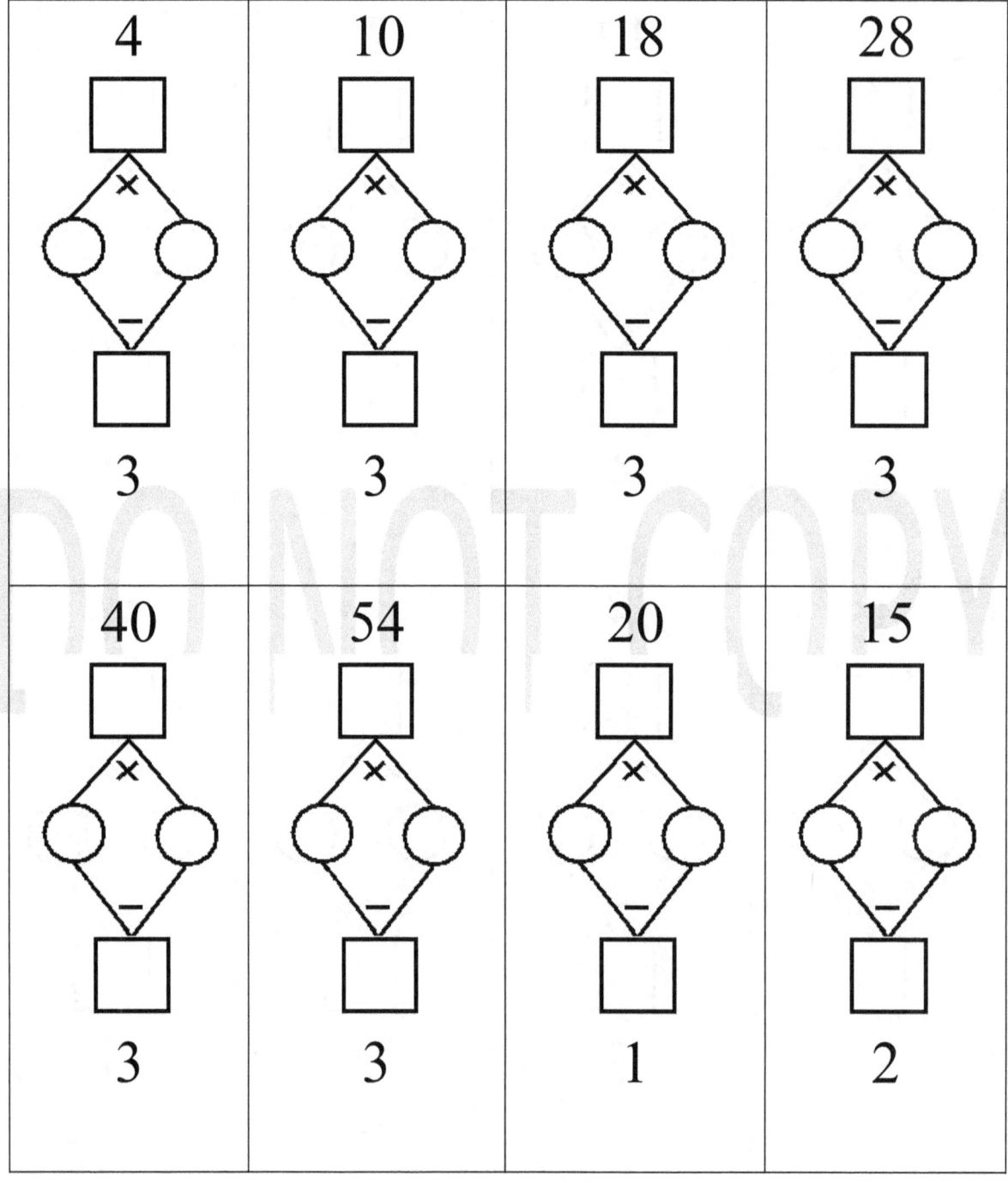

Mom! I Learn Division Using Math-Chess-Puzzles Connection

Ho Math Chess   何数棋谜   妈!我会棋谜式除法啦!

Frank Ho, Amanda Ho © 2004 – 2020, all rights reserved.

Student's Name _____   Date_____

Multiplication and subtraction

Fill in one natural number in each circle.

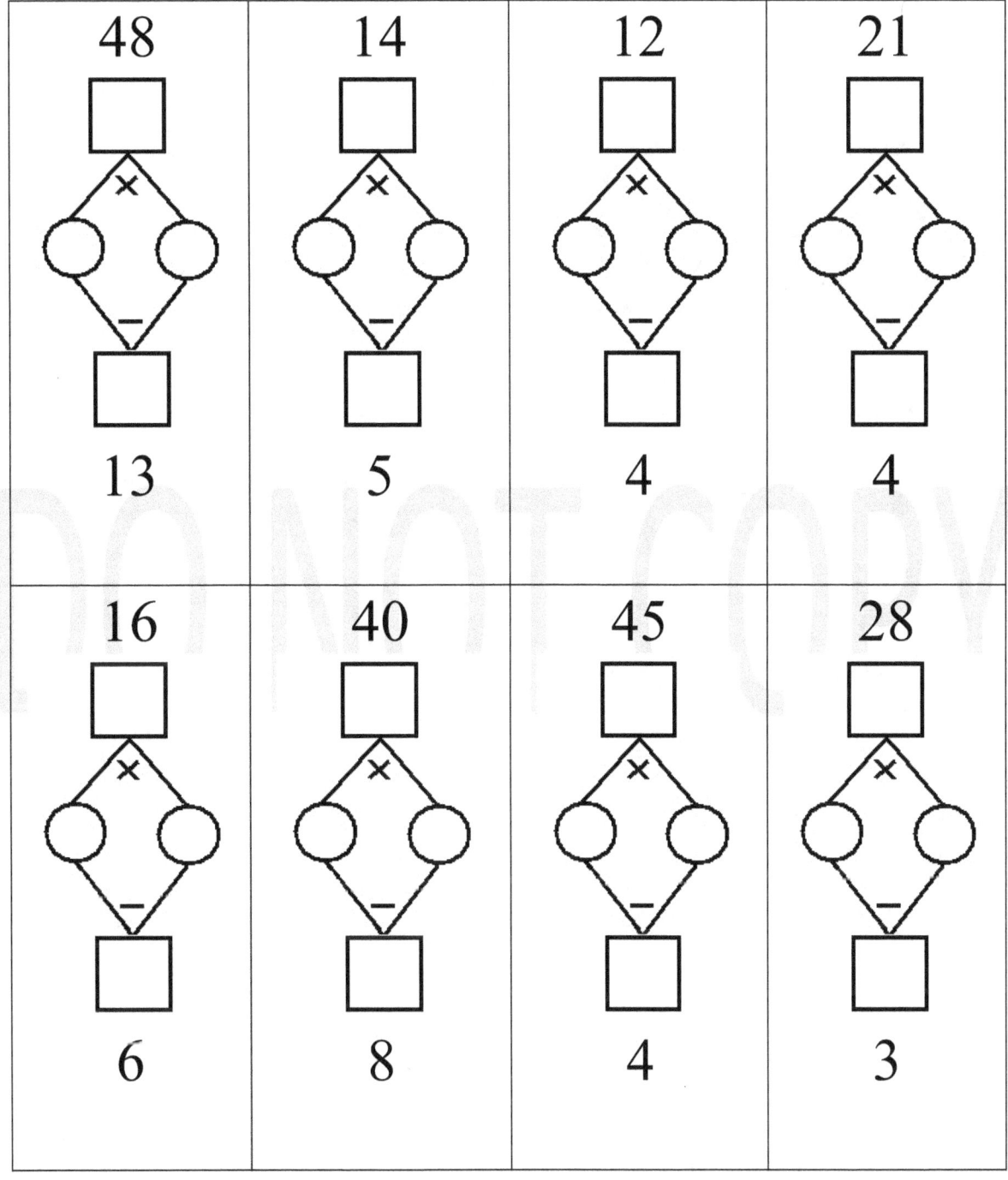

Mom! I Learn Division Using Math-Chess-Puzzles Connection

Division and addition

Fill in one natural number in each circle.

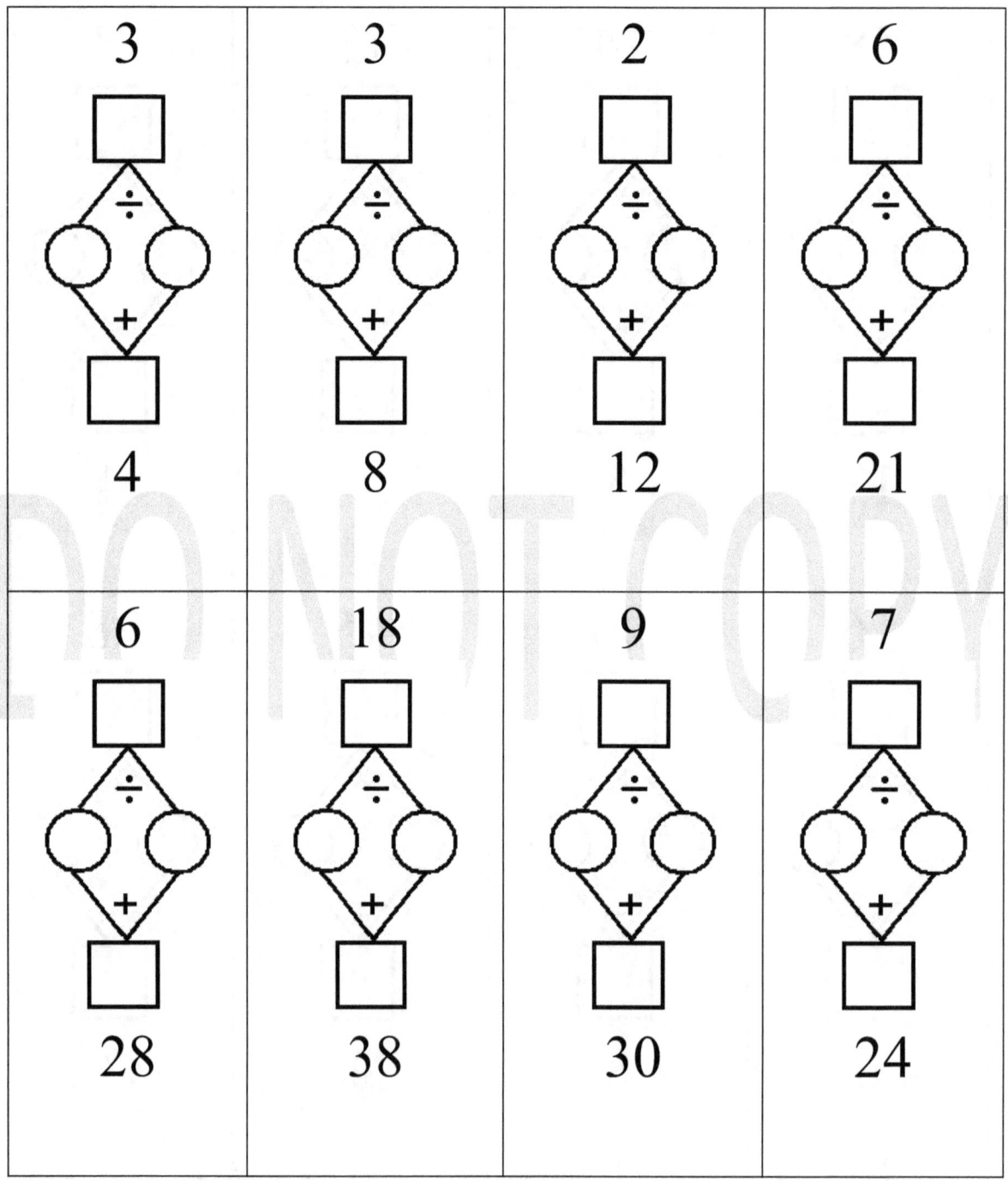

Mom! I Learn Division Using Math-Chess-Puzzles Connection

Ho Math Chess   何数棋谜   妈!我会棋谜式除法啦!

Frank Ho, Amanda Ho © 2004 – 2020, all rights reserved.

Student's Name _____   Date _____

Division and addition

Fill in one natural number in each circle.

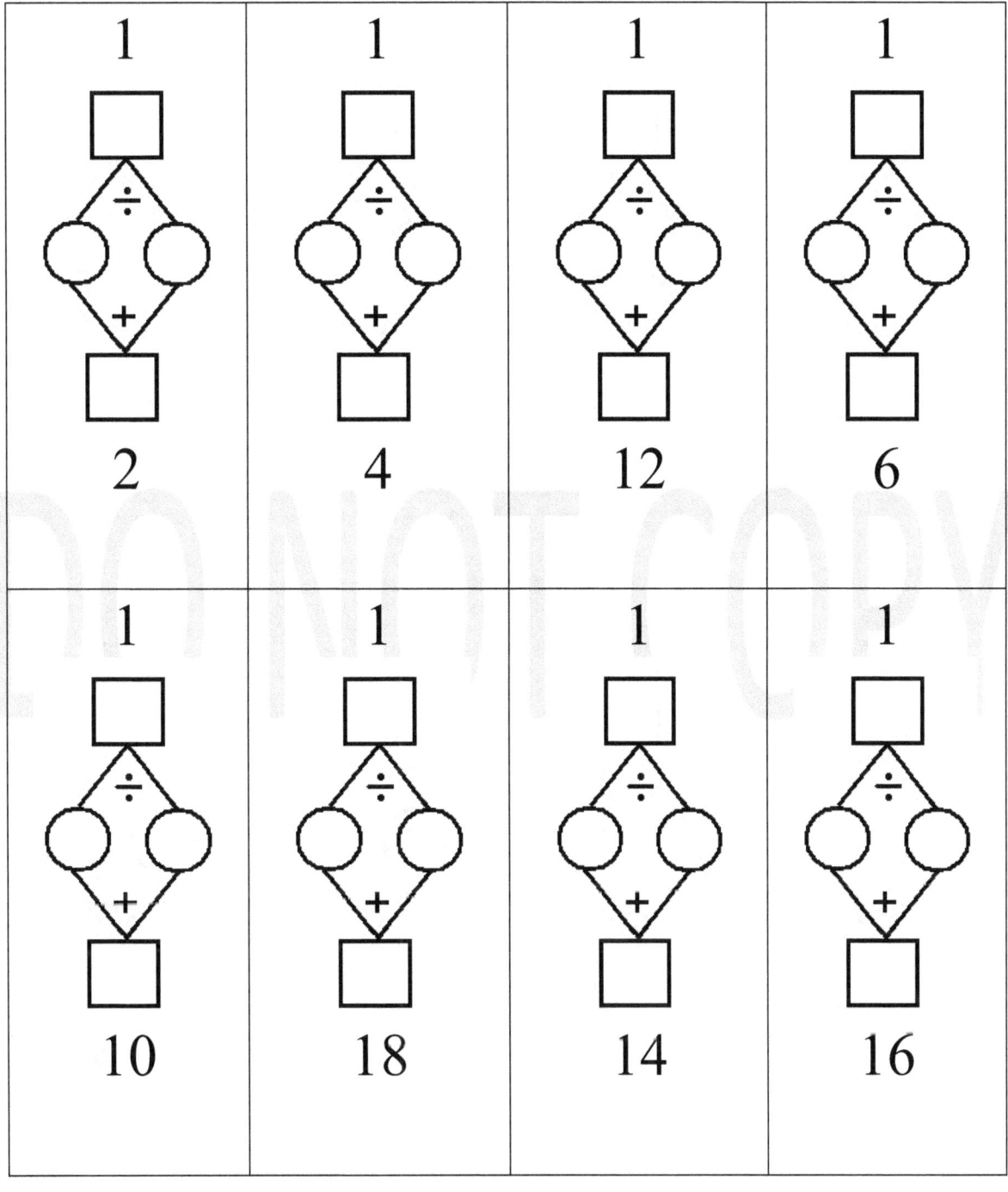

Mom! I Learn Division Using Math-Chess-Puzzles Connection

Division and addition

Fill in one natural number in each circle.

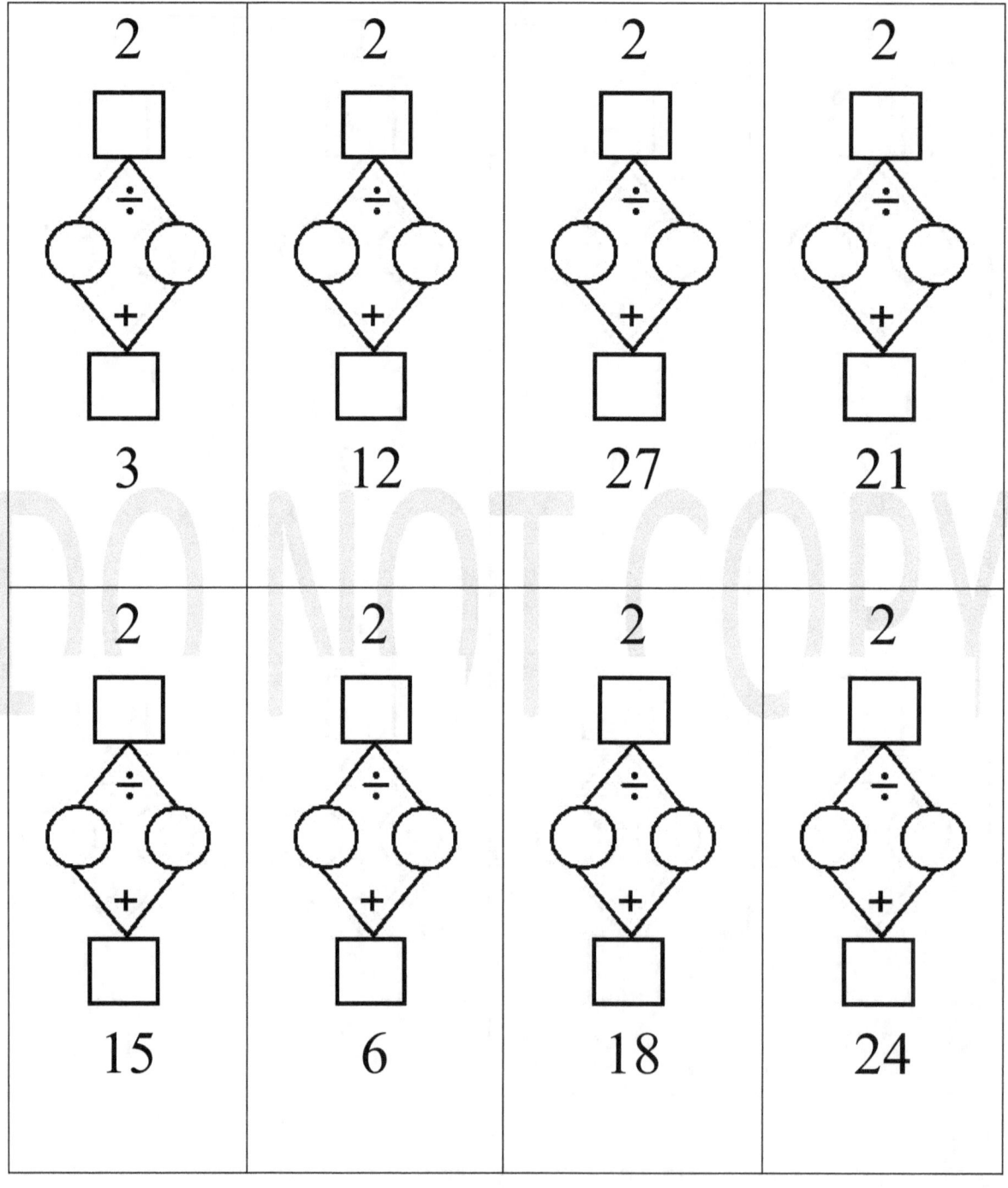

Mom! I Learn Division Using Math-Chess-Puzzles Connection

Ho Math Chess　何数棋谜　妈!我会棋谜式除法啦!

Frank Ho, Amanda Ho © 2004 – 2020, all rights reserved.

Student's Name _____ Date _____

Division and addition

Fill in one natural number in each circle.

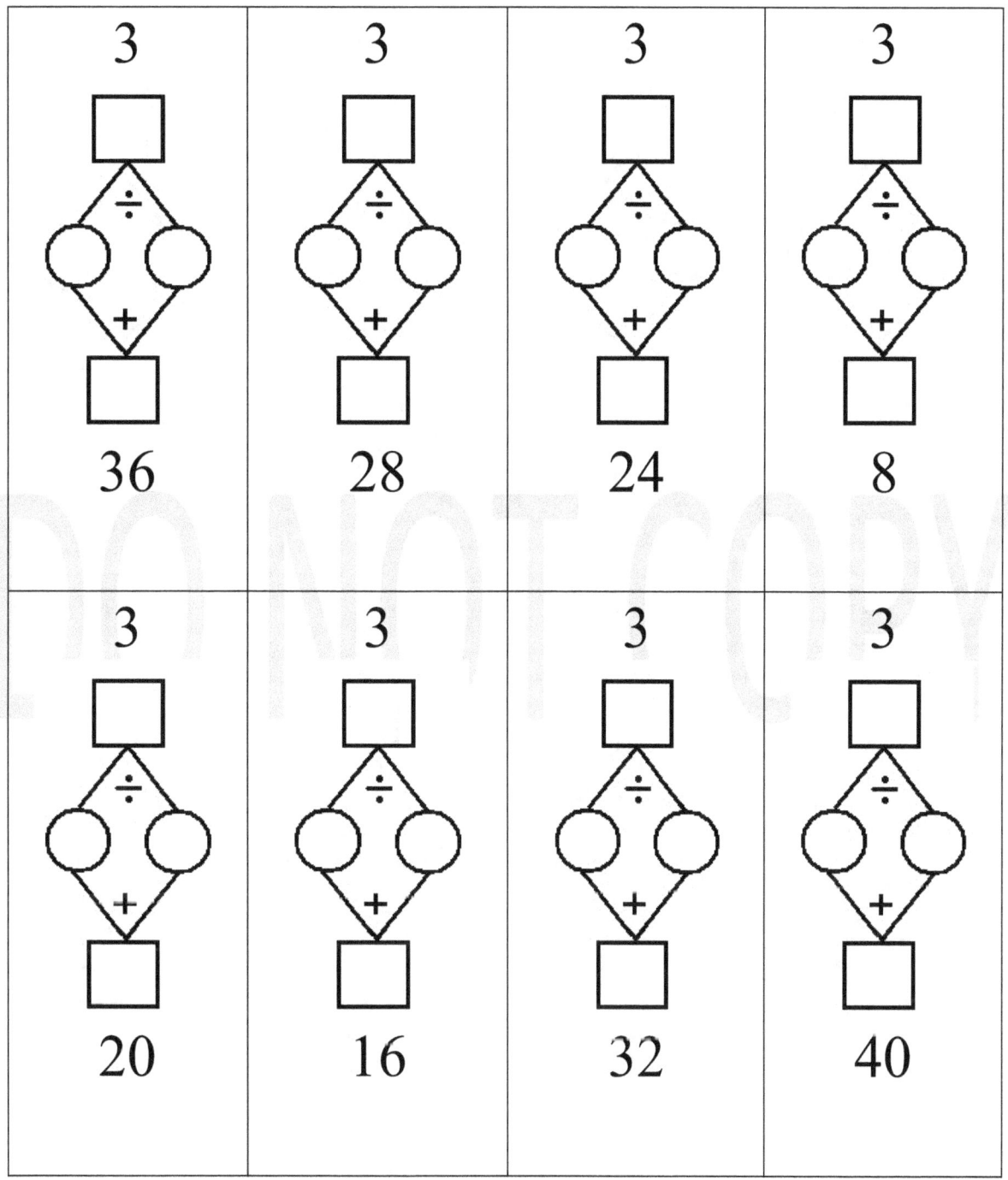

Mom! I Learn Division Using Math-Chess-Puzzles Connection

Ho Math Chess 何数棋谜 妈!我会棋谜式除法啦!

Frank Ho, Amanda Ho © 2004 – 2020, all rights reserved.

Student's Name _____ Date _____

Division and addition

Fill in one natural number in each circle.

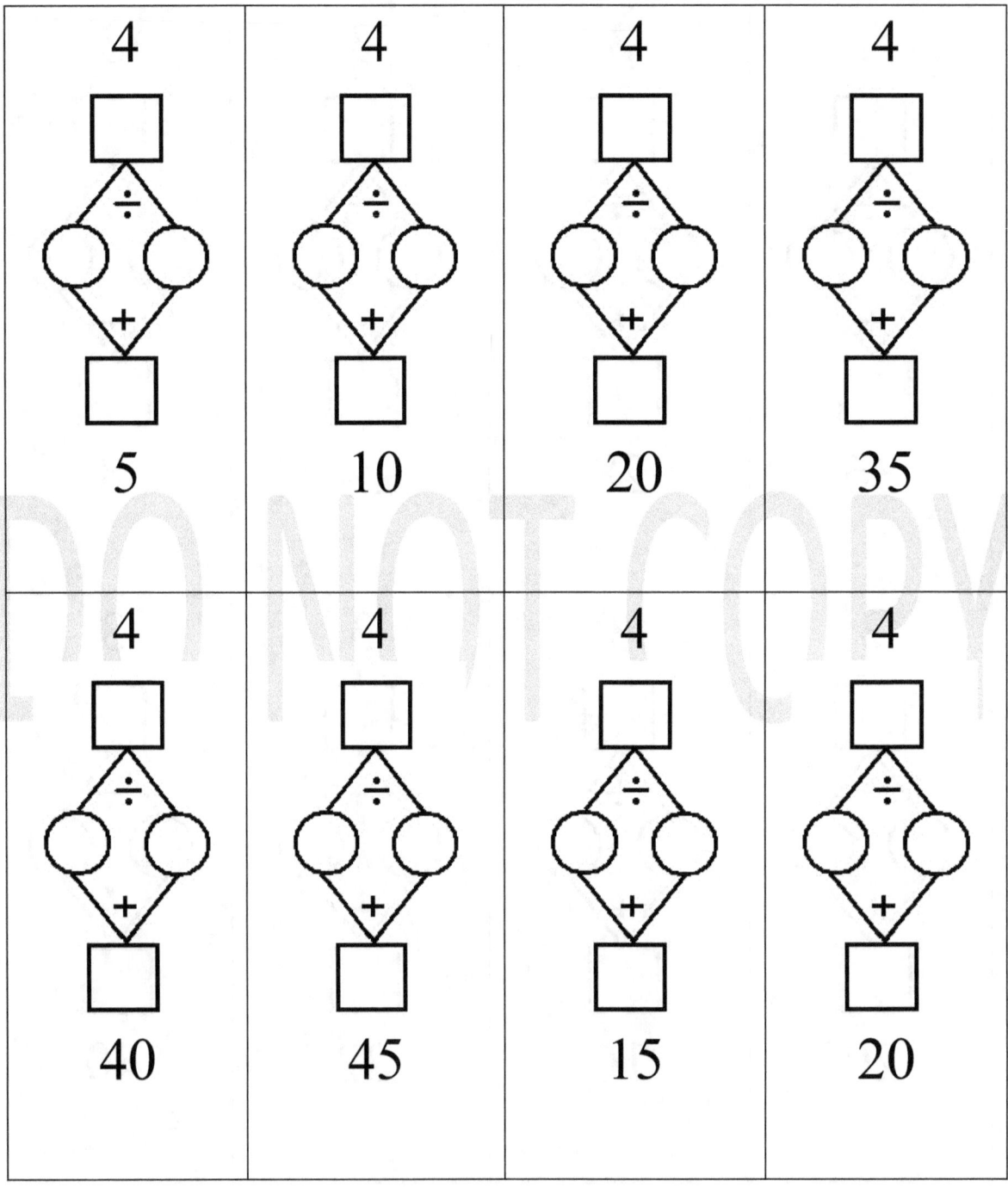

Mom! I Learn Division Using Math-Chess-Puzzles Connection

Ho Math Chess 何数棋谜 妈!我会棋谜式除法啦!

Frank Ho, Amanda Ho © 2004 – 2020, all rights reserved.

Student's Name _____ Date _____

Division and addition

Fill in one natural number in each circle.

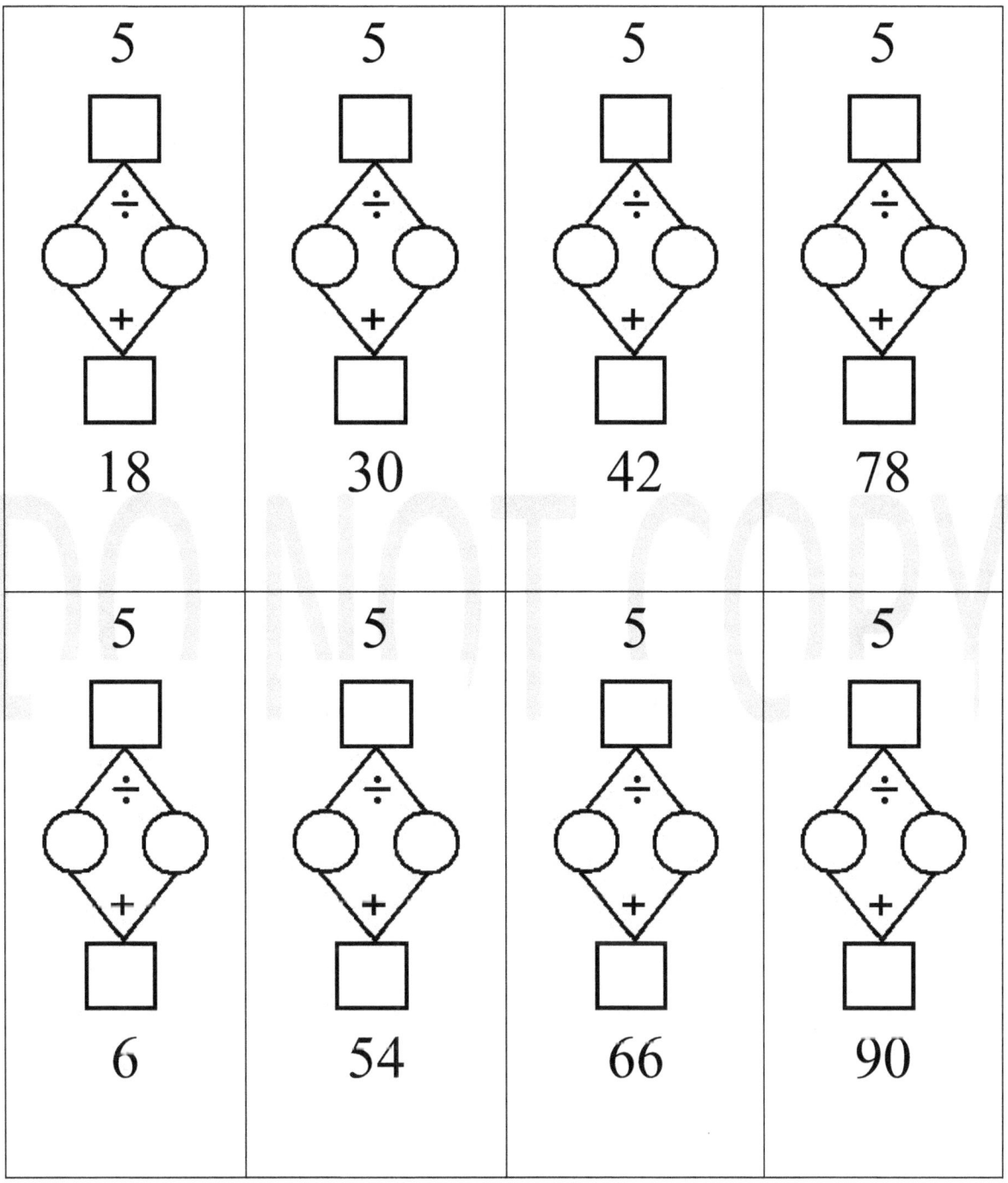

Mom! I Learn Division Using Math-Chess-Puzzles Connection

Ho Math Chess   何数棋谜   妈!我会棋谜式除法啦!

Frank Ho, Amanda Ho © 2004 – 2020, all rights reserved.

Student's Name _____ Date_____

Division and addition

Fill in one natural number in each circle.

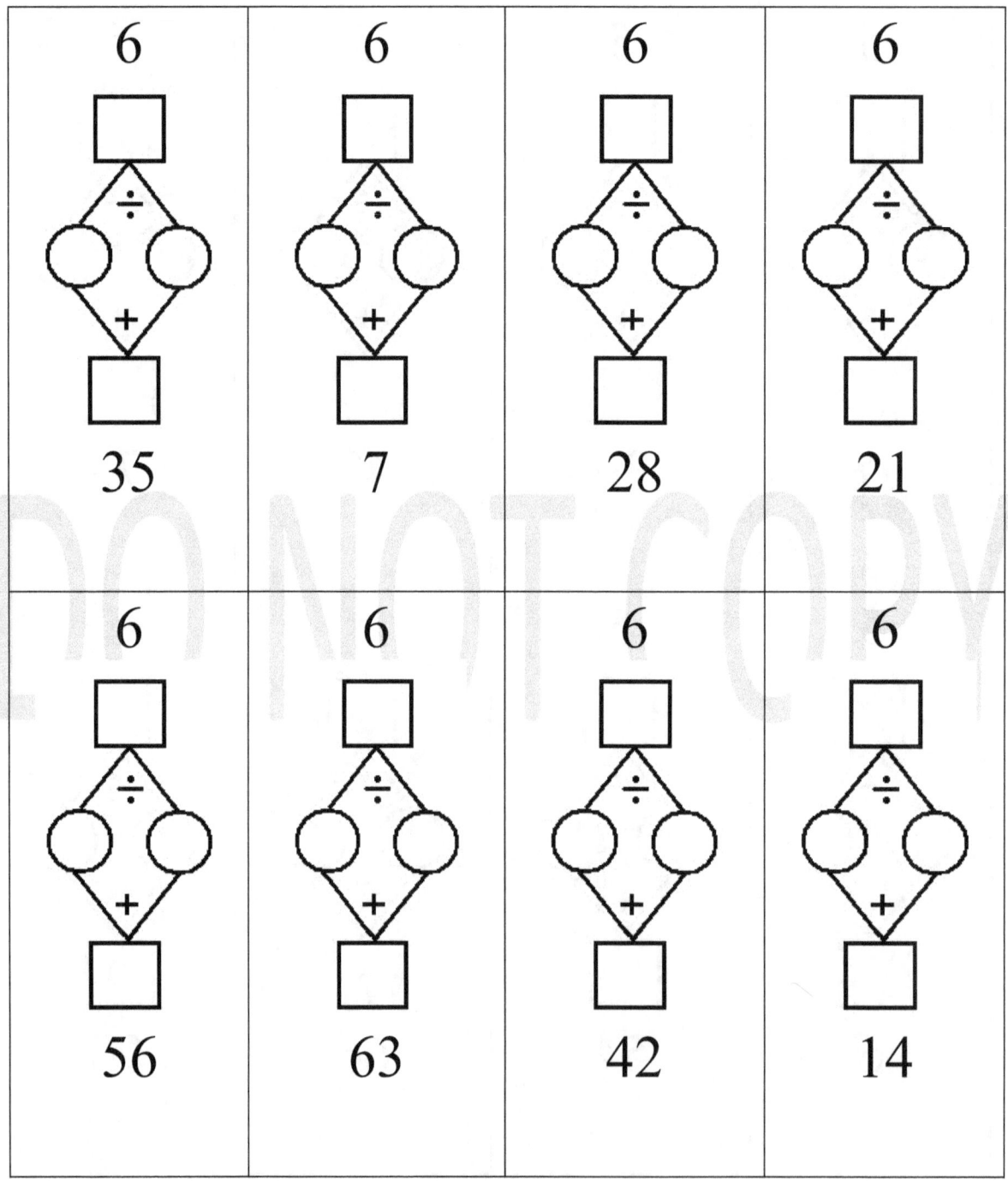

Mom! I Learn Division Using Math-Chess-Puzzles Connection

Ho Math Chess 何数棋谜 妈!我会棋谜式除法啦!

Frank Ho, Amanda Ho © 2004 – 2020, all rights reserved.

Student's Name _____ Date _____

Division and addition

Fill in one natural number in each circle.

□ 7 ÷ ○ ○ + □ = 16	□ 7 ÷ ○ ○ + □ = 8	□ 7 ÷ ○ ○ + □ = 32	□ 7 ÷ ○ ○ + □ = 40
□ 7 ÷ ○ ○ + □ = 72	□ 7 ÷ ○ ○ + □ = 48	□ 7 ÷ ○ ○ + □ = 32	□ 7 ÷ ○ ○ + □ = 24

Mom! I Learn Division Using Math-Chess-Puzzles Connection

Ho Math Chess 何数棋谜 妈!我会棋谜式除法啦!

Frank Ho, Amanda Ho © 2004 – 2020, all rights reserved.

Student's Name _____ Date _____

Division and addition

Fill in one natural number in each circle.

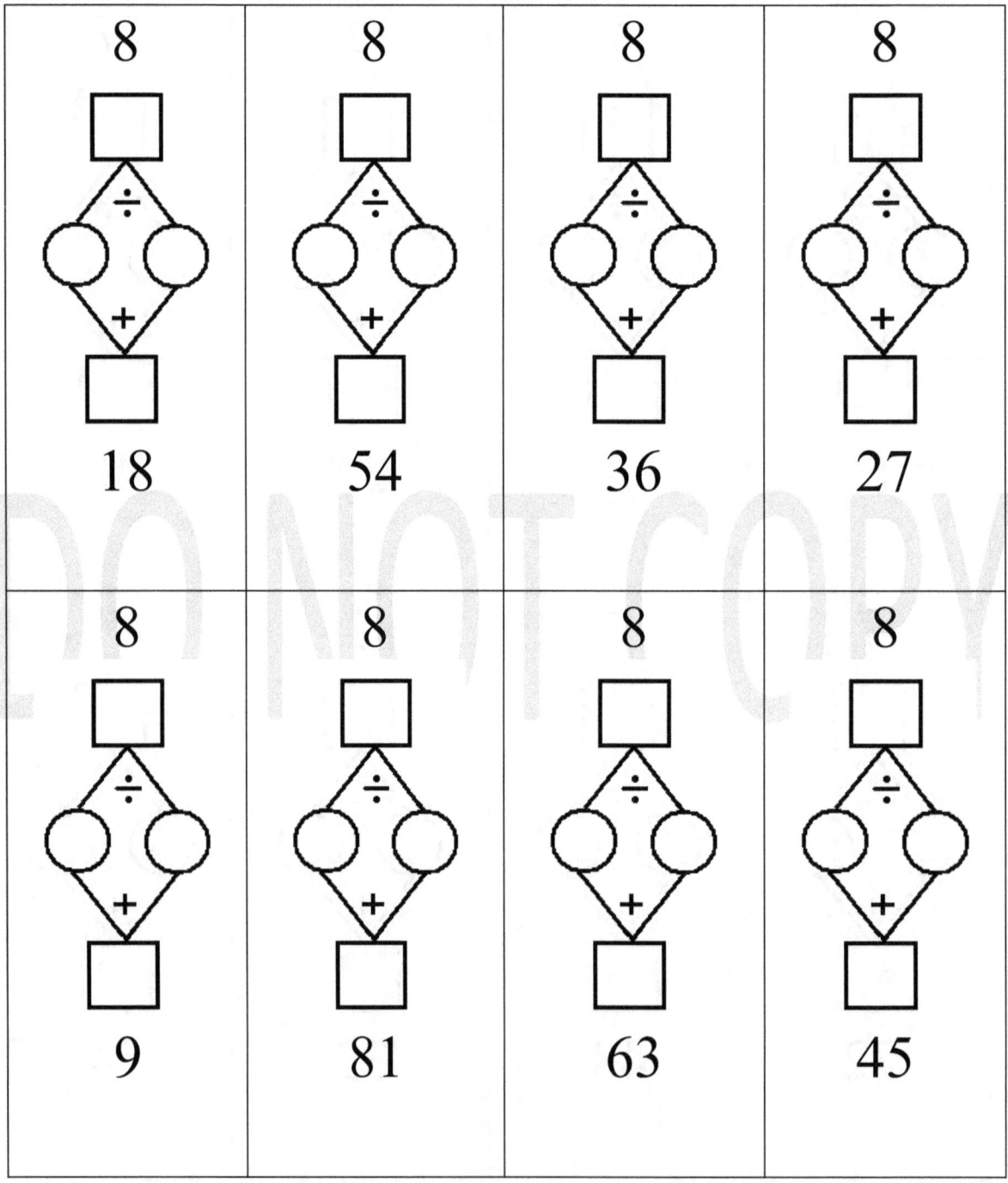

Mom! I Learn Division Using Math-Chess-Puzzles Connection

Ho Math Chess 何数棋谜 妈!我会棋谜式除法啦!

Frank Ho, Amanda Ho © 2004 – 2020, all rights reserved.

Student's Name _____ Date _____

Division and addition

Fill in one natural number in each circle.

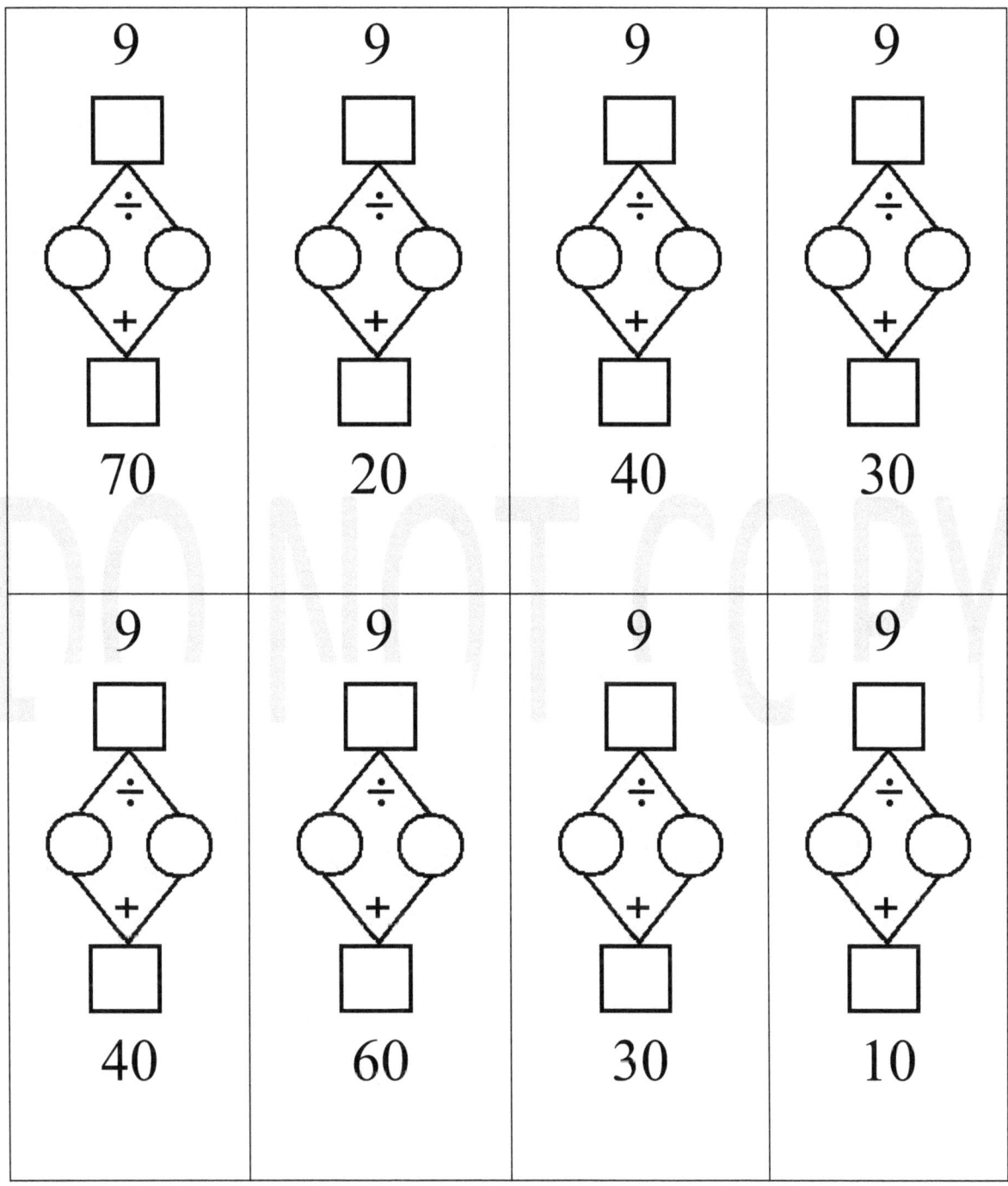

Mom! I Learn Division Using Math-Chess-Puzzles Connection

Ho Math Chess　何数棋谜　妈!我会棋谜式除法啦!

Frank Ho, Amanda Ho © 2004 – 2020, all rights reserved.

Student's Name _____ Date _____

Division and subtraction

Fill in one natural number in each circle.

9 ÷ ○ ○ − = 8	34 ÷ ○ ○ − = 66	12 ÷ ○ ○ − = 88	14 ÷ ○ ○ − = 26
16 ÷ ○ ○ − = 45	18 ÷ ○ ○ − = 34	13 ÷ ○ ○ − = 36	9 ÷ ○ ○ − = 64

Mom! I Learn Division Using Math-Chess-Puzzles Connection

Ho Math Chess 何数棋谜 妈!我会棋谜式除法啦!

Frank Ho, Amanda Ho © 2004 – 2020, all rights reserved.

Student's Name _____ Date _____

Multiplication and division

Fill in one natural number in each circle.

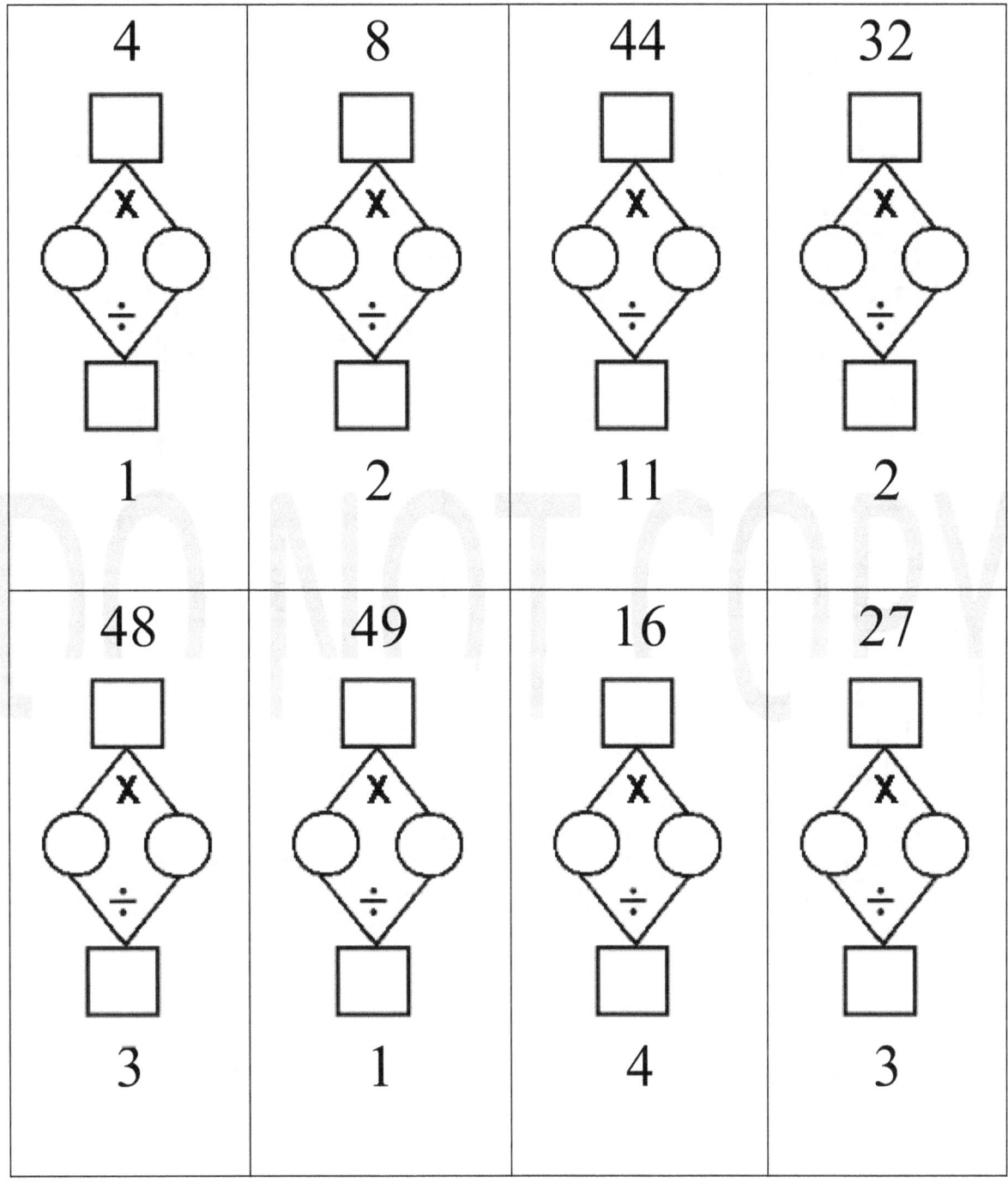

Mom! I Learn Division Using Math-Chess-Puzzles Connection

Ho Math Chess 何数棋谜 妈!我会棋谜式除法啦!

Frank Ho, Amanda Ho © 2004 − 2020, all rights reserved.

Student's Name _____ Date _____

***** Part 4 Decimal division *****

Divide ddd by dd. Round to the nearest hundredth.

16) 282

70) 974

29) 485

36) 543

Page 304

Mom! I Learn Division Using Math-Chess-Puzzles Connection

Ho Math Chess　何数棋谜　妈!我会棋谜式除法啦!

Frank Ho, Amanda Ho © 2004 – 2020, all rights reserved.

Student's Name _____ Date _____

Divide ddd by ddd. Round to the nearest hundredth.

120) 586

241) 876

322) 564

224) 453

4.88, 3.63, 1.75, 2.02
4r106, 3r153, 1r242, 2r5

No part of this publication can be copied, duplicated, or reproduced.

Mom! I Learn Division Using Math-Chess-Puzzles Connection

Ho Math Chess   何数棋谜   妈!我会棋谜式除法啦!

Frank Ho, Amanda Ho © 2004 − 2020, all rights reserved.

Student's Name _____ Date _____

Divide dddd by ddd. Round to the nearest hundredth.

462) 1234

421) 6843

364) 2718

583) 7492

Page 306

ddd ÷ dd. Round the answers to the nearest hundredth.

69)786

78)968

49)576

37)418

ddd ÷ dd. Round the answers to the nearest hundredth.

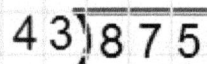

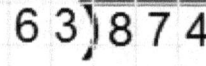

Mom! I Learn Division Using Math-Chess-Puzzles Connection

Ho Math Chess　何数棋谜　妈!我会棋谜式除法啦!

Frank Ho, Amanda Ho © 2004 − 2020, all rights reserved.

Student's Name _____ Date _____

dddd ÷ dd. Round the answers to the nearest hundredth.

Mom! I Learn Division Using Math-Chess-Puzzles Connection

dddd ÷ dd. Round the answers to the nearest hundredth.

Mom! I Learn Division Using Math-Chess-Puzzles Connection

Ho Math Chess 何数棋谜 妈!我会棋谜式除法啦!

Frank Ho, Amanda Ho © 2004 – 2020, all rights reserved.

Student's Name _____ Date _____

ddd ÷ ddd. Round the answers to the nearest hundredth.

224)453

457)678

234)423

398)623

Mom! I Learn Division Using Math-Chess-Puzzles Connection

dddd ÷ ddd. Round the answers to the nearest hundredth.

Mom! I Learn Division Using Math-Chess-Puzzles Connection

Ho Math Chess 何数棋谜 妈!我会棋谜式除法啦!

Frank Ho, Amanda Ho © 2004 – 2020, all rights reserved.

Student's Name _____ Date _____

介紹何数棋谜

何数棋谜=奧数棋谜 + 思唯腦力開發
英文教材, 中英双语教学

什麼是何数棋谜?

上百篇科學論文巳發表國際象棋可以提高兒童問題解答能力.並且訓練他們的專心及耐力.所以我們巳經知道下國際象棋對兒童有好處.但是因為國際象棋與計算能力並無直接開係,所以如何讓兒童能在一個歡樂的環境下也能利用下棋來提高數學的計算呢? 何老師首創並發明有版权的幾何棋藝符號並利用此符號發明了世界第一的独特結合數學与棋谜教材. 何数棋谜讓兒童能利用幾何棋藝符號進行邏輯推理及數字的運算.棋藝與算術的綜合題含蓋了整數,幾何,集合,抽象數,對比異同,函數,座標,多空間圖形資料,及規則性數字分析.並且把棋藝的趣味性和數學的知識性結合在一起.

何数棋谜如何幫助兒童腦力思唯的開發?

很簡單的一個道理就是讓學生自願地去用腦, 何数棋谜首創獨一無二的融合數學與棋谜的独特趣味寓教於樂教材,利用國際象棋訓練右腦的座標,空間分析及圖形處理,並利用發明了整合棋子與數學的圖形語言,讓兒童能利用符號圖形訓練左腦進行邏輯推理及數字的運算.國際象棋與算術的綜合題含蓋了整數,幾何,集合,抽象數,對比異同,函數,多空間圖形資料.所以枯燥無味的計算題變成了謎題,學生需要通過更多的思考.能讓腦去思考愈多則腦力也愈開發.處里訊息,分析資料才能發掘出題目.做這些謎題式數學時可以訓練學生比較會專心及有耐心.

何数棋谜融合數學與國際象棋的教學理論巳在BC省數學教師刊物上發表.科研報告已經證實何数棋谜教學法不但可以提高兒童數學解題及思維能力,還可以開發兒童的腦力,及分析問題的能力並且增加兒童學習的耐力,學生的探索創造精神及求知欲.判斷力,及自信心等,啓發思維訓練機警靈巧及加強手腦眼的靈活運用.

Mom! I Learn Division Using Math-Chess-Puzzles Connection

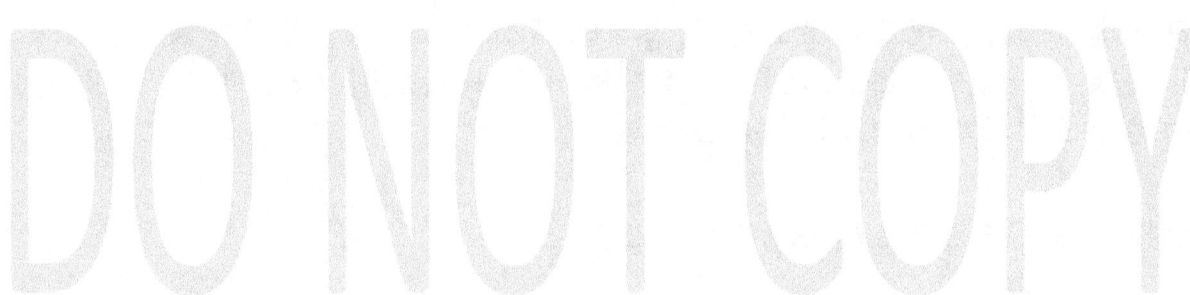

Mom! I Learn Division Using Math-Chess-Puzzles Connection
Ho Math Chess　何数棋谜　妈!我会棋谜式除法啦!
Frank Ho, Amanda Ho © 2004 – 2020, all rights reserved.
Student's Name _____   Date _____

Introducing Ho Math Chess™

Ho Math Chess™ = math + puzzles + chess

Frank Ho, a Canadian math teacher, intrigued by the relationships between math and chess after teaching his son chess started **Ho Math Chess™** in 1995. His long-term devotion of research has led his son to become a FIDE chess master and Frank's publications of over 20 math workbooks. Today **Ho Math Chess™** is the world largest and the only franchised scholastic math, chess and puzzles specialty learning center with worldwide locations. **Ho Math Chess™** is a leading research organization in the field of math, chess, and puzzles integrated teaching methodology.

There are hundreds of articles already published showing chess benefits children and that math puzzles are a very good way of improving brainpower. So, by integrating chess and mathematical chess puzzles together, the learning effect is more significant.

Parents send their children to **Ho Math Chess™** because of they like **Ho Math Chess™** teaching philosophy – offering children problem-solving questions in a variety of formats. The questions could be pure chess, chess puzzles or mathematical chess puzzles in nature of logic, pattern, tree structure, Venn diagram, probability and many more math concepts.

Ho Math Chess™ has developed a series of unique and high-quality math, chess, and puzzles integrated workbooks. **Ho Math Chess™** produced the world's first workbook **Learning Chess to Improve Math.** This workbook is not only for learning chess but also for enriching math ability. This sets **Ho Math Chess** apart from other math learning centers, chess club, or chess classes.

The teaching method at **Ho Math Chess™** is to use math, chess, and puzzles integrated workbooks to teach children fun math. The purposes of **Ho Math Chess™** teaching method and workbooks are to:

- Improve math marks.
- Develop problem-solving and critical thinking skills.
- Improve logic thinking ability.
- Boost brainpower.

Testimonials, sample worksheets, reports, and franchise information can be found at www.homathchess.com.

More information about **Ho Math Chess™** can also be found from the following publications:

1. Why Buy a **Ho Math Chess™** Learning Centre Franchise: A Unique Learning Centre?
2. **Ho Math Chess™** Sudoku Puzzles Sample Worksheets
3. Introduction to **Ho Math Chess™** and its Founder Frank Ho

The above publications can be purchased from www.amazon.com.

www.ingramcontent.com/pod-product-compliance
Lightning Source LLC
Chambersburg PA
CBHW080543230426
43663CB00015B/2692